Reprinted 1985 from the 1888 edition.
Cover design © 1981 Time-Life Books Inc.
Library of Congress CIP data following page 336.

This volume is bound in leather.

MNEMOSYNE

(The Goddess of Memory.)

(FROM A PHOTOGRAPH BY WASHBURNE.)

COLLECTOR'S LIBRARY OF THE CIVIL WAR

When the Civil War began, there were no trained nurses among Southern women, except for a few Roman Catholic nuns. Instead, male nurses were the rule: Attending to the sick and wounded was regarded as too indelicate for "ladies"—a widespread prejudice shared by the majority of surgeons.

Only a few determined and resourceful women managed to break through that barrier to become full-time nurses or medical administrators. Among them was Fannie A. Beers, who served the South as a hospital matron for nearly four years. In 1888, she published *Memories,* a book of vivid recollections of nursing Confederate—and Union—soldiers in Virginia, Alabama and Georgia, on the battlefield, in field hospitals, in a converted hotel, once even in a church. There were times when she supervised more than 1,000 beds filled with the sick and wounded.

Despite her devotion to others, Mrs. Beers evidently chose to remain anonymous in all but the writing of her one major literary effort. No public record remains of her service, of her age at the time, of her maiden name, or even of the dates of her birth and death. Virtually all that is known of her is contained in *Memories.*

She relates that she grew up in a small village in Connecticut, the child of fond parents, who gave her every educational advantage. Sometime in the 1850s, she married Augustus P. Beers, a Southerner educated at Yale. They settled in New Orleans, but retained their ties to Connecticut. The young wife was visiting her mother back home with her son, Georgie, when the War erupted. All too quickly, old friends stopped associating with the "Rebel." Meanwhile, her husband had enlisted in the 1st Louisiana Infantry Battalion and was en route to the fighting in Virginia. Taking Georgie and her servant, Tempe, she headed back to her adopted land in July 1861.

Mrs. Beers volunteered as a nurse in Richmond, despite the protests of a friend that she was "too young, and had been too tenderly raised" for such difficult work. When her husband's unit was transferred to the Army of Tennessee, Mrs. Beers followed and continued nursing where she could at

TIME-LIFE BOOKS INC., ALEXANDRIA, VIRGINIA 22314

least feel closer to him, although the two managed to meet only rarely.

From the outset, the young hospital matron realized "not only that my services were needed, but that my work must be begun and carried on under almost insurmountable difficulties and disadvantages—no comforts, no hospital stores, insufficient nourishment, a scarcity of blankets, even of pillows." To make matters worse, the male nurses with whom she worked usually were convalescing soldiers, and by the time they were properly trained, they were ready to return to combat.

Mrs. Beers remembers some light moments, such as the time she struggled in vain in order to get milk for her patients from a "distrustful" cow. More often she records the dark and terrible scenes, as when she accompanied her chief surgeon to a battlefield where "the dead lay around us on every side, singly and in groups and *piles;* men and horses, in some cases, apparently inextricably mingled. The field we crossed was slippery with blood. The edge of my dress was red, my feet were wet with it." Wielding instruments and applying bandages, and dispensing water, peach brandy and soup, she and her surgeon picked their way among the wounded, "sometimes successful in reviving the patient, sometimes able only to whisper a few words of comfort to the dying."

Once, after most of the hospital attendants had left, she stayed on under rigid quarantine to help fight a smallpox epidemic, working far into the night in "the fever-haunted tents." Late in the War, she chose again to remain with "my boys": Together, they faced the unknown, deserted by all who could pick up a gun and walk or limp to the nearby battle.

At last, however, Mrs. Beers suffered a collapse—not of spirit, but of physical strength. "My health was completely broken down," she relates. "The rigors of the winter, the incessant toil, the hard rations had done their work well. I was no longer fit to nurse the sick." So in February 1865, she sadly made her way to her husband's family in Alabama to await War's end.

—THE EDITORS

★ ★ ★ ★ ★ ★

MEMORIES.

*A RECORD OF PERSONAL EXPERIENCE AND
ADVENTURE DURING FOUR
YEARS OF WAR.*

BY

MRS. FANNIE A. BEERS.

———

PRESS OF J. B. LIPPINCOTT COMPANY,
PHILADELPHIA.
1888.

TO

"THE BOYS WHO WORE THE GRAY,"

WHETHER THE LOFTY OR THE LOWLY;
EQUALLY TO THE SURVIVING HEROES WHO STAND BEFORE THE WORLD IN THE LIGHT
OF A GLORY NEVER SURPASSED, AND TO THE MARTYRS WHOSE PATRIOT
BLOOD AND SACRED GRAVES HAVE FOREVER SANCTIFIED
THE LAND THEY LOVED,

THESE "MEMORIES"

ARE RESPECTFULLY AND LOVINGLY DEDICATED.

PREFACE.

For several years my friends among Confederate soldiers have been urging me to "write up" and publish what I know of the war. By personal solicitation and by letter this subject has been brought before me and placed in the light of a duty which I owe to posterity. Taking this view of it, I willingly comply, glad that I am permitted to stand among the many "witnesses" who shall establish "the truth," proud to write myself as one who faithfully served the defenders of the Cause which had and has my heart's devotion. I have tried to give a faithful record of my experiences, to "nothing extenuate nor aught set down in malice," and I have told the truth, *but not always the whole truth.* A few of these "Memories" were originally written for the *Southern Bivouac,* and are here republished because my book would have been incomplete without them.

I am very inexperienced in the business of making books, but relying with confidence upon the leniency of my friends, and feeling sure that I have no enemy who will savagely rejoice that I have written a book, I make the venture.

CONTENTS.

PART II.

FOR YOUNG PEOPLE.

PART III.

AFTER TWENTY YEARS.

INTRODUCTORY.

Among those who early espoused the Southern Cause, few, perhaps, were more in earnest than my husband and myself. Our patriotism was at the very outset put to a crucial test. The duties of a soldier and a civilian became incompatible. Being in ill health, it was thought best that I should go to my mother at the North for awhile. My husband, after preliminary service with the "Minute Men" and the State troops, as a member of Company A, Crescent Rifles, was, with this company, regularly mustered into the Confederate service in April, 1861, and left for Pensacola, Florida, where the Crescent Rifles, with the Louisiana Guards, Orleans Cadets, Shreveport Guards, Terrebonne Rifles, and Grivot Guards, were organized into the Dreux Battalion. It was then supposed that "the affair" would be "settled in ninety days."

From my house of refuge I watched eagerly the course of events, until at last all mail facilities were cut off, and I was left to endure the horrors of suspense as well as the irritating consciousness that, although sojourning in the home of my childhood, I was an alien, an acknowledged "Rebel," and as such an object of suspicion and dislike to all save my immediate family. Even these, with the exception of my precious mother, were bitterly opposed to the South and Secession. From mother I received unceasing care, thorough sympathy, surpassing love. During this troubled time a

9

little babe was born to me,—a tiny babe,—who only just opened its dark eyes upon the troubled face of its mother to close them forever.

The guns of Sumter, reverberating throughout the North, "stirred a fever in the blood of age" and youth alike. Fanatics raved more wildly than ever, while those who had hitherto been lukewarm hastened to swell the cry of horror and fury which everywhere arose at this "insult to our flag." This feeling found vent in acts of oppression, met by prompt and determined resistance, and thus was inaugurated the fratricidal strife which was for four years to desolate the land.

Rumors of an engagement in Virginia intensified my suspense until it seemed unbearable. One day I received a kindly warning from an old friend concerning a small Confederate flag which had been sent to me by my husband. It was a tiny silken affair, which I kept in my prayer-book. This harmless possession was magnified by the people of the town into an immense rebel banner, which would eventually float over my mother's house. I had still a few friends whose temperate counsel had hitherto protected me. The note referred to warned me that while I retained possession of the flag I might at any time expect the presence of a mob. I would not have destroyed my treasure for worlds, and how to conceal it became a subject of constant thought. The discovery one day of a jar of "perpetual paste" in mother's secretary suggested an idea which was at once carried out. Applying this strongly adhésive mixture to one side of the flag, I pasted it upon the naked flesh just over my heart. One morning the mail brought certain news of a Confederate victory at Big Bethel. This so exasperated the people that on their way from the post-office an excited crowd halted under my window, crying out, "Where's that rebel woman?" "Let's have that flag," "Show your colors," etc. Carried away by intense excitement, I threw open the blinds, and, waving the newspaper above my head, shouted, "Hurrah! Hurrah for Big Bethel! Hurrah for the brave rebels!" A perfect howl of rage arose from below, and greater evil might have befallen but for the timely appearance of the venerable village doctor, who now rode hastily in among the excited men, and, standing up in his buggy, cried out, "Friends, she is but a frail, defenceless woman. Be thankful if your morning's work be not her death." Slowly and sullenly the crowd dispersed, while the good doctor hastily ascended to my chamber. I lay with fevered cheeks and burning eyes among the pillows where my mother had placed me. The terrible excitement under which I labored forbade all blame or any allusion to my act of imprudence. I was soothed and tenderly cared for until, under the influence of a sedative, I fell asleep.

Early next morning the doctor appeared at my bedside. Meantime a change had come over me. I seemed to have lost the nervous excitability of a girl and to have become a *woman*, full of courage and hope. Dr. —— regarded me steadily for a moment; then,—"Ah! better this morning? That's my brave girl." Meeting his gaze fully, I replied, "I shall try henceforth to be brave, as befits the wife of a soldier." A frown appeared upon the doctor's brow. Tenderly placing his hand upon my head, he said, "My child, I fear your courage will soon be put to the test. Your own imprudence has greatly incensed the town people. Danger menaces you, and through you, your mother. Fortunately, the friends of your childhood still desire to protect you; but your only safety lies in giving up the rebel flag which it is said you possess. Give it to me, Fannie, and I will destroy it before their eyes, and thus avert the threatened danger." I only smiled, as I replied: "Dr. ——, since the rebel flag has existed, I have cherished it in my heart of hearts. You may search the house over; you will find no flag but the one I have here," placing my hand on my heart. The good man had known me from childhood, and he could not doubt me. He questioned no further, but took his leave, promising to use his influence with the incensed villagers. They, however, were not so easily convinced. They had been wrought up to a state of frenzied patriotism, and declared they would search the house where the obnoxious flag was supposed to be. Dire threats of vengeance were heard on every side. At last a committee was appointed to wait upon "*the traitress*" and again demand the surrender of the flag. It was composed of gentlemen who, though thorough and uncompromising "Union men," were yet well known to me, and were anxious, if possible, to shield me. They were admitted to the room, where I calmly awaited them. I reiterated the assertion made to the doctor, so calmly, and with such apparent truth, that they were staggered. But they had come to perform a duty, and they meant to succeed. They convinced me that the danger to myself and to the house of my mother was real and imminent, but I only repeated my assertions, though my heart throbbed painfully as I saw the anxiety and trouble in mother's face. Suddenly I remembered that I had in my possession a paper which, just before all mail communication had ceased between the North and South, had been sent to me for the purpose of protection. It was simply a certificate of my husband's membership and good standing in a Masonic lodge, and had a seal affixed. As I called for the portfolio, all eyes brightened with expectation of seeing at last the "rebel flag." Drawing forth from its envelope the fateful document, I said, "I was told to use this only in dire extremity; it seems to me that such a time is at hand. If there be any virtue in Masonry, let it now protect me and the roof which is at present my only shelter!"

Thus speaking, I handed the paper to one whom I knew to be a prominent Mason. The certificate was duly examined and, after a short conference, returned. "We will do our best," said the spokesman of the party, and all withdrew. The day passed without further trouble, and as I sank to sleep that night there came to me a feeling of safety and protection, which was indeed comforting.

Weeks passed, during which I slowly but surely gathered the strength and health necessary to carry out the resolution lately formed, to join my husband, and, if might be, to labor for the cause so loved. The unceasing ministrations of my mother strengthened alike soul and body, but as I read in that dear face a love and devotion which could never fail, my heart felt many a bitter pang at the thought of the parting that must be.

One evening, having found the courage necessary to tell mother of my plans and hopes, to my surprise the noble woman heard me calmly. "I had expected this," she said. "It is right—you must go; but, oh! not now —not soon," and in uncontrollable agitation she left the room. Two days later the subject was resumed. Ways and means were discussed. The mother's face grew paler as that of her child brightened and glowed with returning health and hope. She pleaded to keep my little boy, but fearing lest his young heart might receive, among the enemies of Southern liberty, impressions which could not be effaced, I decided that he must not be left.

Upon the eve of the battle of Manassas we started on our hazardous journey. The utmost secrecy had been observed. No baggage could be allowed. My

2

thoughtful mother converted quite a large sum into gold, which, stitched into a broad belt, was sewed around my waist. One bright morning mother and I, with my boy, seated ourselves in the carriage as if for our usual drive. There was no leave-taking, no appearance of anything unusual. Once on the road, we were rapidly driven to a railroad depot in a distant town; there I took the train, while my poor mother returned homeward alone.

*   *   *   *   *   *   *   *

Arrived in Baltimore, we found ourselves among those whose hearts were filled with ardent love of "the Cause," and bitter hatred for the soldiers who had, in spite of their heroic resistance, so lately passed through the streets of the city on their way to subjugate the South. "The rebel" was enthusiastically received. All were ready to assist her, but at this juncture it seemed impossible to pass the Federal lines.

The great battle of Manassas had been decided. The wildest excitement prevailed. Flying soldiers were everywhere. Almost every hour the sound of fife and drum was heard, as shattered regiments and decimated battalions marched through the streets. Although all expression of feeling, among the citizens, was sternly repressed, the mask of sullen indifference was known to be *but* a mask. Hearts beneath were bounding with pride and joy and hope. Almost without exception, houses were closed and devoid of all appearance of life. Yet behind those closely-shut blinds women embraced each other with tempestuous joy, or paced the floor in uncontrollable agitation, or knelt in earnest prayer, mingling thanksgivings with agonized petitions for those whose fate was yet unknown. Mothers, sisters, wives, strove, with trembling lips, to comfort each other, bidding the voice of patriotism be heard above the "tempest of the heart." In the midst of all this excitement my interests were never lost sight of. Secret meetings were held, and various plans discussed. At last, one day a note was received inviting me to spend a social evening at the house of "one of the faithful." A casual observer would have discovered nothing more than a few lines of invitation, still the paper bore a private mark which made my heart beat with hope.

Arrived at the house indicated, where seemed to be only an ordinary gathering of friends, I found it difficult to appear at ease, and watched eagerly for developments. Not a sign or a word was given, however, until after supper, when the ladies repaired (as usual) to the dressing-room up-stairs to rearrange their toilets. Instead of entering with the rest, the hostess, by a slight pressure of the hand, indicated to me that I was desired to pass on and up a second flight of stairs.

We did so unnoticed, and soon entered a small room in the third story, where were found waiting a few friends, among them a captain and clerk of a steamboat which was expected to leave in three days for Newport News with United States troops to reinforce Colonel Phelps at that point. Here appeared to be a chance, but a hazardous one, since the officers of the boat must not evince any interest in their passenger, and could afford no assistance or protection among the rough soldiers who would crowd every available foot of room. They must appear as good Union men, engaged in transporting troops to assist in quelling "the rebellion." In case of any rough treatment of the "rebel woman," they could only appeal to the officers in charge of the troops, and the result of such an appeal, in the present state of feeling, would be doubtful. The boat was not a passenger steamer, and had only two or three small state-rooms, occupied by its officers. These might be required by the military commanders. Instantly, and unhesitatingly, I decided to make the trial. We ladies then descended to the parlor, while one by one our friends were conveyed out of the house.

A new difficulty at once arose; a friend had applied to General Scott for a pass—unsuccessfully. The precious hours were passing, and failure seemed imminent. This difficulty was increased by the fact that I had undertaken the charge of Jemmy Little, a boy of ten, who, having lingered too long at school in Baltimore, had been cut off from his family in Norfolk, and being desperately unhappy, had implored to be included in the plans formed for me. He was to pass as my brother, and, having once promised, I could not disappoint him, especially as his waking hours were spent by my side, his hand often nestling into my own, his large wistful eyes questioning my face, as if dreading to find there some evidence of hesitation or change of purpose.

One day passed. At evening, as I was anxiously pacing my room, my hostess hurriedly entered, exclaiming, in agitation, " Your brother awaits you in the drawing-room. I *could* not welcome him. I *will not* see him. Only for your sake would I allow a Federal soldier to cross my threshold ; but he is your brother ; go to him."

Trembling with excitement, I descended to the parlor, where I found my brother,—a mere boy yet,—wearing the uniform of a Federal officer.

" Sister !" " Charles !" each cried, and no further greeting passed between us. The boy stood with folded arms, looking proudly, yet tenderly, at me, his only sister, all the brave ardor of a soldier who believes in the cause he serves revealed in his handsome young face. I sank into a chair and covered my face, that I might shut out the sight which so pained me. The interview that followed was long. Finding that my brother not only approved the determination to join my husband, but was able and willing to assist in obtaining the necessary pass, I told him of my wish to have it in possession by the next day, and received his promise to send it, if possible. He was going to " the front," and overcome by the thought that I might never see him again, I threw my arms around his neck, while tears fell fast upon the blue uniform, and so, with a last embrace, we parted.

The pass, embracing " Mrs. Beers, *brother*, and child," was forthcoming next day, and the same afternoon I, with my boys, set forth unattended for the boat. No sign of recognition passed between the captain and ourselves as we were conducted to the upper deck, and seated under the awning. Soon the sound of drum and fife announced the approach of the troops. A regiment of blue-coated soldiers appeared on the wharf, and directly they marched on board. Witnessing their embarkation, I could not repress a feeling of extreme uneasiness, which increased as officers and men appeared on every side. They were so many: I was the only woman on the boat. Sitting motionless, with veil closely drawn, holding my boy on my lap, while poor Jemmy nestled close to my side (valiant in feeling, but of boyish appearance, and looking even smaller beside the tall soldiers), I hoped to pass unobserved, but soon after the boat left the wharf found myself subjected to rude stares and ruder remarks, and at last was forced to seek the clerk to beg that I might find shelter in one of the little state-rooms. All were taken by the officers, who seemed utterly indifferent to the forlorn condition of " Madam Reb." At last the clerk (after a short consultation with one kindly-looking officer, who, however, seemed half ashamed of the kindness of heart which contrasted so finely with the rudeness of his comrades) led the way to a room below,—small, and close, *but a shelter.* Here

b   2*

he placed us, having locked us in to prevent intrusion.
The boys soon fell asleep, but I passed the night in
listening to the ceaseless noises outside.

Morning found the boat at Fortress Monroe, whence,
after a short delay, she proceeded to Newport News.

Under pretence of guarding well the "female rebel,"
the good clerk escorted us to the officers' quarters.
Here my pass was examined closely; many questions
were asked and answered. Still, the result seemed doubtful; means of transportation were wanting. The colonel
in command was inclined to be suspicious and sternly un-
sympathetic. While standing tremblingly before those
whose adverse decision would, I knew, crush all my
hopes, one of the officers espied around my neck a slender
black chain, and demanded to know what it held. Instantly hope returned: I drew from my bosom a small
case enclosing the Masonic document before mentioned.
As at my mother's house, it was examined and returned
without comment. An hour later, however, a plentiful
repast was set before us, after which a covered ambulance
appeared, in which was placed for my comfort the only
arm-chair the camp contained. Soon, attended by an
officer and a guard of Federal soldiers, our little party
entered upon the last stage of our journey to the Confederate lines.

The route lay amid scenes of desolation sadder than
anything I had ever dreamed of. Fields, which a few
short weeks before had given promise of a rich harvest,
were laid waste. Here and there tiny columns of smoke
arose from the smouldering ruins of once happy homes.
The heat and dust were almost insufferable, but as the
sun declined a cool breeze sprang up, and later a flood
of moonlight clothed the landscape with a mystical
beauty. It shone coldly on the few deserted homes
which the hand of the destroyer had spared, and to me

it seemed that its silvery rays were like the pale fingers of a mourner who places white wreaths upon the grave of love. In the soft wind I heard only moans and sighs.

The children slept soundly in the straw at the bottom of the ambulance, and soon the steady, monotonous tramp of the guard lulled me also to rest. We approached the Confederate lines just at sunrise. A flag of truce was unfurled, and at once answered by an officer on picket-duty. A short parley ensued. At a word of command the Federal guard fell back and were replaced by Confederates. A moment later, I, with my charges, descended, to be greeted with enthusiasm, tempered with the most chivalrous respect, by the "boys in gray," who proved to be members of the battalion to which my husband was attached, and who at once relieved my fears by assurances of his safety. It was a supreme moment, such as comes seldom in a lifetime, and yet a time for stern self-repression.

The emotions of a heart at rest, after trials so sore, were too sacred to find expression.

I gazed around me in silent ecstasy. It seemed to me that the sun had never shone so brightly, or on a scene so lovely. Noting the manly faces and noble bearing of those who wore the gray, I felt that the purple and ermine of kings could not have clothed them half so magnificently. And, oh! how delicious and appetizing seemed "the rations," which, though simple, were served under those green trees with the earnest, genuine hospitality which is so well described by the term "Southern."

The camp being several miles distant, nothing remained but to wait patiently for some means of transportation. It was near sunset when the loud singing of a negro driver was heard. Soon he appeared upon a novel conveyance,—a rough, unplaned board or two on wheels and drawn by a single ox. Unpromising as this "*turnout*" appeared, we were informed that it was a "Godsend," so we joyfully mounted the cart, a soldier being detailed to accompany us. My little son was made supremely happy by being invited to sit upon the lap of the driver, whose characteristic songs beguiled the way through the shadowy woods. Within a few miles of camp the challenge of a sentry was heard; half an hour later we found ourselves among the tents of the Dreux Battalion.

My husband was "on guard," perhaps thinking sadly of his absent wife and boy, certainly never, dreaming they were so near. As the ambulance drove into camp it was at once surrounded by soldiers, both officers and privates. As soon as my name was known, some one who evidently appreciated the situation rushed off in hot haste to notify and relieve the soldier most interested. Meantime a dozen hands clasped mine in kindly greeting. To whom they belonged I could not tell, for the dense shade shut out the moonlight, and seen by the light of the camp-fires, disguised as each one was in the rough garb of a soldier, my quondam city friends were quite unrecognizable.

I will leave to the imagination of the reader the happy meeting between long-parted ones and the many caresses showered upon our child.

I had expected nothing better than to spend the night in the ambulance or under a tent, and would have taken great pride in "camping out," but the chivalrous officers in command would not hear of such a plan. Their quarters (two rooms in a little log house) were instantly vacated, and I had scarcely descended from the vehicle when a negro man appeared, to bring a message. "De Major's compliments, mistis, and *de room am ready.*"

I could not have been bidden to a luxurious apartment with more ceremony.

The next morning the shrill sound of the fife and the drum beating the "reveille" aroused us, and we were up with the sun.

The scene was entrancing; to me particularly so, for the white tents gleaming among the trees reminded me that I was among *Southern soldiers.* As they strode to and fro with martial air, fully armed and equipped to answer roll-call, or bent over the camp-fires preparing breakfast, it seemed to me that no such splendid soldiers were ever before seen. Several invitations to breakfast were received; that of the officers' mess, having been first, was accepted.

Major —— came in person to escort his guests to a lovely spot near the cabin, where, under a large shady oak, upon a table of rough boards covered with a nice white cloth, a delicious meal was set, consisting of broiled chickens, omelet, fragrant coffee, buttermilk, corn bread, and batter-cakes. A likely young negro boy attended at table, industriously flourishing a green branch to keep away the flies, and seemingly delighted to show off his company manners.

After breakfast I sat long upon the little gallery of the log cabin entertaining soldier visitors and enjoying the situation with all my heart. I soon discovered, however, an air of sadness and restraint which was unaccountable until my husband told me of the death of the gallant Dreux, the first martyr of the war. Ah! then I *knew.* Struggle as they might, their brave hearts were wrung with anguish, for their gallant leader had succumbed to the only conqueror he ever knew. The impassioned oratory that had never failed to fire the hearts of men was hushed forever. The ardent patriotism ever prompting to deeds of daring was now only a

memory. The brilliant intellect and administrative ability so early recognized, so highly valued, were lost to
the Confederacy.

I no longer wondered that manly brows were clouded,
or that the eyes of soldiers moistened, as, even amidst
pleasant conversation, a sudden remembrance of their loss
overcame them. For them the memory of that death-
scene was fresh. The echo of his last brave words had
not yet died away: " *Steady, boys*, steady," as if he
would have said, "Let not my fate appall; *still* do your
duty."

Before the sun was high the ambulance reappeared to
convey our party as far as Williamsburg, where young
Little was to remain until he could hear from his father;
I and my boy were to go on to Richmond. My husband was granted a furlough of two days that he might
escort his family as far as Williamsburg. As may be
imagined, the ride was most delightful. Although often
oppressed by thoughts of the parting hour so rapidly
approaching, we were, at times charmed into forgetfulness, and keen enjoyment of the beautiful scenery and
the incidents of the journey. I now, for the first time,
began to use from my little store of gold and silver, and
it proved the "open sesame" to much enjoyment.
Watermelons and other fruit, roasting ears, buttermilk,
etc., were purchased without stint, also a chicken. At
noon the little party camped in a grove by the road-
side, where my soldier-husband proudly showed off his
new attainments in the way of cooking. The dinner
was pronounced "just splendid" by the appreciative
guests. Our boy having gorged himself, fell asleep upon
the grass; the negro driver was sent off to buy a few
dainties to send back to friends in camp, and the two so
lately reunited—so soon to part—enjoyed for the first
time an uninterrupted talk relating to the adventures

that each had met with since our parting in New Orleans.
I unfolded my plans for the future, receiving the full
permission and sympathy of my husband.

Soon after the journey was resumed two horsemen
appeared on the road coming from the direction of
Williamsburg. I was quite unprepared to recognize a
Confederate officer of high rank in either of the riders
who now approached, as neither were very handsomely
uniformed.

The one who most attracted my attention appeared of
middle age, was rather stout, of florid complexion, and
(as I thought) looked very cross. He wore a sort of
fancy jacket or roundabout, profusely trimmed with
gold lace.

"There is General Magruder!" exclaimed my husband,
and, as the officers came near, saluted. Bringing the
ambulance to a halt with an imperious gesture, the
general sharply questioned him as to his absence from
camp, his name, command, destination, length of time
he expected to be absent, etc. I was then introduced,
and began to express my pleasure at the meeting, etc.
The grim visage of the general did not relax. My
pleasant talk was cut short by another question, this
time, of importance. I then found myself subjected to
a series of questions so searching that all I had seen or
heard while passing through the enemy's lines was im-
parted to General Magruder before I quite realized the
situation.

What woman, denied the pleasure of talking, would
not have felt and expressed, as did my discomfited self,
great indignation in view of a deprivation so severe.
But upon being reminded of the heavy responsibility
resting upon the mind and heart of the patriot who
could not withdraw his attention from the great and
all-absorbing interests committed to his guidance long

enough to think of, much less to practise, the amenities of life, I felt ashamed of my hasty anger, and remembered only that I had been permitted to see and converse with the hero of the battle of Bethel, the first Confederate victory of the war.

At Williamsburg, under the roof of the queer, old-fashioned, but comfortable inn, excellent accommodations were found, and here the soldier partook heartily of the "square meals" which he knew were his last for many a day.

A few hours of happiness was all that could be accorded to us. A battle seemed imminent. My husband must return to his post. I, with my little boy, proceeded to Richmond, where unbounded kindness and hospitality awaited me.

Here began the realization of the dream which had haunted me while yet compelled to linger among the foes of the South. Joining at once the noble army of women who untiringly ministered to the sick and wounded, I entered upon the performance of a vow to devote myself to this work if only the opportunity were accorded me.

MEMORIES.

PART I.

CHAPTER I.

ALPHA.

Richmond in 1861–62.

Who that witnessed and shared the wild excitement which, upon the days immediately following the victory at Manassas, throbbed and pulsated throughout the crowded capital of the Southern Confederacy can ever forget?

Men were beside themselves with joy and pride,—drunk with glory.

By night the city blazed with illuminations, even the most humble home setting up its beacon-light,—a sure guide to where loyal, devoted hearts were throbbing with patriotism.

In the general rejoicing the heavy price of victory was for a time unheeded. But Richmond had sent forth to battle her best beloved, and, alas! many were the "unreturning braves."

The dazzling light fell upon many dwellings only to reveal the utter darkness that reigned without and within. No need to ask why. All knew that in each darkened home stricken hearts filled with an agony of desolation struggled in vain to remember that they were mothers and wives of heroes, but could not yet lift their eyes from the ghastly wounds—the bloody graves of their dead.

Ah! the lovely, joyous, hopeful, patriotic days of that summer of 1861. The Confederate gray was then a thing of beauty,—the outer garb of true and loyal souls. Every man who wore it became ennobled in the eyes of every woman. These boys in gray were strangers to none. Their uniform was a passport to every heart and every home. Broad Street was thronged with them all day long.

Officers of all grades rode hither and thither, or congregated on the steps of the hotels. Squads of soldiers promenaded, gayly chatting with acquaintances whom they chanced to meet. Occasionally the sound of drum and fife or the fuller music of a brass band would herald the appearance of a company or regiment, perhaps just arrived from some distant State, eager to reach the front. On more retired streets, at their homes, humble or luxurious, sweet young girls welcomed with kindly words and sunny smiles officers and private soldiers, extending equal courtesy to both. The elegant mansions on Clay Street and elsewhere were never without soldier guests. Impromptu meals were served whenever needed. In elegant dining-rooms stately servants supplied the wants of soldiers. No one asked who they were, whence they came. They were Confederate soldiers—that was quite enough.

In the cool drawing-rooms pleasant chat beguiled the summer hours, sweet songs floated out upon the air, or the more stirring notes of " Dixie" or " The Bonnie Blue Flag," played with a spirit and vim which electrified every listener.

If these warriors who lingered here could have chosen

for themselves, they would never have thus quietly rested upon the laurels won at Manassas. Contrary to their wishes, they had been recalled from the pursuit of the flying foe and consigned to temporary inactivity.

As the new companies or regiments came in they were marched into camp in the suburbs or temporarily provided for in the immense tobacco warehouses which were numerous all over the city. Passing one of these, at every window appeared laughing or discontented faces of soldiers newly arrived, full of ardor, ready and expecting to perform prodigies of valor, yet ignominiously shut up within four brick walls, with a sentinel guarding every door.

The evening drills at the camp-grounds were attended by hundreds of ladies. So enthusiastic were these, so full of pride and admiration for the braves who had come to defend their homes and themselves, so entirely in accord with the patriotic spirit which burned in every manly heart, that not a soldier, no matter how humble, came near or passed before a group of these animated beauties who was not literally bathed in the radiance of kindly smiles,—transformed into a demigod by the light of gloriously flashing eyes.

No pen can do justice to the scenes I would fain describe. Language is quite inadequate to express the feeling which then lived and had its being in the hearts of all Southern women towards the heroes who had risen up to defend the liberties of the South. Exalted far above mere sentiment, holding no element of vanity or selfishness,—idolatrous, if you will, yet an idolatry which inspired the heart, nerved the hand, and made any sacrifice possible. No purer patriotism ever found lodgment in human breast. No more sacred fire was ever kindled by human hands on any altar than the impulse which imperatively called men from the peaceful avocations of life to repel the threatened invasion of their homes and firesides. They were actuated by no spirit of hatred or revenge (*then*). They sought not to despoil, to lay waste. But, when justice was dethroned, her place usurped by the demon of hate and prejudice, when the policy of coercion and invasion was fully developed, with one heart and voice the South cried aloud, "*Stand!* The ground's your own, my braves."

Swift as a meteor, yet clear and unwavering, flashed and burned the beacon-light first kindled in South Carolina. A million torches lighted at this flame were borne aloft throughout the Southland.

And now the invader had been met and foiled in his first attempt to conquer and desolate the homes of Virginia. Who can wonder that their brave defenders were the idols of a grateful people? Their valor, having been fully tested, had far surpassed the expectations of the most sanguine. "Hope told a flattering tale." Alas! *too* flattering, for the confidence begotten by this first success inspired a contempt for the foe quite undeserved.

Meanwhile, the summer sun still brightened the unharmed capitol. The summer wind still bore aloft on the dome in Capitol Square the flag of the new Confederacy, the "stars and bars." Here, after sunset and in the moonlight, came young men and maidens, matrons and children. Old men, too, who, baring their silvery heads to the cool breeze, gazed upward at the bonnie flag, with a look half triumphant, half sad; for the love of the "star-spangled banner" had grown with their growth and strengthened with their strength, and it had been hard to tear it from their hearts.

To young eyes the new flag seemed an emblem of glory. Young hearts glowed with pride as often as they looked upon it. The story of the eventful hour when it first replaced the "stars and stripes" and floated over the capitol building in full view of the whole city, hailed by acclamations from many thousand voices, is still told with pride by the citizens of Richmond.

The moment it was known that Virginia had passed the ordinance of secession, the cheering, enthusiastic crowd which had for hours surrounded Mechanics' Institute, made a rush for the State-House to "haul down" the old flag, and run up the "stars and bars." Upon making the attempt, it was found impossible to move the United States flag, some one having either nailed or driven it with staples to the staff. Two boys, burning with zeal, started for the cupola to cut loose the flag. One of these, although a lad of eighteen, was a member of the Richmond Howitzers. Hoping to outstrip the other, he climbed hand over hand up the lightning-rod. Just as he reached the goal of his ambition, however, the staples securing the rod pulled out and the boy was left swaying back and forth in mid-air, while the crowd upon the top of the capitol and on the ground below looked on in horror. The lightning-rod was one of the old-fashioned sort, and more than an inch in diameter. One after another the staples gave way under the weight. The rod swayed gently back and forth as if uncertain which way to fall, but finally lurching towards the up-town side. Every one expected that the lad would be so disconcerted and appalled when he struck the edge of the roof, that he would be unable to look out for his own safety. One of the party resolved to attempt a rescue, although by so doing his own life would be endangered. Throwing himself flat on the roof like a bat, he slid down headforemost to the gutter, which, fortunately, was very wide. Placing himself on his back in this gutter so as to be able to arrest the other poor boy in his fall, he waited until the lightning-rod

3*

struck the roof, then called out loudly, "Let go; I'll catch you." The boy obeyed, and as he slipped down the roof in an almost unconscious condition, his rescuer in the gutter grasped and held him until he recovered his self-possession, when both pulled off their shoes and climbed the steep roof to the skylight. Both boys were gallant soldiers, but perhaps neither was ever again in greater danger than when excess of patriotism cost the one that hazardous ride on the lightning-rod, the other to assume the equally dangerous but noble position of rescuer.

Both are still living,—veterans now. One, occupying a position of honor and of public trust, is a personal friend of the writer.

To me the Confederate flag was an object of profound love and passionate devotion. It represented hopes that I thought could never fail, possibilities so glorious that imagination was dazzled. I used to go to the square before sunrise, leading my little boy, trying vainly to make him understand and share in some degree my own enthusiasm, but instead he only busied himself in trying to steal near enough to pounce upon one of the many little birds flitting from spray to spray with happy songs. Approaching the beautiful monument where the statues are so lifelike as to appear real companions, sentient and cognizant of one's presence, I chose always a seat where I could gaze upon the face of Patrick Henry, recalling his stirring words, trying to imagine what he would have thought and said *now*, and almost daring to wish that soul of fire might come, if only for a moment, to animate the cold form; that the silent lips might speak, the eyes look upward to where the breeze of morning stirred the sacred flag which my own heart saluted. Lingering thus until the first rays of the sun came to glorify its waving folds, I drank in deep draughts of patriotism and love for the holy cause, sweet, inspiring, elevating; a tonic powerful and lasting in its effects, bracing mind and soul to persevere in the course I had marked out for myself, to tread unfalteringly a path beset by difficulties then undreamed of. Not long afterward the capitol square became forever sacred to Southern hearts; for here, standing upon the steps of the beautiful monument, beneath the bronze statue of George Washington, the first President of the Southern Confederacy took upon himself the solemn vows of office, and at the same time the stirring airs of " Dixie" and " The Bonnie Blue Flag" received the stamp of nationality. Ah! then how overwhelming the applause. But no one dreamed of a time in the far future when the Southern Confederacy should have become a thing of the past; of a time when the first faint notes of " Dixie" would have power to sway the hearts of thousands, to turn quiet crowds into excited, surging masses of men who would rend the air with cheers and the dear old " rebel yell," of women who, unable to control their feelings, would testify by applauding hands, waving handkerchiefs, and streaming eyes how precious were the memories awakened.

One moonlight evening I stood again before the statue of that grand patriot and statesman, Patrick Henry. My companions were Mrs. Frances Gawthmey, of Richmond, and Commodore Matthew F. Maury, a man whom the scientific world delighted to honor, and of whom it may be well said, " We ne'er shall look upon his like again." When Virginia cast her fortunes with the Southern Confederacy, he held a distinguished position under the United States Government. Had he sought self-aggrandizement, renown, the fullest recognition of valuable services to the Government, the way was open, the prospect dazzling. But he was not even tempted. Beloved voices called him,—the voices of love and duty. He listened, obeyed, laying at the feet of the new Confederacy as loyal a heart as ever beat,—a resplendent genius, the knowledge which is power.

In the days of my childhood I had known *Captain* Maury, and had been taught to revere him. When we met in Richmond, *Commodore* Maury was still my friend and mentor. His kindly offices were mine whenever needed, and his care followed me through all vicissitudes, until, after many months, the varying fortunes of war separated us, never, alas! to meet again in this world.

On the evening referred to above, Mrs. Gawthmey and myself, escorted by Commodore Maury, passed through the square on our way to the hotel, where we expected to meet a brilliant circle of distinguished Southerners. Arrived in front of the monument, we paused involuntarily. The same thoughts which had before come to me seemed to possess all our minds. Mrs. Gawthmey remarked, "If Patrick Henry had been living, I reckon Virginia would have stepped out of the Union side by side with South Carolina." "Well," replied Commodore Maury, "he would have acted as he thought. There would have been no 'pros and cons,' and his irresistible eloquence would have carried all before it." Then baring his head, while the moonlight seemed to glorify his grand intellectual countenance, he repeated a portion of that grand oration of Mr. Henry ending, "Give me liberty or give me death." As these immortal words fell from his lips all remained silent, though wrought up to the highest pitch of patriotic excitement. After a moment we walked on very quietly, until, passing out of the mellow moonlight, we entered the brilliantly-lighted parlors of the Spottswood Hotel.

The hum of conversation, the sound of careless, happy

laughter, the music of a band playing outside, soon brought us down from the heights of enthusiasm to the delightful realities of the present. For, spite of battle and death and perplexities, even certain trouble ahead, Richmond was gay, hopeful, and "all went merry as a marriage bell." The gaunt spectres of privation, want, disease, death, of ruined homes, starving families, and universal desolation, were shadows which fled before the legions of hope pressing so gladly and gayly to the front. Here in one corner laughing girls bewitched and held in thrall young soldier boys,—willing captives,—yet meeting the glances of bright eyes with far less courage than they had shown while facing the guns upon the battle-field. Thrilling tales of the late battle were poured into credulous ears : "*We* were *here*. *We* were *there*. *We* were everywhere. *Our* company accomplished wonderful deeds of valor ;" and if Beauty's smile be indeed a fit reward, truly these young heroes received it.

Our party exchanged greetings with several groups, seating ourselves at last within the brilliant circle surrounding Judge and Mrs. Hopkins, of Alabama. Here were several ladies, wives of distinguished officers in the Confederate service, members of the Cabinet, and others, and splendid-looking officers in handsome uniforms were constantly coming and going, exchanging courteous greetings, lingering for a few moments in conversation, grave or gay. Here, perhaps, a stately form strode up and down the large rooms so engrossed in thought as to be regardless of all that was passing. There, in deep converse, stood a group equally regardless of their surroundings, whose grave faces and earnest questions showed the importance of the subject under discussion. Among those who upon that evening and afterward, " many a time and oft," were met together in those brilliant rooms there was not one heart untouched by

c

the fire of patriotism,—a flame fed by every thought, word, and action, burning ever with steadily-increasing brightness.

I fail to recall many of the illustrious names which on that night sounded like stirring music in my ears; but as often as memory reverts to that scene, the forerunner of repeated pleasures, I seem to feel anew the pressure of friendly hands, unforgotten *faces* appear through the mists of the past, still aglow with "the light of other days."

Judge Hopkins was rather an invalid, but his high position, fine appearance, his pleasant conversational powers, marked him as one worthy of attention from all.

To Mrs. Hopkins had been entrusted the duty of caring for the sick and wounded soldiers from Alabama. Two State hospitals had already been established by her, and she had full power to control all matters connected with these hospitals, except such as came within the province of the surgeon in charge.

I have never seen a woman better fitted for such a work. Energetic, tireless, systematic, loving profoundly the cause and its defenders, she neglected no detail of business or other thing that could afford aid or comfort to the sick or wounded. She kept up a voluminous correspondence, made in person every purchase for her charges, received and accounted for hundreds of boxes sent from Alabama containing clothing and delicacies for the sick, and visited the wards of the hospitals every day. If she found any duty neglected by nurse or surgeon or hospital steward, her reprimand was certain and very severe. She could not nurse the sick or wounded personally, for her whole time was necessarily devoted to executive duties, but her smile was the sweetest, I believe, that ever lit up a human face, and standing by the bedside of some poor Alabamian, away from home, and wretched as well as sick, she must have seemed to him like an angel visitant. A more decided woman in dealing with all who came within her influence or control I never knew, yet she was kindly withal, though never expecting or brooking opposition. To her husband alone she deferred in all things, and was gentleness itself.

On meeting her for the first time she called me to her side, saying, in her abrupt way, "I like you, you are so in earnest; do you really mean to nurse our sick soldiers during the war, as Mr. Maury tells me?" I replied, as I distinctly recollect, with great fervor, "I do, God helping me."

"But you are not strong enough, and you are too young."

Again I replied, "I feel that I am called to the work, and strength will be given me."

She laid her hand kindly upon my shoulder, smiling as she said, "I may put you to the test some day; be ready."

This conversation occurred on the evening of my visit to the hotel with my friends. On the way home an earnest protest against my "quixotic idea" was made by both, which ended in a truce of a few days, during which it was hoped I would repent and rescind my determination.

On the corner of Clay and Twelfth Streets stood the pleasant and commodious residence of Mr. and Mrs. Booker.

My friend Mrs. Gawthmey resided here, and here the greater part of my time was spent when "off duty" (of which more anon).

This model Virginia household was so true a type of the homes of Richmond as they were at that time, that its description will present to the reader *all*, for the same spirit pervaded every one. As in almost every case, the young men of the family were in the Confederate service (the sons of this household were of the Richmond Howitzers). The father, in feeble health, yet lavished his means and his little strength upon every patriotic duty which arose. The mother, far more youthful, active, and energetic, full of enthusiasm for the cause, exceeding proud of the brave boys whom she had freely sent out to battle, loving and serving all soldiers with heart and hand, was seconded with equal ardor and wonderful ability by her sweet young daughters. The spare sleeping-rooms were always daintily prepared, and at the service of any *soldier* who needed care and rest. *Soldiers* feeble from recent illness were encouraged to recline awhile in restful arm-chairs in the cool flower-scented parlors, while the girls often entertained them with music or pleasant conversation.

Not a meal was set in that house unshared by one or more *soldiers*. The table was always as attractive as finest linen damask, elegant china and glass, and handsome silver could make it. The meals were abundant and nourishing, but plain. Delicacies of all kinds were prepared constantly in that " Virginia kitchen," and daintily arranged in the pantry by the ladies' own hands, but only to be sent to the sick and wounded strangers lying in the numerous hospitals.

Opposite to the home just described arose the spacious but unpretentious residence of President Davis, the Confederate " White House" (in this case only in a figurative sense, for the executive mansion was of dark brown stone or stucco). As nearly as I can remember, the main entrance was on Clay Street. On one side the windows opened on Twelfth Street, on the other lay a beautiful garden extending quite to the edge of "'Shokoe

Hill," which overlooked the classic valley of "Butcher-
town," through the midst of which ran "Shokoe Creek."
The boys of this region, from generation to generation,
had been renowned for exceeding pugnacity. Between
them and the city boys constantly-recurring quarrels
were so bitter that sometimes men were drawn in
through sympathy with their boys. The law seemed
powerless to put an end to this state of things.

Regular arrangements were made, definite challenges
were given and accepted, and fights took place between
successive sets of boys as they grew old enough to throw
down or take up the gauntlet. Richmond was at that
time considered a law-abiding city, and had only a few
policemen, whom the boys found it easy to elude. The
appearance of officers Chalkly and Tyler, however,
generally served to close the fight *until next time.*

Within the Presidential mansion was no magnificence
of furniture or appointments,—nothing in the style of
living calculated to create dissatisfaction or a sense of
injustice in the minds of those who, equally with their
chosen leader, had already sacrificed much, and were
willing to give their *all* to the cause. No pomp and
circumstance chilled loyal hearts.

Jefferson Davis, the *statesman* to whose wisdom had
been entrusted the destinies of the South; the *patriot*
who merged his ambition, his hopes, *himself*, in his devotion to the right; the *Christian*, who humbly committed
his ways unto the Lord, whose dignity enhanced prosperity, whose fortitude conquered adversity,—Jefferson
Davis, the chosen exponent of undying principles, was
yet in his own house simply a Southern gentleman,—a
kindly, genial host, extending genuine hospitality to all.

Of Mrs. Davis my recollections are very pleasant.
Always meeting from her a cordial reception, admiring
the unaffected courtesy which put her visitors at their

ease, I yet became distinctly conscious that in her the feelings of wife and mother were stronger than any other; that no matter into what station of life it should please God to call her, devotion to these womanly duties would be paramount.

From the very first there was among the people of the South an earnest dependence upon God, a habit of appeal to His mercy and loving-kindness, and a marked attention to religious duties. On Sundays the churches were crowded with devout worshippers. Every service was attended by more or less Confederate soldiers, generally in squads, but sometimes even in companies, marshalled by some of their officers.

The first Sunday after my arrival in Richmond, kneeling in St. James's Church, I heard for the first time the *changed* prayer for the "President of the *Confederate* States and all others in authority." A death-like silence prevailed during the most solemn and impressive reading of the prayer. Then from every mouth welled forth a fervent, heartfelt "Amen!" The earnest, manly voices of the soldiers added depth and volume to the sound which thrilled every pulse of one's being. It did not seem to us that we were merely going through a form of prayer for one of "those in high places," but that our President was one of ourselves, and all hearts went out toward him, earnestly desiring for him heaven's choicest blessings,—the all-wise guidance he was so sure to need.

Scattered all over the city in many a shady nook were cosey, pleasant retreats, where wounded or sick soldiers were gladly welcomed,—private hospitals presided over by ladies, sustained by their constant attention and unbounded liberality. One lady generally had direction of the affairs of one particular hospital, assisted by others whose duties lay just there, and who devoted each in turn on successive days their entire care and attention to this labor of love. For instance, on Monday certain ladies sent in all the cooked food needed by the patients. Others personally nursed the sick. Still others attended to the distribution of the food or superintended the servants, and so with all duties required. On Tuesday another set of ladies were on duty, and so on.

My whole heart and soul went out toward the sick soldiers. My days were mostly spent in visiting the hospitals.

At first the larger ones attracted me, because there seemed to be so many sufferers and more need of nurses. My timid advances (never amounting to a direct application, but only a suggestion as to my qualifications as a nurse) were condescendingly smiled down by the surgeons in charge. My youthful appearance was against me. Besides, there really was no need for other nursing in many of the State hospitals, notably that of Louisiana, than the angelic ministrations of the Sisters of Charity, whose tireless vigils knew no end, whose skill and efficiency, as well as their constant devotion, environed the patients committed to their care. Occasionally I was allowed the blessed privilege of fanning a sick hero or of moistening parched lips or bathing fevered brows. But somebody always came whose *business* it was to do these things, and I was set aside. One day, however, by a happy chance, I found in a ward of one of the hospitals a poor fellow who seemed to have been left to die. So forlorn, so feeble, so near death did he seem, that my heart yearned over him, for he was only a boy, and I knew he was *some* mother's darling. He had, like many other soldiers, been unwilling to go to a hospital, and remaining in camp while broken out with measles, took cold and provoked an attack of pneumonia. In addition to this, terrible abscesses had formed under each ear, and his eyes were swollen and suppurating. His surgeon said there was little hope of his recovery; none at all unless he could be removed to some more quiet place, and receive unremitting care and watchfulness as well as excellent nursing. "Can he be removed if I promise to fulfil all these conditions?" said I. "It is a risk, but his only chance," replied Dr. ——. "Then I will go at once and prepare a place." As I spoke, the suffering boy grasped my hand with all his feeble strength, as if afraid to let me leave him. Reassuring him as well as I could, I rushed off to the "Soldiers' Rest," where I knew I should find friends ready and willing to help me. My tale was soon told to the ladies in charge, who at once and with all their hearts entered into my plans. One vacant cot temptingly clean and white was moved into a secluded corner and assigned to me for the use of my "sick boy." The loan of an ambulance, readily obtained, facilitated his removal. That same evening I had the satisfaction of seeing him laid carefully upon the comfortable bed so kindly prepared by the ladies of the Soldiers' Rest, exhausted, but evidently not worse for the change.

Right here began my career as a nurse of Confederate soldiers. This was my first patient,—*my very own,*—to have and to hold until the issues of life and death should be decided. All facilities were accorded me by the ladies. Dr. Little gave his most careful attention and his greatest skill, but the nursing, the responsibility, was mine.

I may as well state that I came off with flying colors, earning the precious privilege, so ardently desired, of being enrolled among those ready for duty and *to be trusted.* My patient recovered, and returned to his command, the —— Mississippi Regiment. His name was D. Babers, and twenty years after the war I met him once more,—a stalwart, bearded man, as unlike as possible the pale young soldier who had lived in my memory.

His delight and gratitude and that of his family seemed unbounded, and so I found the bread once cast upon the waters very sweet when returned to me "after many days."

Finding that my desultory wanderings among the larger hospitals were likely to result in little real usefulness, and that the ladies attached to the Soldiers' Rest would be glad of my help, I became a regular attendant there. This delightful place of refuge for the sick and wounded was situated high up on Clay Street, not very far from one of the camps and parade-grounds. A rough little school-house, it had been transformed into a bower of beauty and comfort by loving hands. The walls, freshly whitewashed, were adorned with attractive pictures. The windows were draped with snowy curtains tastefully looped back to admit the summer breeze or carefully drawn to shade the patient, as circumstances required. The beds were miracles of whiteness, and clean linen sheets, in almost every case, draped and covered them. Softest pillows in slips of odorous linen supported the restless heads of the sick. By the side of each cot stood a small table (one or two old-fashioned stands of solid mahogany among them). Upon these were spread fine napkins. Fruit, drinks, etc., were set upon them, not in coarse, common crockery, but in delicate china and glass. *Nothing was too good for the soldiers.* The school-house contained three rooms. The school-room proper was quite large, and here were ranged about thirty beds. One of the recitation-rooms was set apart for patients who might need special attention or seclusion. The other was occupied by the ladies whose duty it was to receive and distribute the delicate and nutritious supplies of food which unfailingly arrived at stated hours, borne by aristocratic-looking colored servants, on silver waiters or in baskets covered with snowy damask. During every hour of the day, gentle women ministered untiringly to the sick. They woke from fevered dreams to behold kindly faces bending above them, to feel the touch of soft hands, to receive the cooling draught or welcome food. Every evening brought carriage-loads of matrons and young girls laden with flowers or fruit, bringing books, and, better than all, smiles and pleasant words. The sick soldiers were objects of interest to all. All hearts yearned over them, all hands were ready to serve them. As night came on, the ladies who had served during the day were replaced by others. No one ever failed to meet her self-imposed duties. No patient was for a moment neglected.

I cannot recall the names of all the ladies who attended at the Soldiers' Rest. Those whom I knew best were Mrs. Gawthmey, Mrs. Booker, Mrs. Grant, Miss Catherine Poitreaux, Mrs. Edmond Ruffin, and Miss Susan Watkins.

A few steps below, between Ninth and Tenth Streets, was another private hospital, similar in almost every respect to the one just described, organized and presided over by Mrs. Caroline Mayo. She also was assisted by several ladies, but had entire direction, and threw herself into the work with all her soul. Her patriotism was boundless, her courage and endurance unfailing. Not only at that time, but for three years, every hour of her time, every thought of her heart, was given to the sick and wounded Confederates.

Sometimes, alas! the care and nursing lavished upon the sick was unavailing. Death often invaded the "Rest." In every case the rites of burial were accorded. Women remembered tenderly the far-distant mother or wife, and therefore honored their dead.

For a few days after my patient had ceased to need special nursing I continued to serve with the ladies attached to the little hospital on Clay Street, still long-ing, however, for a larger sphere of usefulness.

One morning, just as I had arrived there and was preparing to begin my daily duties, a carriage stopped at the door, from which Mrs. Judge Hopkins descended, and, hastily entering the hospital, announced to the ladies that she had "*come for Mrs. Beers.*" They strongly demurred, and I felt at first great hesitation in obeying so hasty a summons. But Mrs. Hopkins was very much in earnest. "Indeed, you *must* come," said she, "for I have great need of you. A large number of sick and wounded Alabamians will arrive this morning. I have found a place to put them, but some one must be there to prepare for their accommodation, to receive hospital supplies, and direct their arrangement, while I make purchases and attend to other matters. Come," holding out both hands towards me; "no *hireling* can fill the place. Come, *now;* with me: we have no time to lose." I hesitated no longer, but entered the carriage. We were at once driven down-town, stopping to order cots, mattresses, etc., then to the corner of —— and —— Streets, where stood an immense tobacco factory, owned by Messrs. Turpin & Yarborough.

Arrived here, a pitiful sight met our eyes. Perhaps fifty sick men had arrived unexpectedly, and were sitting or lying about in every conceivable position expressive of feebleness, extreme illness, utter exhaustion. Mr. Yarborough, having given up the keys to Mrs. Hopkins, was impatiently pacing in and out among the prostrate men. Coming upon this scene, both Mrs. Hopkins and myself at once realized all that lay before us, and braced our nerves to meet the emergency.

The men were soon under shelter, but no beds had yet arrived. Mrs. Hopkins led me into the factory, introduced me to Dr. Clark, who had come to take charge as surgeon, and placed me under him at the head of affairs as her deputy. A corps of nurses, hastily summoned, were ordered to report to me.

Meantime immense boxes arrived from the depot, sent by the people of Alabama. These contained pillows, comforts, sheets, as well as wines, cordials, and every delicacy for the sick, also quantities of shirts, drawers, and socks, old and new. The boxes were wrenched open, pillows placed quickly under the heads of the sickest, and cordials administered. As the beds came in they were placed, made up, and the worst cases first, others afterward, were transferred to them, until all were lying comfortably between clean sheets and clad in clean shirts and drawers. There was no lack of food, both substantial and of a kind proper for the very sick.

I do not believe that a squad of sick soldiers arrived in Richmond, at least during the first year of the war, who were not discovered and bountifully fed shortly after their arrival. In this case waiter after waiter of food was sent in, first from the house of Mr. Yarborough and afterward by all the neighborhood. Hospital supplies having been ordered as soon as it was known the sick men were expected, all necessaries were soon at hand, while the boxes referred to supplied many luxuries. The large room into which all these were huddled presented for days a scene of "confusion worse confounded." The contents of two of the largest boxes were dumped upon the floor, the boxes themselves serving, one as a table for the drugs, the other as a sort of counter where the druggist quickly compounded prescriptions, which the surgeons as hastily seized and personally administered. Carpenters were set at work; but of course shelves, etc., could not be magically produced, so we placed boards across barrels, arranging in piles the contents of the boxes for ready use.

Mrs. Hopkins, sitting upon a box, directed these matters, while I had my hands full attending to the poor fellows in the wards where they had been placed.

Four of our sick died that night. I had never in my life witnessed a death-scene before, and had to fight hard to keep down the emotion which would have greatly impaired my usefulness.

At the end of a long, large wing of the factory were two excellent rooms, formerly the offices of the owners. These were comfortably fitted up, the one as a bedroom for myself, and the other as a sitting-room and private office. A female servant was specially assigned to me, who slept on a mattress on the floor of the sitting-room, and whose duty it was to accompany me through the wards and render any special or personal service required. A long hall ran along this wing, connecting the offices with the main building. The long, broad room opening out of this hall was fitted up as a ward specially mine, for the reception of my own friends and very ill patients who needed my special attention day and night. This favor was granted me because I had shown some unwillingness to place myself in any position where I could not nurse any Louisiana soldier friends or others who might desire or be permitted to come to me. As soon as matters were somewhat settled, my little son joined me in my new quarters, and thus the Third Alabama Hospital became our home for many a month. The little fellow spent very little time there, however. My Richmond friends never lost sight of me for one day during my service in that city. Nearly every day my little boy was sent for to play among happy children, far away from the impure atmosphere of the hospital, which was soon filled with patients suffering from almost every form of disease.

As the demand for more room became pressing, the

three stories of the main building were successively utilized, as well as a large storage-room in the yard. The ground-floor contained the surgeons' and steward's offices, store-rooms, etc., while the second and third formed two immense sick-wards. The first floor of the long wing before mentioned was occupied by the kitchen and sleeping apartments for servants.

Mrs. Hopkins and I thought exactly alike regarding the disposition of the delicacies continuously sent from all points in Alabama for the sick and wounded. None but the sick should have them. Nothing but the simple though plentiful rations were ever served at the meals, which the resident surgeons and druggists shared with me. Yet, by the never-ceasing kindness of friends outside, I was well supplied with luxuries enough for myself, and to share with my messmates each day.

Having the care and responsibility of so many sick, my time was fully occupied. I seldom went out. I could not stop to talk to visitors, but often led kind ladies to the bedsides of those whom I knew would enjoy and be benefited by their bright presence and kindly words, as well as by their offerings of flowers, fruit, or dainties.

Amid disease and suffering, battling always with death (too often, alas! the conqueror), I was yet happy and content. The surgeons were skilful and devoted; the means at hand to supply the wants, even the caprices of my patients, as soon as expressed.

I loved very dearly these heroes whom I served, and felt that I was as well beloved. Welcoming smiles, eager greetings, grateful words, blessed me as unfailingly as the sunlight and dew the earth. Every hour of toil brought its own rich reward. These were Confederate soldiers. God had permitted me to work for the holy cause. This was enough to flood my whole being with content and deepest gratitude.

Next to Commodore Maury one of my most faithful friends was Dr. Little, of Richmond. He was surgeon of the Soldiers' Rest, and also attended the sick soldiers at many private houses in the city and at some of the larger hospitals.

Small in stature, in extremely delicate health, he was yet a giant as far as skill and work were concerned. An earnest Christian, a polished gentleman, of quiet and unassuming yet elegant manners, interesting in conversation, a true, firm friend, an unflinching patriot, what more could be added to indicate an almost perfect character? His care and watchfulness, combined with rare skill,—directed by the All-merciful Father,—saved the life of my little boy, who was brought to death's door by an attack of typhoid fever during the fall of 1861.

Meantime, as the months rolled on, it became evident that the victory at Manassas could not be considered as a criterion of future success. Everywhere there was fighting. Varying fortune attended the Confederate arms. *Un*varying glory, unsurpassed, magnificent bravery so dazzled the eyes of the nation that none saw or admitted defeat anywhere. Yet valuable territory had been surrendered. Homeless refugees flocked into Richmond, but even these were hopeful and defiant, almost proud of their early martyrdom, ready to serve the cause by "doing all their hands found to do with their might."

If anything had been needed to inspire hope, to arouse patriotic pride, the appearance of Johnston's army as it passed through Richmond on its way to the Peninsula to foil once more the "On-to-Richmond" plans of the enemy would have more than sufficed.

Oh, what days were those, which came *unheralded*, to write their history in letters of fire upon the records of the city of Richmond!

General Johnston had kept his own counsel. Says Pollard : " With such consummate address was this move managed, that our own troops had no idea of what was intended until the march was taken up." Soldiers had been continually passing through the city, but by companies or regiments, each in its turn admired and enthusiastically cheered. Now, when seemingly countless legions swept by with martial tread, their resounding footsteps and splendid appearance equally with the roll of many drums and the clash of regimental bands stirred the hearts of the multitude thronging the sidewalks, crowding every door-way and gallery, " mounting wall and battlement, yea, even to chimney-top ;" not, indeed, to see a "great Cæsar," but to hail with wildest delight a magnificent army, of which the humblest soldier was a " greater than Cæsar," inasmuch as he was ready to sacrifice upon the altar of patriotism all that the Roman conqueror held most dear first of all,—*personal ambition.*

Among the crowd, side by side with the ladies resident in Richmond, stood mothers, wives, sisters, from other Southern States, looking eagerly for the well-known uniform worn by *their own,* proudly pointing them out as they passed, even to utter strangers, sure of warmest sympathy, following them with longing eyes until they were lost to sight, hundreds, alas ! *forever.*

Among the gayly-fluttering banners borne proudly aloft some were ragged and torn by shot or shell. As each of these appeared men shouted themselves hoarse, women drew shuddering sighs and grew deathly pale, as if realizing for the first time the horrors of war and the dangers their loved ones had passed.

For several days this excitement was kept up. All night heavy artillery rumbled along Broad Street. At any hour of the night I could see from my window shadowy figures of mounted men, could hear the ceaseless tramp of cavalry horses. Every day the sun shone upon the glittering bayonets and gay flags of swiftly-passing soldiery. The air was flooded with music until the last strain died away, and the calm which preceded a terrible storm of battle fell upon the city.

The glorious scenes of the past few days had engendered a sense of protection and security. All felt that this splendid army *must* prove invincible.

In the Valley of Virginia brave troops under Stonewall Jackson were actively engaged in keeping the enemy at bay. Forced marches, insufficient food, the want of tents to shelter them from the weather while they slept, continually decimated this army.

The number of wounded in our wards increased daily. Sick men poured into the hospital. Often they came too late, having remained at the post of duty until fever had sapped the springs of life or the rattling breath sounded the knell of hope, marking too surely that fatal disease, double pneumonia. Awestruck I watched the fierce battle for life, the awful agony, trying vainly every means of relief, lingering to witness struggles which wrung my heart, because I could not resist the appealing glance of dying eyes, the hoarse, whistling whisper that bade me stay,—because I must try to comfort the parting soul, must hope to catch some last word or message to comfort the loved ones at home.

Since then I have witnessed every form of suffering and death, but none more appalling than the fierce struggle for breath, when the lungs are filling up by sure degrees, in the last stages of the disease. Never has the Death Angel seemed to me more merciful than when he took in his icy grasp the fevered hands wildly beating the air, closed the starting eyes, silenced the gasping breath.

c   d   5

Fortunately, I then had ample means at my command to relieve suffering, in many cases even to indulge the caprices of the sick. In this I only acted as the almoner of devoted, generous women in far-away homes, who deprived themselves of every luxury to benefit the sick soldiers. There seemed to be no end to the arrival and unpacking of boxes.

To nearly every one of numberless pairs of socks and gloves was pinned a paper upon which was written some kindly message, a few words of cheer, generally signed with the name of the donor. Strange as it may seem, it is perfectly true that I found among these (not once, but several times) the name of one of my patients, and at a venture bearing the article to his bedside, watched his delight, the eager grasp, the brightened eyes, the heaving breast of some poor fellow who had thus accidentally received a gift and message from his own home.

Although relieved of all unnecessary fatigue, having at my command nurses and servants to carry out my plans for the sick, the burden of their suffering lay heavy upon my own heart. The already full wards of the hospital now became crowded. For many of the gallant men who a few weeks before had marched so gayly to their doom were brought back bearing horrible, ghastly wounds.

Anxious responsibility murdered sleep. A shuddering horror, a consuming pity, possessed me as often as dreadful groans from the operating-room reached my ears. No one could have convinced me then that I should ever *get used to it,* as I *did* later.

Mrs. Hopkins watched over me with the tenderness of a mother. But she also had hands and heart full. Her cautions, with those of other friends, bore not a feather's weight in comparison with the increasing de-

mands of my sick. But one day I fell fainting while
on duty. Thus began a severe attack of nervous fever,
which brought me very low. Can I ever forget the
tender, devoted nursing of some of the ladies of Richmond! Truly it seemed as if "God had sent angelic
legions," whose sweet faces bent above me day after
day, whose kindly voices pervaded my feverish dreams.
The same care usually given to sick soldiers was now lavished upon me. After several days I was able to leave
my bed, but, finding myself totally unfit for duty, and
being unwilling to remain a burden upon my kind
friends, I decided to go to my husband's relatives in
Alabama, though fully intending to return to my labors
in Richmond as soon as my strength should be restored.

My husband having been transferred to the Army of
Tennessee, where he continued to serve until the close
of the war, this plan was changed. I have never since
revisited the scene of my earliest service to the Confederacy. Perhaps it is as well that I did not, for memory
preserves at least this one picture, more full of light than
shadow, because always softly illumined by the beautiful star which had not then begun to wane,—"the star
of Hope."

CHAPTER II.

"Here we rest."

THE hoarse panting of the steam-pipes, the clangor of bells, the splashing of the paddle-wheels, died away in the distance as I stood upon the landing watching the receding boat steaming down the Alabama River on its way to Mobile.

Ah, how lovely appeared the woodland scenery around me! The sombre green of pines, and the equally dark though glossy foliage of oaks, were beautifully enlivened by lighter greens, and by the brilliant hues of the sassafras-tree. Here climbed in tantalizing beauty—tempting as insidious vice, which attracts but to destroy—the poison-oak vine. Cherokee roses starred the hedges, or, adventurously climbing the highest trees, flung downward graceful pendants. Upon the edge of the bank stood a lofty pine, branchless and dead, but, by the law of compensation which nature delights to execute, clothed to the very top with closely-clinging vines of mingled green and brightest red.

Standing upon the bluff above the river, drinking in the beauty of the scene, listening to the murmur of waters, the song of birds, the weird music of the pines, I repeated to myself the sweet name *Alabama* with a new sense of its fitness: sweet quiet and restfulness seemed to belong to the spot.

Surely, the noise of battle, the suffering and sorrow I had so lately witnessed, could never invade this abode of peace. Walking towards the house where I was to

52

await conveyance to the plantation of my uncle, I heard the moaning of one apparently in deep distress. At the door the lady of the house appeared, with red eyes and a sorrowful countenance. Said she, "Just listen at Mrs. ——. Her son went off on the boat to join the army, and 'pears like she can't get over it. *She kept up splendid until after he got off.*" I sat listening, not daring to intrude upon such sorrow.

Over the lovely landscape before me fell the shadow of the future, a shadow soon to darken every fair domain, every home in all the South.

After a time the grieving mother passed out, and, entering her carriage, was driven away to her desolate home.

Later, I, too, accomplished the last ten miles of my journey, arriving at my destination in time for supper, and meeting with a cordial welcome from my friends.

* * * * * * *

Let none give undue praise to the women to whom during the war Almighty God vouchsafed the inestimable privilege of remaining near the front, even though they may have endured untold hardship, hours of agony while listening to the noise of battle, fully realizing the extreme danger of beloved fathers, husbands, or sons.

Never until my visit to Alabama had I fully realized the horrors of suspense,—the lives of utter self-abnegation heroically lived by women in country homes all over the South during the dreary years of the war.

Every day—every hour—was fraught with anxiety and dread. Rumor was always busy, but they could not hear *definitely :* they could not *know* how their loved ones were faring.

Can imagination conceive a situation more pitiable ?

Ghastly visions made night hideous. During the day, the quick galloping of a horse, the unexpected appear-

ance of a visitor, would agitate a whole household, sending women in haste to some secret place where they
might pray for strength to bear patiently whatever
tidings the messenger should bring.

Self-denial in all things began from the first. Butter,
eggs, chickens, etc., were classed as luxuries, to be collected and sent by any opportunity offering to the
nearest point of shipment to hospital or camp. Fruits
were gathered and made into preserves or wine "for
the sick soldiers." Looms were set up on every plantation. The whirr of the spinning-wheel was heard from
morning until night. Dusky forms hovered over large
iron cauldrons, continually thrusting down into the
boiling dye the product of the looms, to be transformed
into Confederate gray or *butternut jeans.*

In the wide halls within the plantation-houses stood
tables piled with newly-dyed cloth and hanks of woollen or cotton yarns. The knitting of socks went on
incessantly. Ladies walked about in performance of
household or plantation duties, sock in hand, "casting
on," "heeling," "turning off." By the light of pine
knots the elders still knitted far into the night, while to
young eyes and more supple fingers was committed the
task of finishing off comforts that had been "tacked"
during the day, or completing heavy army overcoats;
and painfully these toiled over the unaccustomed task.

When a sufficient number of these articles had been
completed by the united efforts of ladies for miles
around, a meeting was held at one of the churches,
where all helped to pack boxes to be sent to "the front."
I attended one of these meetings, the memory of which
is ever fresh.

We started from the plantation in the early morning.
Our way lay along the red clay roads which in many
parts of Alabama contrast so beautifully with the vari-

ously-shaded green of the woods and the brown carpet beneath the pines. The old negro driver, "Uncle George," sitting upon the box, looked solemnly out from the enormous and stiff shirt-collar which helped to support his dignity.

I believe the old man always drove his beautiful horses under protest. It was either too early or too late, too hot or too cold, the roads either too muddy or too dusty.

This particular morning was so lovely that even the horses seemed to enjoy it, and for some reason "Uncle George" was less pompous and more gentle than usual. Perhaps the anxious faces of the ladies touched his heart, or he may have been softened by the knowledge of the perils his young masters were being subjected to.

As often as we passed horseman or carriage on the road a stop was ordered, while the ladies made eager inquiries for news from Richmond.

The battle of Shiloh, and afterwards that of Seven Pines, had desolated many homes in the vicinity. The fate of some was yet uncertain. Strong fellow-feeling knit all hearts. *Any* passer-by, even if a stranger, asked or answered questions.

A drive of eight miles brought us to the church, a simple, lowly building, the "Grove Church" I believe it was called. Here beneath the shade were drawn several carriages, and at the door a few plantation-wagons waited, some laden with straw, others with articles to be sent off. In the vestibule, boxes were being rapidly filled. It was a busy scene, but by no means a gay one. A few unconscious children "played at party" in the pews, setting out on leaves or bits of bark their luncheon, broken into fragments, and serving in acorn cups cold water for tea. Unmolested and un-reproved, they ran up and down the steps of the high,

old-fashioned pulpit, half-fearfully sitting down upon
the minister's chair, or standing on tip-toe to peep over
the sacred desk at the busy group below. Young girls
moved silently about "helping." Over their pale lips
not a ripple of laughter broke. The fire of youth
seemed to have died out of their sad eyes, quenched for
a time by floods of bitter tears.

To kindly question one of these replied, "Mamma
is well, but of course utterly prostrated, and does not
leave her room. Papa is still in Virginia nursing Buddie Eddie. We have no tidings of brother yet; he is
reported 'missing,' but we hope he may have been
taken prisoner."

Some familiar faces were absent. And of these it
was told that one had lost a husband, another a son,
and so the sadness deepened. Presently the trot of a
horse was heard. In another moment the good minister
stood among his people. Alas! he could only confirm
the fearful tales of battle and carnage. But from the
storehouse of mind and heart he brought forth precious
balm, won direct from heaven by earnest prayer and
simple faith. With this he strove to soothe the unhappy, anxious ones who looked to him for comfort.
His heart yearned over his little flock, wandering in a
pathway beset with sharpest thorns. But upon his
troubled face was plainly written, "Of myself I can do
nothing." A few faltering words he essayed, but, as if
conscious of the utter uselessness of any language save
that of prayer, he raised imploring hands to heaven,
saying, simply, "Let us pray."

Calmer, if not comforted, all arose from their knees,
and, having finished their labor of love, separated, to
return to the homes which had known beloved forms
and faces, but would know them no more for years, perhaps forever.

Upon reaching once more our own home, we crept, one by one, to a darkened chamber, where lay a martyred mother whose son had been slain at the battle of Seven Pines. Pale as death she lay, her Bible clasped to her breast, the sad eyes closed, the white lips murmuring always words of prayer for patient submission to God's will, the nerveless hands never losing their grasp upon the " rod and staff" which comforted her.

Of this family, every man, and every boy old enough to handle a gun, had long ago joined the Confederate army. The dear boy whom our hearts now mourned had just graduated with the highest honors when the war broke out. Never a blind enthusiast, but an intelligent patriot, he had been among the first to lay ambitious hopes and literary aspirations upon the altar of his country. His brothers were cadets at the Virginia Military Institute, and afterwards did good service under Stonewall Jackson. Our slain hero joined the Third Alabama Regiment, and, notwithstanding his tender age and delicate health, had already made his mark as a soldier, brave as the bravest, never succumbing for a moment to unaccustomed hardship. His record as a son was all that a mother's heart could desire. He had been seen by a comrade during the terrible battle, sitting up against a tree, shot through the breast and mortally wounded. The enemy swept over the ground and he was seen no more. Not even the poor comfort of knowing that his last hours were rendered comfortable or where his grave was made, was vouchsafed to this distracted mother. Two more brave boys of the household were still unheard from, but believed to be unhurt, as they were not reported " dead," " wounded," or " missing." And yet the noble women of this as well as of numberless families so situated in every State of the new Confederacy never intermitted,

even for a day, their work for "the soldiers,"—left no
domestic duty unattended to,—in many instances taking
the place and doing the work of the men whom patriotism had called to the field.

Much as I admired and revered this "noble army of
martyrs," I lacked moral courage to emulate their example. Such a life of anxiety and suspense would have
driven me mad. The pitiful faces of the sick and
wounded haunted me every hour. I yearned to be
with them. I felt sure that I was called to this work.
My health being restored, I could no longer remain idle.
But where to go, how to begin, I knew not.

One day there appeared in the Selma paper a letter
from Surgeon W. T. McAllister, Army of Tennessee,
describing the dreadful condition of hundreds of sick
and wounded men, who, after the terrible battle of
Shiloh and the subsequent evacuation of Corinth, had
been huddled into hospital-quarters at Gainesville, Alabama, and inquiring for a "lady" to assist him in organiz-
ing, and in caring for the sick. Here was a chance for
me. I applied for the position, and, receiving a favorable
answer, proceeded without delay to Gainesville, leaving
my little boy at the plantation in charge of his father's
relations.

CHAPTER III.

BUCKNER HOSPITAL, GAINESVILLE, ALABAMA.

HAD I yielded to the almost irresistible impulse which tempted me to fly from the painful scenes and fearful discouragements which met me at Gainesville, Alabama, these "Memories" would have remained unwritten.

I had stipulated that while I would not receive compensation for nursing sick Confederates, and was quite willing to live on the government rations, I must always be provided with a sleeping-room in some respectable private family, apart from the hospital. This was promised; and this arrangement continued as long as I remained at the "Buckner."

Dr. McAllister, surgeon in charge, being unavoidably absent, I was met at the depot by Dr. Minor, assistant surgeon. His look of surprise, almost consternation, when I appeared gave me an uneasy sensation; but, assuming an extra amount of dignity, I calmly accompanied him to a most comfortable-looking house, where my room had been engaged. The hostess was unmistakably a lady. I met with a pleasant reception, and was soon seated at supper with several officers and their wives. During the meal I had an uneasy consciousness that curious glances were bent upon me from all sides. The evening, however, was spent agreeably. After I had gone to my room, a kind old lady came to me to beg that I would reconsider my determination to accept the position of matron, but, finding me firm and somewhat dignified, left me to my fate.

The next morning, escorted by Dr. Minor, I went through the hospital.

For the first time my heart utterly misgave me, and I felt that my courage was inadequate to the task before me. I must premise that this was not a *State* hospital, but under the direction of the Confederate Government, which, at that time, was full of perplexity and trouble, yet, like all new governments, exceedingly tenacious of forms. Dr. Minor told me that the time and attention of Dr. McAllister had been fully occupied in untying, one after another, *knots of red tape*, and that, so far, perfect organization had been impossible.

I entered the wards expecting to find something of the neatness and order which in the Richmond hospitals had charmed every visitor.

Alas! alas! were *these* the brave men who had made forever glorious the name of Shiloh?

Hospital supplies were scarce; beds and bedding could not be often changed. Here were rooms crowded with uncomfortable-looking beds, on which lay men whose gangrened wounds gave forth foul odors, which, mingled with the terrible effluvia from the mouths of patients ill of scurvy, sent a shuddering sickness through my frame. In one room were three or four patients with faces discolored and swollen out of all semblance of humanity by erysipelas,—raging with fever, shouting in delirious agony.

The hospital had formerly been a large hotel, and was divided into many rooms, all crowded with sick. The wounded men who were not gangrened were carefully kept apart from those who were. Some of these were frightfully disfigured in the face or head, and presented a ghastly appearance. In rooms filled with fever-patients old men and mere boys lay helpless, struggling with various forms and stages of disease, hoarsely raving, babbling sweetly of home, vainly calling remembered names, or lying in the fatal stupor which precedes death.

Although many convalescents paced gloomily up and down the halls, or lounged upon the spacious galleries, I noticed few male nurses. Perhaps half a dozen women met us at the doors of different wards, jauntily dressed, airily "showing off" their patients, and discoursing of their condition and probable chances of life, in a manner utterly revolting to me. I caught many a glance of disgust bent upon them by the poor fellows who were thus treated as if they were stocks or stones. These women were, while under the eye of the surgeon, obsequious and eager to please, but I thought I saw the "lurking devil in their eyes," and felt sure they meant mischief.

Dr. McAllister arrived that night. The next morning I was regularly installed. But I could not help feeling that there was a reservation of power and authority, a doubt of my capacity, due to my youthful appearance. Very helpless and friendless I felt, as, escorted by the "surgeon in charge," I once more made the rounds. He left me at the door of one of the fever-wards. This I entered, and stood for a moment looking upon the scene of suffering humanity, wondering how and where to begin the work of alleviation. Suddenly a faint voice called "Milly! *Oh*, Milly!" I turned to meet a pair of blue eyes regarding me with a look of pleased recognition, although it was at once evident that I had been mistaken for some "loved one at home" through the delirium of fever. Humoring the fancy, I stepped to his bedside and gave my hand to the hot clasp of the poor fellow, a man of middle age, whose eyes, fever-bright, still devoured my face with a happy look. "Howdy, Milly! I've been looking for you every day. I'm mighty glad you've come. The roar of the guns has hurt my head *powerful.* Get some water from the far spring and bathe my head, Milly."

6

It so happened that one of his own company, of some Georgia regiment, a convalescent, had by his own request been detailed to nurse the sick man. He soon brought me water, and I bathed the hot head, face, and hands, until the patient fell asleep.

This little incident encouraged me greatly. Passing on among the sick, I found no lack of work, but sadly missed the facilities, comforts, and luxuries which in Richmond had been always at my command.

Lest it seem strange that such a state of things should have existed, I will here ask the reader to remember that military movements of tremendous importance were then taking place. An immense army was executing, " with admirable skill and precision," a change of base. Upon this army depended the destinies of a large portion of the Confederacy. Means of transportation for the troops and their military supplies, including, as an important precautionary measure, medical stores, became an imperative necessity. The wounded and sick had also been moved, and at least placed under shelter. Surgeons, however, were unable to obtain either suitable diet or needed medicines. Requisitions failed to be promptly filled, and hence the state of things I have tried to describe.

Dr. McAllister was absent most of the time in the interests of the unfortunates under his charge. Meantime, I struggled to perform my duties among the sick, and to exert authority, of which, as I soon discovered, I possessed but the semblance. Nothing was left undone by the women before referred to to thwart and annoy me. They had evidently determined I should not remain there. I had ample evidence that they were neglectful and unscrupulous in their dealings with the patients.

In one of the rooms, separated from the other patients,

I found a man who had been brought in several days before, suffering from excessive drinking. Not being able to obtain whiskey, he had managed to get hold of a bottle of turpentine emulsion from a table in the hall, and had drank the whole. Dr. Minor and I worked for hours with this unfortunate and hoped he would recover, but other patients required looking after, and during my absence whiskey was smuggled in to him, of which he partook freely. After that, nothing could save his life. A patient suffering agonies from gastritis was also placed under my special charge. I was to feed him myself, and avoid giving water, except in the smallest quantities. I did my best, but he grew worse, and just in time I found under his pillow a canteen full of water, which had been procured for him by the woman who attended in his ward. If I called for a basin of water to wash the face and hands of neglected men, one of these women would laugh insultingly and say, "Perhaps ye'll wait till I get a nagur to bring it to you, or a silver waiter." They would insist that the surgeon had ordered them to do this or that, and stop to argue against my directions, until I was fain to save the sick further noise and clamor by leaving the ward.

Not wishing to begin my work by complaining, or reporting to the surgeons these daily-recurring annoyances, I struggled to hold my own and to break down opposition by patient endurance. But one morning the "last straw" was added to my burden. I found my Georgia soldier apparently dying,—breathing heavily, and as cold as death already. His comrade was in great distress, but ready to do all in his power, and together we went to work in earnest. I sent for brandy and a box of mustard. Pouring through the white lips spoonful after spoonful of the stimulant, rubbing hands, arms, and legs with mustard, applying plasters of the same, as well as bottles of water, to restore warmth to the body, I soon had the satisfaction of seeing a faint color tinge the cheeks and lips,—the clammy sweat superseded by returning warmth. Working earnestly, thinking of nothing but the human life that hung in the balance, I failed to observe the presence of the most disagreeable of the female nurses, who was standing, with "arms akimbo," looking on, until, with an insulting leer, she remarked, "It seems to me ye're taking great liberties *for an honest woman.*" Paralyzed with surprise and indignation, I knew not how to act. Just then the surgeon in charge of the ward, who had been summoned, appeared.

After a hasty examination, "Madam," said he, "you have saved your patient."

Leaving the case in his hands, I fled to my room, resolving never to enter the hospital again. Forthwith I wrote my resignation, and demanded transportation back to Alabama.

Meantime, the comrade of the sick man had reported to the surgeon the whole matter. The next morning I received a visit from Surgeons McAllister, Minor, and —— (whose name I am sorry to have forgotten), of the ward I had fled from. A letter had been received from Dr. Little, of Richmond, whose name I had given as reference. The ill behavior of the nurses having come to the knowledge of the surgeon in charge, he at once acted with his usual promptness and decision. The obnoxious women had already been discharged and furnished with transportation to Mobile; the men who had aided and abetted them were ordered to their regiments. I was urged to remain, on my own terms, and offered a position of trust, responsibility, and honor,—my authority to be second only to that of surgeon in charge in general matters; in the wards, to that of the ward

surgeons. Under these circumstances I could not refuse to withdraw my resignation.

The next day the work of reorganization commenced.
Then and there I was invested with full power and
authority, and received from Dr. McAllister assurances
of entire confidence and thorough co-operation, which
were accorded in the highest degree during the whole
term of my service in the Buckner Hospital, and the
prestige of which gave me great advantages in other
fields of labor.

Aside from profoundest love of "the Cause," and (as
I firmly believed) the *inspiration* which directed my
efforts to serve it, I had nothing to offer. "With all
my soul, with all my heart, with all my strength," I was
ready to serve; but this would have availed little had
not my *right* to do so been officially acknowledged, had
I not acquired *power* to follow out the dictates of reason
and heart for the benefit of my patients.

As the organization begun at Gainesville, and the rules
and regulations then adopted, were fully perfected soon
after we reached the next "post," and remained in full
force as long as the Buckner Hospital existed, it may
be as well to briefly describe them here.

Convalescents were turned over to the steward, and
their meals were attended to by him and his assistants.
I had only to see that their mess-room was kept in order
and that their rations were cooked to the best advantage. For the sick I had my own kitchen, my own
cooks and other servants, my own store-room, also
liberty to send out foragers. Every morning I sent to
each surgeon a list of such diet as I could command for
the sick. With this in hand he was able to decide
upon the proper food for each patient. Each bed was
numbered. The head-nurse kept a small book, into
which he copied each day's diet-list. He was also ex-

e   6*

pected to have ready every morning a fresh piece of
paper, upon which the surgeon wrote the numbers of
the beds, and opposite, F. D., H. D., L. D., V. L. D., or
S. D. (full diet, half diet, light diet, very light diet, and
special diet). If special directions were needed, the surgeon brought the list to my business-room. If not, it
was left with the head-nurse, and when I made my own
rounds it would be my guide in consulting the tastes
of the patients themselves as to the kind of food they
preferred and its preparation. Of all this I made notes.
I made it a point to feed the very ill patients myself.
Others were served from a distributing-room, where at
regular meal-times I always presided, sitting at the end
of a long table, having a pile of tin numbers before me
corresponding to the numbers on the beds in the wards.
There was an under-steward whose business it was to
supply the plates; also two helpers. The head-nurse
from Ward No. 1 having come down with his subordin-
ates would call out, "No. 1, full diet," or as the case
might be. As the plate was filled, I handed out the
corresponding number, which was put upon the plate.
The plates having been placed upon large wooden trays,
were carried off to the ward. Then came No. 2, and
so on, all the special patients having been attended to
previously.

Everything relating to the bedding, clothing, and the
personal belongings of the sick and wounded I found
in a fearful state. In one room down-stairs perhaps
two or three hundred knapsacks, haversacks, canteens,
etc., were thrown upon the floor in large piles. No one
knew to whom they belonged, no one seemed to care,
and it appeared to me *impossible* to bring any degree of
order out of the chaotic mass of wet, half-dry, rough-
dry, in some cases mildewed clothing lying everywhere
about. Prompt measures were taken with the washer-

woman, which resulted, in a day or two, in a procession
of darkies, each bearing a pile of clothing embracing
almost every article of men's apparel. A "linen master" having been detailed, a "linen-room" set apart and
shelved, the articles were placed upon large tables to be
sorted and piled upon the shelves, ready for reclama-
tion by the convalescents and others who were not too
ill to identify their own. Some of these clothes were
torn and buttonless. My detailed men could not sew.
The demands of the sick and the duties of general
supervision left me no time. Taught by my experience
of the devoted women of Virginia and Alabama, I resolved to visit some of the ladies of Gainesville, and to
solicit their aid. The response was hearty and immediate. Next day the linen-room was peopled by bright,
energetic ladies, at whose hands the convalescents
received their renovated garments with words of
warm sympathy and encouragement that cheered their
hearts.

The lack of clean bedding being made known, these
generous, patriotic women sent in soft, clean old sheets,
pillow-slips, etc., also a few old shirts,—some of them
even bearing with me the horrors of the scurvy and gangrene wards to assist in making the sufferers more comfortable. Details for all purposes were made as soon as
I asked for them, and as "many hands make light work,"
order and system began to pervade all departments. A
baggage-master, with several temporary assistants, found
work for several days in disposing of the knapsacks,
haversacks, blankets, etc. As fast as they were claimed,
they were ticketed with the number of the ward and
bed of the claimant, and piled away to await his return
to his regiment. Those unreclaimed and known to have
belonged to the dead were labelled as far as possible
with the name and date of death, company, and regi-

ment, and stored until friends should come or write for them.

The work of organization was not nearly complete, when Dr. McAllister received orders to report with his hospital staff at Ringgold, Georgia. The sick were to be removed elsewhere,—at any rate were not to accompany us. Hospital stores would be supplied at Ringgold. The doctor and his attendants awaited transportation, which seemed difficult to obtain. Many bodies of soldiers crowded every train,—passenger, freight, and even cattle cars.

Dr. McAllister decided to send his wife and myself by private conveyance to Marion, Alabama, to remain there until we should receive final directions. Two servants belonging to Mrs. McAllister accompanied us. Our kind hostess had put up a basket of provisions.

I took a sad leave of the patients who had become so dear to me, and one bright morning we drove rapidly out of Gainesville on our way to Marion.

The ride was a perfect delight, over excellent roads, or through aisles of the forest, where the healthful odor of the pines perfumed the air, and myriads of birds made sweetest music. Stopping beside some sparkling spring to lunch and dine, chatting gayly all day, growing thoughtful and silent, as, borne upon the breeze of evening, there came to us the whispering voices of memory, renewing the sorrow of parting, awakening afresh anxious fears for the absent.

We slept at any house along the road where night overtook us, always expecting and finding a welcome. In these homes, as everywhere else over the South, sorrow and care had taken up their abode. Haggard, weary-looking women, from whose hearts and homes joy had departed with the dear ones who had gone forth to battle, plied us with eager questions. We related to them all we knew of military movements. But it was very little, and we could give them no tidings of their own.

The third day brought us to Marion, where, at the pleasant home of Mrs. McAllister, we awaited further orders.

I have very pleasant recollections of Marion, and of the elegant homes where I was so delightfully entertained. But already love for my chosen work had reached (so people told me) the height of infatuation. Between me and every offered pleasure appeared the pale, reproachful faces of the suffering soldiers. My place was beside them, and I longed for the summons.

A letter from Dr. McAllister to his wife announced the establishment of a hospital post in Ringgold, Georgia, but counselled our waiting until "things could be straightened out." I *could not* wait, so left the same evening, arriving in time to organize my own department, which, as the assistants had not been changed, and fell easily into their places, was not so difficult as at Gainesville. Besides, we received a fair supply of hospital stores, and were enabled to make patients very comfortable.

CHAPTER IV.

RINGGOLD.

THE hospitals established at Ringgold, Georgia, early in the fall of 1862, received the wounded and the not less serious cases of typhoid fever, typhoid pneumonia, dysentery, and scurvy resulting from almost unparalleled fatigue, exposure, and every kind of hardship incident to Bragg's retreat from Kentucky. These sick men were no shirkers, but soldiers brave and true, who, knowing their duty, had performed it faithfully, until little remained to them but the patriot hearts beating almost too feebly to keep soul and body together. The court-house, one church, warehouses, stores, and hotels were converted into hospitals. Row after row of beds filled every ward. Upon them lay wrecks of humanity, pale as the dead, with sunken eyes, hollow cheeks and temples, long, claw-like hands. Oh, those poor, weak, nerveless hands used to seem to me more pitiful than all; and when I remembered all they had achieved and *how* they had lost their firm, sinewy proportions, their strong grasp, my heart swelled with pity and with passionate devotion. Often I felt as if I could have held these cold hands to my heart for warmth, and given of my own warm blood to fill those flaccid veins.

Every train brought in squads of just such poor fel-. lows as I have tried to describe. How well I remember them toiling painfully from the depot to report at the surgeon's office, then, after being relieved of their accoutrements, tottering with trembling limbs to the beds from which, perhaps, they would never more arise. This hospital-post, as nearly as I remember, comprised only two hospitals, the Bragg and the Buckner. Of the Bragg, Dr. S. M. Bemis was surgeon in charge; assistant surgeons, Gore, of Kentucky; Hewes, of Louisville, Kentucky; Welford, of Virginia; Redwood, of Mobile, Alabama, and some others whose names I cannot now recall. Dr. W. T. McAllister was surgeon in charge of the Buckner. Of the assistant surgeons I can only remember Dr. W. S. Lee, then of Florida, now a successful practitioner and an honored citizen of Dallas, Texas; Dr. R. D. Jackson, of Selma, Alabama, who since the war has lived a well-beloved physician and druggist in Summerfield, Alabama; Dr. Reese, also of Alabama, and Dr. Yates, of Texas, now dead. For a few months Dr. Francis Thornton, of Kentucky, was surgeon of the post. He was a fiery, impetuous, *manly man*, a rigid disciplinarian, but always compelled to fight against the dictates of his large, warm heart when duty compelled him to execute severe justice.

Mrs. Thornton was one of the most lovable women I ever knew; impulsive and earnest in her friendship, of a sunny, cheerful temperament seldom clouded. Her pride in her husband and her happiness in being with him was pleasant to see. While she remained in Ringgold we were warm friends. To her thoughtful kindness I owed many an indulgence in dainties not supplied by the Confederate Government. My room was in the same house where the surgeons and their wives were boarding. Often returning late from the hospital, weary and dispirited, her sweet voice would "*halt*" me at the foot of the stairs, a kindly arm impelling me to her cheerful room, where a cup of tea and a nice little supper was in readiness, made far more enjoyable by her loving service and pleasant talk so full of cheer. The other ladies were just as kind-hearted, but none had the sweet, winning grace that characterized Mrs. Thornton, except, perhaps, Mrs. Lee, wife of the surgeon above mentioned. She was also one of the dearest and kindest of friends. My enthusiasm in regard to Mrs. Lee was almost like that of a lover. She was a beautiful woman, tall, majestic, graceful, towards the world at large dignified and, perhaps, a little reticent; to those whom she honored with her love or friendship, irresistibly fascinating. Her eyes were—not magnificent, but just "the sweetest ever seen," and combined with a perfect mouth to make her smile a caress. In addition, rare intelligence and fine conversational powers rendered her a delightful companion. Dr. Lee was by birth a South Carolinian, a polished gentleman, and, though in general self-contained and of quiet manners, proved a warm friend and a most pleasant host. Mrs. Lee used to search for me through the wards, and, having found me, would flourish a "prescription," made out in due form, for "an hour of leisure, to be repeated twice every week before retiring." These hours spent at the pleasant quarters of Dr. and Mrs. Lee were, indeed, "a feast of reason and a flow of soul," often diversified by funny experiments in disguising the remains of the day's rations by cooking recipes familiar in ante-bellum days, but which generally failed because substitutes would never produce the same results as the real ingredients.

Dr. Lee was some months afterwards transferred to Cherokee Springs as surgeon in charge of one of the convalescent hospitals, of which Mrs. Lee volunteered to act as matron. We parted with real regret, but truly her patients gained by our loss. For she was most competent, faithful, and well-beloved by those to whom she ministered.

The autumn passed quickly, some pretty severe days giving us a foretaste of the rigor of a winter in North Georgia. By November 1 it was not only bitterly cold, but snow covered the ground to the depth of six inches, and the roads were furrowed and frozen. Terrible accounts reached us from Bragg's army, who were without shoes, blankets, or clothes, and suffering fearfully. Officers and men were alike destitute. General Patton Anderson determined to make an effort to supply his division, and for this purpose selected Lieutenant J. A. Chalaron, Fifth Company, Washington Artillery, as one in every way qualified to carry out such an undertaking, who was therefore ordered to Savannah and other places to secure the needed supplies.

He cheerfully accepted the charge, although it involved deprivation of the rest so greatly needed, and the continuance of hardship already extended almost beyond human endurance. But the young officer was every inch a soldier, and one of a company which had already won a name for itself not less for invincible courage than for soldierly bearing and devotion to duty. That so young a soldier was selected to conduct such an undertaking proved how surely he had deserved and won the confidence of his superior officers. In those days railroad travelling was far from pleasant. The train upon which Lieutenaut Chalaron embarked at Knoxville was a motley affair,—perhaps a single passenger-car, rough and dilapidated (crowded with those who, though ill, made shift to sit up or recline upon the seats), box-cars and *cattle-cars* filled with suffering men helplessly sick. In order that these might not be crowded, Lieutenant Chalaron, with one or two others, rode on the top of a box-car for twelve hours, from Knoxville to Chattanooga, exposed to the inclement weather which he was ill prepared to meet, having shared the inexpressible hardships of the Kentucky campaign, including destitution of suitable clothing. I take pleasure in recording this noble act, because Lieutenant Chalaron was from **New Orleans** (also my own beloved home). The impulse of self-sacrifice, and of chivalrous devotion towards the helpless and suffering, sprung from a heart pulsating with the knightly blood of the Creole of Louisiana. Ah, that impetuous blood which stirred at the first call to arms, which was poured out in continual libations to Southern liberty, from the time it gushed from the breast of the first martyr of the war (our Charlie Dreux), until almost in the "last ditch," piled high with masses of Confederate dead, lay the gory body of *Edgar Dreux*, the very topmost man, proving how invincible was the courage that quailed not at the sight of that ghastly altar of sacrifice!

The large brick court-house in the centre of the town of Ringgold was especially devoted to my use. The court-room occupying the entire upper floor was fitted up for fifty patients. This was facetiously called "the nursery," and its occupants "Mrs. Beers's babies." In this ward were placed, as far as its capacity permitted, patients who needed to be visited very often, and for whose proper nourishment and the prompt administration of medicine I was responsible. For instance, if one of the fever-patients was taking veratrum, I must see it dropped and given, and note the pulse. If one was just struggling through dysentery, I must attend to his nourishment, and generally fed him myself. Down-stairs was one large room, and three of good size, but smaller. The large one was also a ward My business-room opposite was also the linen-room of the hospital. Shelves ran from floor to ceiling, a counter in front of them. In one corner stood my desk, and beside it a large country rocking-chair; in another a rough lounge for the convenience of visiting patients. In front of the immense fireplace (where there was always a cheerful fire) stood a table and chairs for the surgeons, who came in after each round through the wards, to leave special directions and diet-lists. Through the day this room was a cheerful place. I seldom entered it without finding one or more visitors, especially in the morning, when the surgeons always met there, and their wives generally joined them. On the other side of the hall was the distributing-room in one corner, in the other a store-room, where, also, under my own lock and key, I kept the effects of dead soldiers, labelled and ready for identification by their friends. I was assisted in this work, in keeping the linen-room in order, and in various other ways, by a young German who had been detailed for that purpose. He was a well-educated young man and a fine musician,—in fact, had been a professor of music before the war, had entered the service intelligently, desiring to remain in active service, but some disability caused his detail. His position was no sinecure: he was expected to keep a full account of all stores in my department, all bedding, hospital clothing, all clothing of the patients, and a great many other things, having full charge of the laundry and the laundresses, with whom he was always in " hot water." For this reason he was dubbed by the surgeons *General Blandner*, and his employees were called *Blandner's Brigade*. He was methodical in all things. His books were exquisitely kept. I had been a good musician, and now used often to sing to Blandner's lute, which he played in a masterly manner. His improvisations were a great delight to me, and, finding me so appreciative, he composed a lovely set of waltzes, " *The Hospital Waltzes*," which were dedicated to me, but never published, only exquisitely written out on pieces of wall-paper by the composer. After the war, Mr. Blandner obtained through Dr. McAllister the position of professor of music at the female college at Marion,

Alabama, but removed later to Philadelphia, where he now resides, still as a professor and teacher of music.

The cold increased, and the number of patients grew larger. Snow and ice rendered it difficult for me to get to the wards, as they lay quite far apart. The boarding-house at first occupied by the surgeons' families was now vacated and fitted up for officers' wards, a room being found for me in a log house, owned by an old lady, Mrs. Evans, whose sons, except the youngest, a mere lad, were in the Confederate army.

It was nearly a quarter of a mile from the court-house. The road thither, lying through a piece of piney woods, was almost always blocked by drifted snow or what the Georgians called "slush" (a mixture of mud and snow). I must confess that the freezing mornings chilled my patriotism a little, but just because it *was* so cold the sick needed closer attention. One comfort never failed me: it was the watchful devotion of a soldier whom I had nursed in Gainesville, Alabama, and who, by his own request, was now permanently attached to my special corps of "helpers." No matter how cold the morning or how stormy, I never opened my door but there was "Old Peter" waiting to attend me. When the blinding storms of winter made the roads almost impassable by night, Peter would await my departure from the hospital with his lantern, and generally on very stormy nights with an old horse which he borrowed for the occasion, savagely cutting short my remonstrances with a cross "Faith, is it now or in the mornin' ye'll be lavin'?" He would limp beside me quite to the door of my room, and with a rough "Be aisy, now," in reply to my thanks, would scramble upon the horse and ride back.

"I know not is he far or near, or that he lives, or is he dead," *only this*, that my dreams of the past are often haunted by the presence of this brave soldier and humble, loyal friend. I seem to see again the lined and rugged face ("harsh," others thought, wearing always for me a smile which reminded me of the sunlight brightening an old gray ruin,) and the toil-hardened hands which yet served *me* so tenderly. I seem to hear once more the rich Irish brogue which gave character and emphasis to all he said, a *naughty* character and a most *unpleasant* emphasis sometimes, I must admit, fully appreciated by any who chanced to displease him, but to me always as sweet and pleasant as the zephyrs blowing from "the groves of Blarney." Peter was an Alabama soldier. On the first day of my installation as matron of Buckner Hospital, located then at Gainesville, Alabama, after the battle of Shiloh, I found him lying in one of the wards badly wounded, and suffering, as were many others, from scurvy. He had been morose and fierce to all who approached him. At first I fared no better. "Sure, what wad a lady be wantin' in a place like this?" said he, crossly. "Why, comrade," I replied, "I thought you would *like* to have a lady to nurse you?" "Divil a wan," growled he, and, drawing the coverlid over his face, refused to speak again. I felt disheartened for the moment, but after a consultation with Dr. McAllister, surgeon in charge,—than whom a better disciplinarian or a kinder-hearted man never lived,—it was decided that Peter should be induced or compelled to receive my ministrations. For several days, however, he remained sullen and most unwilling to be nursed, but this mood softened, and long before he was well enough to leave the ward the warm Irish heart had melted, and I had secured a friend whose unalterable devotion attended me through all the vicissitudes of the war.

Being permanently disabled, by reason of his wound,

7*

from service in the field, Peter was detailed for hospital service, and by his own request attached to my special corps of assistants. He could and did in a hundred ways help me and contribute to my comfort. No matter how many times I met him during the day, he never passed without giving me a military salute. If I was detained by the bedside of one very ill or dying, hoping to save life, or at least to receive and treasure "for the loved ones at home" some word or message, I was sure to hear Peter's limping step and his loud whisper, "Sure it's dying he is; can't ye lave him in the hands av God, an' go to your bed?" He constituted himself, in many cases, my mentor, and deeply resented any seeming disrespect towards me.

I recall a case in point which highly amused the whole "post." While located at Ringgold, Georgia, it was considered desirable to remove some of the convalescents to a camp hospital at Cherokee Springs, some three miles out of town. It became my duty to see these patients every evening, and I rode out on horseback attended by Peter. Riding into camp one evening, I dismounted near a tent in front of which a group of officers were standing, in conversation with Dr. ——, of Kentucky. We exchanged a few words of greeting as I passed on to attend to my patients. Returning, to mount my horse, I noticed that Peter rather rudely pushed before Lieutenant ——, who came forward to assist me. I also noticed that his face wore the old sullen look, and that his manner was decidedly unpleasant. Before we had gone far, he broke out with, "'Dade, ma'am, ye'll go there no more, if ye plaze." Amazed, I questioned why? "Sure, thim fellers was makin' game av ye an' callin' ye out av yer name." "Why, Peter," cried I, "you are crazy: *who* called me names, and what did they call me?" "Thim offshurs. ma'am. Sure, I couldn't make out their furrin worruds, but I belave 'tis a *sinner* they called ye. Faith, an' if *ye're* a sinner, where wad the saints be?" Of course, woman-like, I became furious, and, on our arrival at headquarters, indignantly reported the "off-shurs" to the surgeon in charge, who promised to investigate.

The sequel is most amusing. It turned out that Peter had overheard a conversation between the officers above mentioned and Dr. ——. They having made some kindly remark as to my hospital service, Dr. —— as kindly replied, "Yes, she is a *sine qua non.*" My amusement was mingled with chagrin at my hasty anger, but Peter remained unconvinced and never forgave the offenders. Upon another occasion I was compelled to interfere to protect an innocent victim of Peter's wrath. One of my "boys" about returning to his command came to take leave of me and to offer a little keepsake. This was, or appeared to be, a crochet-needle prettily carved and having *one end fringed out.* I took it with thanks, saying, "I hope I may use this needle to crochet a pair of mittens for you." Cried the donor, "That ain't no crochet-needle." "No? Well, what is it?" "It is a dipping-stick; don't you chaw snuff?" Upon my indignant denial, the crestfallen man exclaimed, "Well, Lor', lady, I made sure you did, you're so yaller complected" (I had shortly before recovered from an attack of jaundice). Now, it chanced that Peter, knowing my fondness for a pine-knot fire, had collected a quantity of knots, which he just then brought in, and, hearing the uncomplimentary remark of my soldier-friend, turned upon him with the utmost fury, and such a tirade of abuse as followed baffles alike my power to recall the words or to describe the rage which prompted them. I was compelled to interfere and order Peter out of the room.

" When, in the course of human events," those who
for four years had shared the fortunes of war separated
to seek their several homes, I lost sight of my devoted
friend.

He was "*Old* Peter" then, and, in all probability, no
longer lives, save in my memory.   If he be dead,
"peace to his ashes."   If living, may God bless and
sustain him in the days that are "full of trouble."

*   *   *   *   *   *   *

In the midst of this terrible winter, on one of the
most bitter days, there came about noon an order from
" the front" to prepare for two hundred sick, who would
be down late the same night.   There was not a bed to
spare in either of the hospitals.   Negotiations were at
once opened for the only church in Ringgold not already occupied by the sick.   The people declined to give
it up.   But, " necessity knows no law;" it was seized
by Dr. Thornton, the pews being taken out and piled
up in the yard.   Fires were then kindled in both stoves
to thoroughly warm the church.   There was, however,
not a single bunk,—no time to make any; all the empty
ticks when filled with straw and placed upon the floor
fell far short of the number required.   For the rest
straw was littered down as if for horses, and when the
pillows gave out, head-rests were made by tearing off
the backs of the pews and nailing them slantwise from
the base-board to the floor, so that knapsacks, coats,
etc., could be used for pillows.

The order had reached Ringgold about noon; it was
ten at night before the rough preparations were completed.   Meantime, such nourishment as hot soup, coffee,
and tea, milk, egg-nog, and milk-punch (prepared with
home-made peach or apple brandy), were kept in readiness.   Near midnight I stood in the church awaiting
the arrival of the train.   Candles were scarce, but light-

wood-fires outside gave sufficient light. The candles
were not to be used until needed by the surgeons, who
were now at the depot waiting to receive the sick. At
last the train arrived,—departed; shortly thereafter
there poured through the doors of that little church a
train of human misery such as I never saw before or
afterward during the war, and pray God I may never
see again. Until that night the tale of the retreat from
Moscow had seemed to me overdrawn; ever since I can
well believe "the half has not been told." They came,
each revealing some form of acute disease, some tottering, but still on their feet, others borne on stretchers.
Exhausted by forced marches over interminable miles of
frozen ground or jagged rocks, destitute of rations, dis-
couraged by failure, these poor fellows had cast away
one burden after another until they had not clothes
sufficient to shield them from the chilling blasts of
winter. Not one in twenty had saved even a haversack,
many having discarded coats and jackets. One man
had gained possession of an india-rubber overcoat,
which, excepting his underclothing, was his only gar-
ment. Barefooted,—their feet were swollen frightfully,
and seamed with fissures so large that one might lay a
finger in them. These were dreadfully inflamed, and
bled at the slightest touch; others were suppurating.
The feet of some presented a shining, inflamed surface
which seemed ready to burst at any moment. Their
hands were just as bad, covered with chilblains and
sores. Many were tortured with wounds which had at
first seemed slight, but by neglect and exposure had
become sources of exquisite torture. The gleaming
eyes, matted hair and beard hanging about their
cadaverous faces, gave to these men a wild, ghastly look
utterly indescribable. As they came in, many sunk exhausted upon the pallets, some falling at once into a

f

deep sleep, from which it was impossible to arouse them, others able only to assume a sitting posture on account of the racking, rattling cough which, when reclining, threatened to suffocate them. Few would stop to be undressed: food and rest were all they craved. Those who crowded to the stoves soon began to suffer from their frozen feet and hands, and even ran out into the snow to ease their pain. The surgeons worked faithfully, and the whole force was in requisition. But, alas! alas! death also was busy among these unfortunates. The very first man I essayed to feed died in my arms, two others during the night. The poor wounded feet I tried to handle so tenderly bled at every touch. The warmth of the room, while it sent some into a sound sleep which seemed death's counterpart, caused terrible agony to others, who groaned and screamed. It seemed to me just as if these men, having previously kept up with heroic fortitude under trials almost too great for human endurance, had, as soon as the terrible tension was loosened, utterly succumbed, forgetting all but the horrible pain that racked them.

Fever running riot in the veins of some found expression in delirious shouts and cries, which added to the horror. My courage almost failed me. About half-past two, Dr. Thornton, yielding to my earnest entreaties, went home and brought Mrs. Thornton to share my vigil, although, as a general thing, he was opposed to her going into the hospital wards. Together we labored through that long night. Soon after daylight next morning, passing into the church porch, we stood for a few moments silently, hand in hand, for, although both hearts were too full for speech, our labor of love had drawn us very near together.

Everywhere the snow lay white and glittering. In the church-yard, upon some of the pews arranged for the purpose, had been placed the lifeless bodies of the three men who had died during the night. There they lay, stark and stiff. Upon these cold, dead faces no mourners' tears would fall; no friends would bear with reverend tread these honored forms to their last resting-place. Rough pine boxes would soon cover the faces once the light of some far-away home, careless hands would place them in their shallow graves, without a prayer, without a tear. Only the loving hand of nature to plant flowers above them.

For months after entering the service I insisted upon attending every dead soldier to the grave and reading over him a part of the burial-service. But it had now become impossible. The dead were past help; the living *always* needed succor. But no soldier ever died in my presence without a whispered prayer to comfort his parting soul. Ah me! The "prayers for the sick, and those near unto death," are to this day more familiar to me than any other portion of the Prayer-Book, and at no time can I hear unmoved the sacred old hymns so often sung beside dying beds. Passing to my office along the path traversed last night by the incoming soldiers, I found the snow along the whole distance stained by their bare, bleeding feet, and the sight made my heart ache sorely. I think I never in all my life felt so keen a sense of utter dependence upon a higher Power, or understood so thoroughly how "vain is the help of man," than when, in the seclusion of my own room, the events of the night passed in review before me. With a heart aching with supreme pity, ready to make any sacrifice for the noble martyrs who, for my sake as well as for that of all Southern women, had passed unshrinking through inexpressible suffering, never faltering until laid low by the hand of disease,—I could yet do nothing. I could not save them one moment of agony, I could not stay the fleeting breath, nor might I intermit the unceasing care imperatively demanded by those whom timely ministrations might save, to give due honor to the dead.

Only an hour or two of rest (broken like the sleep of those of a household who retire from the side of beloved sufferers, leaving them to the care of others while they snatch a few moments of the repose which is needed to prepare them for fresh exertions) and I was once more on my way to the wards. At the gate of the boarding-house stood one of the nurses. Again, as often before, I was summoned to a bed of death. A soldier who had come in only two days before almost in the last stages of pneumonia was now dying. I had left him at eight o'clock the night before very ill, but sleeping under the influence of an opiate. His agony was *now* too terrible for *any* alleviation; but he had sent for me; so I stood beside him, answering by every possible expression of sympathy his imploring glances and the frantic clasp of his burning hand. Finding that my presence was a comfort, I sent for Dr. McAllister, and, requesting him to assign my duties to some one else for a while, remained at my post, yielding to the restraining grasp which to the very last arrested every movement away from the side of the sufferer. A companion of the sick man lay near. From him I learned the excellent record of this young soldier, who, during the frightful "retreat," had contracted the cold which culminated in pneumonia, but would not consent to leave his regiment until too late.

I had feared an awful struggle at the last, but the death angel was pitiful, bringing surcease of suffering; and so, peacefully sped the soul of John Grant, of the —— Mississippi Regiment, happily unconscious of the end, and murmuring with his last breath, of home and mother.

I remember with great distinctness his face,—suffering while he yet struggled with death,—happy and tranquil, when he stood upon the threshold of life eternal. Almost the very saddest and most trying portion of my Confederate service was just here. Only that my record must be faithful, I would fain bid memory pass with flying feet and veiled eyes over the scenes of that terrible winter at Ringgold, when my very soul was steeped in pity so painful that every night I was fain to cry out, "It is too hard! I *cannot* bear it!" and every morning my heart, yearning over "my boys," gave itself with renewed ardor to "the Cause" and its defenders.

Returning to my patients in the church about noon, I found a change for the better in many cases; in others it was but too evident that days, even hours, were numbered. Two soldiers in particular attracted my attention. One was an Irishman, of an Alabama regiment, the other from Arkansas. The Irishman was fast passing away, and earnestly desired to see a priest. There was none nearer than twelve miles. One of our foragers, himself a Roman Catholic, volunteered to go for him and by permission of Dr. McAllister rode off through the snow, returning after nightfall to report that Father —— had been called in another direction, and would not return home until the next day. Finding the poor fellow, though almost too far gone to articulate, constantly murmuring words of prayer, I took his prayer-book and read aloud the " Recommendation of a soul departing," also some of the preceding prayers of the " Litany for the dying." He faintly responded, and seemed to die comforted and satisfied. Afterwards I never hesitated to use the same service in like cases.

The Arkansian was a devoted soldier and a pronounced " rebel." He had preserved through all vicissitudes a small Confederate flag, made for him by his little daughter

"Annie," now alas torn and shattered. When he came into the church on that terrible night, although almost destitute of clothing, he bore the flag safely pinned inside of his ragged flannel shirt. A few days afterwards I found the poor, emaciated frame propped up in bed, with a crumpled sheet of paper spread upon a piece of pine board before him, while, with unaccustomed hand and unaccustomed brain, he toiled over some verses of poetry addressed to "Annie." After a week or two, when he lay dying, I received from his hand the flag and the verses pinned together, and addressed to "Miss Annie ——," in some part of Arkansas; but as I hoped to retain, and finally to deliver safely, the articles so addressed, I did not tax my memory with it, and when afterwards, in Macon, all my belongings were taken by the raiders, I had nothing left to recall the name, and only remember one of the verses, which ran thus:

> "Your father fought under this flag,
>   This bonny flag so true,
> And many a time, amidst the fray,
>   The bullets whistled through——
>   *So, Annie, keep the flag.*"

The verses were headed, "Annie, Keep the Flag," and each one ended with the same words.

The sad days of winter passed slowly away; with the spring came changes. Dr. Thornton was ordered to another post (I had forgotten just where), and of course Mrs. Thornton accompanied him. Everybody connected with the post regretted their departure, especially the loss of Mrs. Thornton, who was a general favorite. We had not ceased to miss her when tidings came of Dr. Thornton's death, and of the wild grief of the stricken wife, which resisted all control. A messenger had been despatched to call me to her side. I found her clinging to the body of her murdered husband, stained with his blood, yet resisting all attempts to remove her. Dr. Thornton having severely punished a case of insubordination, the culprit swore vengeance, and had fulfilled his oath in a most complete though cowardly manner. Just after dark, as the doctor was sitting at supper with his wife, a voice at the gate called his name. He answered the summons at once, followed closely by Mrs. Thornton, who, standing upon the doorsteps, saw and *heard* the murderous blow which laid him dead at her feet, stabbed to the heart. For many hours horror and grief dethroned the reason of the wife. After I had persuaded her to go to her room, she continually insisted upon washing her hands, which she shudderingly declared were red with *his blood*. Subsequently she struggled successfully for composure, pitifully saying, "He liked me to be brave; I *will try*," and with remarkable fortitude she bore up through the trying ordeal which followed. In my ministration to Mrs. Thornton I was assisted by a lady whose name is well known and well beloved by the soldiers of the Army of Tennessee, —Mrs. Frank Newsome. Of remarkable beauty, sweet and gentle manners, deeply religious, and carrying the true spirit of religion into her work, hers was indeed an angelic ministry. We had never met before, but in the days of my early girlhood I had known her husband, Frank Newsome, of Arkansas, who, with Randal Gibson, of Louisiana, Tom Brahan, of Alabama, and my own husband (then my lover), studied together under a tutor in preparation for the junior class of Yale College; they were room-mates at a house in the same village where my mother resided, and I had known them very well. Dr. Newsome had died some time before, but his having once been my friend proved a bond of sympathy between his widow and myself. Although our pleasant intercourse was never again renewed, I continued

through the years of the war to hear accounts of Mrs.
Newsome's devotion to the Confederate soldiers. Duty
requiring my presence at the hospital, I was compelled
to leave Mrs. Thornton, who soon after returned to
Kentucky. I never met her again, but remember her
with unchanged affection.

Dr. Gamble, of Tallahassee, Florida, succeeded Dr.
Thornton as surgeon of the post at Ringgold. He was
one of the most thorough gentlemen I ever knew, as
courteous to the humblest soldier as to General Bragg,
who was then and during the summer a frequent visitor.
His wife lay for some months very ill at some point
near Ringgold. Mrs. Gamble, who, with her lovely
children, was domiciled at Cherokee Springs, three miles
distant, was also a delightful addition to our little circle.
She was thoroughly accomplished, of charming manners,
although perfectly frank and outspoken. Her musical
talent was exceptional, and her lovely voice, coined into
Confederate money, was freely given in aid of all chari-
table objects. She was a frequent visitor at my office,
walking into town in the evening to ride out with her
husband. During the summer, Mrs. Bragg passed many
days of convalescence at the lovely cottage-home of Dr.
and Mrs. Gamble, at Cherokee Springs, but she was
quite too feeble to come into town very often. Religious services were frequently held in the beautiful
grove at the Springs; these I attended as often as I
could be spared, Mrs. Gamble always sending for me
and sending me back in the ambulance. Later a convalescent camp was established there, and then I rode
out on horseback every evening to look after my "boys,"
until the transfer of Dr. Lee as surgeon in charge and
Mrs. Lee as matron rendered my services no longer
necessary. Very pleasant memories cluster about the
room in the court-house at Ringgold assigned to my

special use. I often seem to hear once more the sweet
music of "General Blandner's lute," sometimes accompanied by the clear soprano of Mrs. Gamble, sometimes
by our blended voices. I remember as distinctly as if
it were only yesterday the kindly faces and cheerful
voices that smiled upon and greeted me as I ran in
from the wards to take a few moments' rest. I had
collected and kept on the shelves in my office a great
many books for the use of convalescents, who were my
most constant visitors. The mantelpiece was decorated
with articles of curious workmanship and miracles of
beautiful carving (the gifts of my patients), variously in-
scribed. There were cups and saucers, with vines running over and around them, boxes which simulated
books, paper-cutters, also rings made of gutta-percha
buttons, with silver hearts let in like mosaic. I was
as proud of them as a queen of her crown-jewels, and
always kept them on exhibition with the precious notes
of presentation attached. Had I retained possession of
these treasures, I would have proudly bequeathed them
to my children; but, alas! these, like everything else,
fell into the hands of raiders. Many officers of distinction visited my little sanctum,—not only surgeons from
other posts, but men of military distinction, clergymen,
and others. General Bragg came frequently for a time,
also Bishop Beckwith, and many others whose faces
come to me while their names elude the grasp of
memory. I welcomed them all alike, for I have never
felt a prouder heart-throb in the presence of an officer,
no matter how exalted his rank, than while viewing
the shadowy forms of my convalescents or answering
their earnest greetings as they passed in and out of my
office, or rested awhile in my one easy-chair, or, still
better, came with buoyant step and bright eyes to bid
me farewell when ready to report for duty, never fail-

8*

ing to leave with me the "God bless you!" so precious to my soul.

Some of the poor fellows who were wounded at the battle of Murfreesboro' now began to suffer from gangrene. Tents were pitched outside the hospital for such cases, and it was often my fate to stand beside these sufferers while the surgeon removed unhealthy granulation with instruments or eating acids, or in other ways tortured the poor fellows to save life.

The establishment of an officers' ward added to my cares. As in most cases they were waited upon by their own servants, I could do a great deal by proxy. If any were very ill, however, as often was the case, I attended them myself. Among those whom I nursed in Ringgold was Captain E. John Ellis, of Louisiana. If I am not mistaken, he had been slightly wounded at the battle of Murfreesboro'. At any rate, he was for a time very ill of pneumonia, and received all his nourishment from my hand. Often since the war, as I have seen him standing with majestic mien and face aglow with grand and lofty thoughts, or have listened spellbound to the thrilling utterances of "the silver-tongued orator," memory, bidding me follow, has led me back to a lowly room where, bending over a couch of pain, I saw the same lips, fevered and wan, open feebly to receive a few spoonfuls of nourishment. "Aye! and that tongue of his which now bids nation mark him and write his speeches in their books" cried faintly, "Give me some drink."

Captain Ellis recovered rapidly, but insisted on rejoining his command while yet pale and weak.

The incident I shall here relate is intended to illustrate and emphasize the thoroughly gentlemanly qualities of our Southern soldiers, their unvarying respect and courtesy toward women, and their entire appreciation and perfect understanding of my own position among them. I presume all will comprehend my meaning when I assure them that the occasion referred to was the only one during four years of service when even an unpleasantness occurred. In the same ward with Captain Ellis were three officers,—one, Colonel ——, of Alabama (very ill), another just able to sit up, and one, Lieutenant Cox, of Mississippi, only suffering from a bad cold which had threatened pneumonia. My constant habit was to carry into the wards a little basket containing pieces of fresh linen, sponges, and a bottle of Confederate bay-water (vinegar). Invariably I bathed the faces and hands of the fever-patients with vinegar and water, but as soon as they were well enough to dispense with it gave it up. One day, upon entering the ward above mentioned, I found Captain Ellis up and standing before the fire, his back towards it. It struck me at once that he looked worried, and at the same time appeared to be struggling between vexation and a desire to laugh. Lieutenant Cox was covered up in bed, rolling and holding his head, seemingly in dreadful agony. Approaching, I asked a question or two regarding his sudden seizure, but he only cried, "Oh, my head! my head!" at the same time shaking as if with a violent chill. Turning down the sheet, I placed my hand upon his head, which was quite cool. As soon as I caught a glimpse of his face, I saw that he was laughing, and, glancing at the others, realized that all were full of some joke. Drawing myself up haughtily, I said, "I see I have made a mistake; I came here to nurse *gentlemen;* I shall not again lend myself to your amusement," and out I swept, nor ever while in Ringgold entered the officers' quarters again, except to nurse very sick or dying men. It seems that Lieutenant Cox had received a box from home containing, among other dainties, a bottle of home-made wine. One day he said to the other occupants of the ward, " Mrs. Beers never bathes *my head.* I believe I'll get up a spell of fever, and see if I can't get nursed like you other fellows." The others declared that he could not deceive me, and he offered to bet the bottle of wine that he would have me bathe his head at my next visit. The result has been described. I had hardly reached my office, when a special patient and friend of mine, Charlie Gazzan, of Mobile, Alabama, arrived with an apology from Lieutenant Cox, a few words of explanation from Captain Ellis, signed by all the officers in the ward, and *the bottle of wine,* sent for my acceptance. I would not accept the wine or read the note, and in this course I was upheld by Dr. McAllister, who severely reprimanded Lieutenant Cox, and excused me from future attendance upon that ward.

I have said that Charlie Gazzan was a special patient and friend; perhaps the expression needs explanation. A few weeks before, he had been brought to me one night from the ambulance-train, a living skeleton, and seemingly at the point of death from dysentery. His family and that of my husband were residents of Mobile, Alabama, and intimate friends. He seemed almost in the agony of death, but had asked to be brought to me. There was not, after the battle of Murfreesboro', a single vacant bed. He begged hard not to be put in a crowded ward, so, until I could do better, he was placed upon the lounge in my office. One small room in the officers' ward being vacant, I asked and obtained next day the privilege of placing him there. He recovered very slowly, but surely, and during his convalescence made himself useful in a hundred ways. My sick boys owed many a comfort to his wonderful powers of invention; even the surgeons availed themselves of his skill. He often relieved me of a task I had sometimes found very wearisome, because so constantly recurring,—that of writing letters for the sick. He made his own pens and his own ink, of a deep green color, and seemingly indelible. A more gentle, kindly, generous nature never existed, and yet his soldierly instincts were strong, and almost before he could walk about well he "reported for duty," but was soon relegated to his room and to special diet.

Spring proved hardly less disagreeable in Upper Georgia than winter had been. The mud was horrible, and I could not avoid it, as the wards were detached, occupying all together a very wide space. The pony was no longer available, because he splashed mud all over me. Old Peter brought me one day an immense pair of boots large enough for me to jump into when going from one place to another, and to jump out of and leave at the entrance of the sick wards. With these, an army blanket thrown over my shoulders and pinned with a thorn, and my dress kilted up like a washerwoman's, I defied alike the liquid streets and the piercing wind. My "nursery" was at this time filled to overflowing. My mind's eye takes in every nook and corner of that large room. It is very strange, but true, that I remember the position of each bed and the faces of those who lay there at different times. As I said before, they were principally the youngest patients, or those requiring constant supervision. I seem to see them now, lying pale and worn, their hollow eyes looking up at me as I fed them or following with wistful gaze my movements about the ward. Some bear ghastly wounds, others sit upon the side of the bed, trembling with weakness, yet smiling proudly because they can do so much, and promising soon to pay me a visit downstairs, "if I can *make* it; but I'm *powerful weak* right *now*." I remember two brave Texas boys, brothers, both wounded at Murfreesboro', who lay side by side in this ward. One of them was only fifteen years old. When he was brought in, it was found that a minie-ball had penetrated near the eye, and remained in the wound, forcing the eye entirely from the socket, causing the greatest agony. At first it was found difficult to extract it, and it proved a most painful operation. I stood by, and his brother had his cot brought close so that he could hold his other hand. Not a groan did the brave boy utter, but when it was over, and the eye replaced and bandaged, he said, " Doctor, *how soon can I go back to my regiment?*" Poor boy! he *did* go back in time to participate in the battle of Chickamauga, where he met his death. Twenty years after, I met his brother at a reunion of Confederate soldiers, in Dallas, Texas, and he could hardly tell me for weeping that Eddie had been shot down at his side while gallantly charging with the —— Texas Cavalry. Another youth, —— Roundtree, of Alabama, lingered in that ward for many weeks, suffering from dysentery, and, I believe, was finally discharged.

Dr. Gore, of Kentucky, took the deepest interest in my nursery, and sometimes asked permission to place young friends of his own there, a compliment which I highly appreciated. Dr. Gore was one of Nature's noblemen. In his large, warm heart there seemed to be room for everybody. His interest in his patients was very keen, and his skill greatly enhanced by extreme tenderness and unfailing attention. He was an earnest Christian (a Methodist, I believe), but upon one occasion I saw him so excited and distressed that he " fell from grace," and gave vent to a fearful imprecation. He had brought to me a boy of seventeen very ill of dysentery. For days it seemed that he must die. Dr. Gore and I watched him and nursed him as if he had been very near and dear. A slight improvement showed itself at last, and of course his craving for food was insatiate. As this was a special ward, the nurses had been forbidden to admit visitors without a permit, and no stranger was ever allowed to feed the patients except when some particularly nourishing and suitable food was brought, when I used to take a great delight in the mutual pleasure of patient and visitor, hardly knowing which was more happy, the giver or receiver. Our sick boy continually craved and talked about some "apple *turnovers*," such as his mother used to make, but of course was denied. One day, during my absence, an old lady gained access to the ward, and when she heard the boy's desire for "turn-overs" promised him some. The next day she found an opportunity to keep her promise. At midnight, Dr. Gore and I having been hastily summoned, met at the bedside of the poor fellow, who was in a state of collapse, and died before morning. Dr. Gore was so overcome that he actually wept. The boy had been a patient of his from his infancy, and in a piteous letter, which I afterwards read, his mother had implored the doctor to watch over him in case of sickness. When, under the dead boy's pillow, was found a portion of the apple-pie, revealing the cause of his death, the doctor's anger knew no bounds, and he gave vent to the imprecation above mentioned.

As the summer waned, our commissary stores began to fail. Rations, always plain, became scant. Our foragers met with little success. But for the patriotic devotion of the families whose farms and plantations lay for miles around Ringgold (soon, alas! to fall into the ruthless hands of the enemy), even our sickest men would have been deprived of suitable food. As it was, the supply was by no means sufficient. One day I asked permission to try *my* fortune at foraging, and, having received it, left Ringgold at daylight next morning, returning by moonlight. Stopping at every house and home, I told everywhere my tale of woe. There was scarcely one where hearths were not lonely, hearts aching for dear ones long since gone forth to battle. They had heard mischievous and false tales of the surgeons and attendants of hospitals, and really believed that the sick were starved and neglected, while the hospital staff feasted upon dainty food. Occasionally, perhaps, they had listened to the complaint of some " hospital rat," who, at the first rumor of an approaching battle, had experienced " a powerful misery" in the place where a brave heart should have been, and, flying to the rear, doubled up with rheumatism and out-groaning all the victims of *real* sickness or horrible wounds, had remained huddled up in bed until danger was over. After having been deceived a few times by these cowards, I became expert at recognizing them, and paid them no attention whatever. I really believe that in some cases it was a physical impossibility for men to face the guns on a battle-field, and I have known instances of soldiers who deliberately shot off their own fingers to escape a fight. These men were conscious of their own defects, and often, smarting under a knowledge that the blistering, purging, and nauseating process pursued in such cases by the surgeons was intended as a punishment, grew ugly and mischievous, seeking revenge by maligning those in authority. I do not know what abuses may have existed in other hospitals of the Confederacy ; I can, however, say with entire truth that I never saw or heard of a more self-sacrificing set of men than the surgeons I met and served under during the war. With only two exceptions, they were devoted to their patients, and as attentive as in private practice or as the immense number of sick allowed them to be. These exceptions were both men who were unwilling to get up at night, and if called were fearfully cross. At one time I had a fierce contest with a surgeon of this kind, and fought it out, coming off victorious. I was called up one night to see a patient who had required and received the closest attention, but who was, we hoped, improving. Finding him apparently dying, I sent at once for Doctor ——, meanwhile trying, with the help of the nurse, every means to bring back warmth to his body, administering stimulants, rubbing the extremities with mustard, and applying mustard-plasters. The poor fellow was conscious, and evidently very much frightened; he had insisted upon sending for me and seemed to be satisfied that I would do everything in my power. Doctor —— came in, looking black as a thunder-cloud. "What the devil is all this fuss about? what are you going to do with that mustard-plaster? Better apply it to that pine table; it would do as much good;" then to the nurse, "Don't bother that fellow any more; let him die in peace." My temper was up, and I rushed at once into battle. "Sir," said I, "if you have given the patient up, *I have not* and *will not*. No true physician would show such brutality." He was nearly bursting with rage. "I shall report you, madam." "And I, sir, will take care that the whole post shall know of this." He went out and I remained with the soldier until he was better (he eventually recovered). The next morning, bright and early, I made *my* report to Dr. McAllister, who had already received an account of the affair from the nurses and other patients of the ward. He reprimanded the surgeon instead of gratifying his desire to humble me.

But to return to my expedition: Fortunately, I was able to disprove the false tales which had prejudiced the country people. Their sympathy being thoroughly aroused, they resolved to make up for lost time; and after this ladies rode in town every day, arranging among themselves for different days, and bringing for the convalescents the fresh vegetables which were so valuable as a palliative, and preventive of scurvy; for the sick, chickens, eggs, fresh butter, buttermilk, and sweet milk. Country wagons also brought in small supplies for sale, but never in proportion to the demand. Many of the ladies, after one visit to a ward or two, were utterly overcome by the ghastly sight, and wept even at the *thought* of looking upon the misery they could not relieve. Others seemed to feel only deepest pity and a desire to " do *something* for the poor soldiers." As there were so many, it was difficult to distribute impartially: some must be left out. The ladies, finding so many craving buttermilk, sweet milk, home-made bread, etc., did not well know how to manage; but the soldiers themselves soon settled that. " I ain't so *very* bad off," one would say, " but that little fellow over yonder needs it *bad;* he's *powerful weak*, and he's been studying about buttermilk ever since he came in."

All the time his own emaciated frame was trembling from exhaustion, and, spite of his courage, his eyes greedily devoured the dainties which he denied himself. This was but one of a thousand instances of self-abnegation which go to make up a record as honorable, as brave, as true as that of the glorious deeds which such men never failed to perform whenever opportunity offered.

During this foraging trip, and once afterwards during a spell of fever which lasted a week, I was cordially received and elegantly entertained at the house of Mr. and Mrs. Russell, who lived about ten miles from Ringgold. This aged couple were eminently and most intelligently patriotic.

Their sons were in the Confederate service. Their

time and their substance were literally at the disposal
of all who served the cause. The silver-haired mother
knitted and spun incessantly for the soldiers. The
father superintended the raising of vegetables, and sent
wagon-loads to the hospitals.

Miss Phemie, a lovely young girl, was a frequent visitor to the hospitals, and often herself dispensed the
golden butter and rich buttermilk prepared under her
own direction; she would even dispense with the carriage
and ride in town on the wagon, that she might bring
plenty of vegetables, fruit, etc. Convalescents were entertained royally at the old homestead; those who could
not go so far were often treated to pleasant and invigorating rides.

To me Miss Phemie's friendship and kindness brought
many comforts, and I remember gratefully the whole
family.

Through the summer frequent skirmishes and fights
were heard of, and sick and wounded men came in every
day, and every few days squads of men who had "reported for duty" took their places at the front. At last,
about the first of September, 1863, appeared the never-
failing forerunner of a real battle near at hand,—a
small brigade of "hospital rats," distorted, drawn up,
with useless crippled fingers, bent legs, crooked arms,
necks drawn awry, let us say by—*rheumatism.* A day
or two later was fought the sanguinary and fiercely-con-
tested battle of Chickamauga. I could not if I would
describe this or any other battle, nor is it necessary, for
historians have well accomplished this duty. The terrible results to the brave men engaged only appeared to
me, and these guided me to an opinion that among the
horrible, bloody, hard-fought battles of the war none
could exceed that of Chickamauga, and afterwards
Franklin. From the lips of my boys, however, I often

gained knowledge of deeds of magnificent bravery which cannot be surpassed by any which adorn the pages of history. These jewels have lain undiscovered among the débris of the war. Would I could reclaim them all. Seen in the aggregate, they would even out-shine the glory already known and visible. Finding memory a treacherous guide while searching for these hidden treasures, I have called upon my comrades to aid me in clearing away the dust and cobwebs,—the accumulation of years,—but only in a few instances have they responded. I shall here relate one incident of the battle of Chickamauga never before published, but which is true in every particular.

Austin's Battalion of Sharpshooters, composed of two companies, the Continental Guards and Cannon Guards, both from New Orleans, was as well known to the Army of Tennessee as any organization in it, and commanded the respect and admiration of all the army. The following lines from the pen of a gallant soldier in Fenner's Louisiana Battery truly portray the sentiments of their army comrades towards the famous battalion :

" In the Army of Tennessee, Austin's Battalion always occupied the post of honor in the brigade (Adams's and Gibson's Louisiana) to which it belonged. In the advance, that battalion was in the front; in the retreat, it hung upon the rear, a safeguard to the Confederates, and a cloud threatening at every step to burst in destructive fury upon the advancing enemy.

"Who is on the front?" "Austin's Battalion." "Then, boys, we can lie down and sleep." Such were the words heard a hundred times among the troops of the Army of Tennessee, to which was attached Austin's Battalion of Sharpshooters. Whose tongue could so graphically picture to the mind's eye a soldier and a hero as do these brief questions and answers interchanged between battle-scarred veterans in the gathering gloom of the night, when they knew not, until they were assured Austin's Battalion was in the front, if they could snatch a few hours of repose from the toil and danger of battle? Austin's Battalion, famous throughout the armies of the Confederacy for its discipline and fighting qualities, was formed out of the remnants of the Eleventh Louisiana Regiment, which distinguished itself at Belmont, and which was literally shot to pieces at Shiloh. The battalion is well known to all the survivors of the Army of Tennessee as a fighting organization. During the active campaign of the army, it was almost continually under fire, and Ned Austin, on his little black pony, was always in the advance, "fooling the enemy, or in the retreat fighting and holding him in check."

As the title of the battalion indicates, it was always in the front, on the advanced skirmish-line, pending a battle. It will be remembered by all the heroes of the Army of Tennessee that nearly every regiment in that army at the time of the battle of Chickamauga had on its battle-flag "cross-cannon," which signified the regiment's participation in the capture of a battery, or part thereof, at some time and place. Austin's Battalion had not won that honor when it commenced its destructive fire upon the enemy early Saturday morning, September 19, 1863. Sunday, the 20th, the battalion, on the extreme right of the army, moved forward upon the skirmish-lines of the Federals about eight o'clock in the morning, driving them rapidly back towards their main lines, leaving many dead and wounded on the ground, and many prisoners in the hands of the enthusiastic advancing Confederates. It was published in general orders after the battle that Austin's Sharpshooters captured three times as many prisoners as they had men in their whole battalion. The Continentals, on the right of the battalion, commanded by Captain W. Q. Loud, suddenly found themselves in range of and close quarters to artillery, as shells were singing through the woods directly over their heads. Still advancing as skirmishers, they saw on the road two pieces of artillery, supported by perhaps a small company of infantry, about one hundred yards from their advanced position in the woods. The command, "Rally," was given by Lieutenant William Pierce, commanding first platoon, and as the word was passed along by the sergeants all within hearing jumped to the command, and as "Forward, charge!" was given, in a minute the gallant Confederates had forced back the Federals and had possession of the guns, Lieutenant Pierce striking one of them with his sword, proclaiming the right of the battalion to have *cross-cannon* at last on its beloved flag. Although the battalion, as was just and correct, participated in and enjoyed the proud honors of the capture, it will cause no feeling of envy among the members of Company B living to-day to give the exclusive credit of the capture of those guns to the first platoon of the Continental Guards. The Federals, seeing how few were the numbers of the foe who had driven them from their guns, rallied, advanced, and fired a volley into the victorious Confederates, who were still surrounding the pieces. Three men were wounded by the volley, among them Lieutenant William Pierce, whose leg was so badly shattered that amputation was necessary. The boys in gray retired to the first line of trees, leaving their lieutenant under the guns, surrounded by the boys in blue. It was for a short moment only: a volley which killed three and wounded more of the Federals, a yell and a charge, and the lieutenant's comrades again had possession of the guns, and soon were carrying him and dragging the guns to the rear, making the captured Federals assist in both duties. The advancing brigade was more than a quarter of a mile from where the guns were captured. It is very doubtful whether the history of the war will record a similar capture of artillery supported by infantry, disclosed suddenly by an advance-line of skirmishers who unhesitatingly charged, took possession of, and carried to the rear the guns. One would have supposed that Lieutenant Pierce, having suffered amputation of a leg, might have rested upon laurels won so gloriously. Ah, no! his gallant soul was yet undismayed. At the earliest possible moment he returned to his command, there receiving a rich recompense for past suffering. Imagine his great pride and satisfaction when, following his comrades to the quarters of the gallant Major Ned Austin, he was shown the battalion flag with its "honored and honorable" cross-cannon liberally displayed.

The survivors of the Continental Guards, returning to New Orleans after the war, have clung together like true brothers, retaining their military organization and the name they bore so gallantly. Of the veterans, not many remain; these are known and revered by all. Captain Pierce is fondly beloved and highly respected by his former command, as well as by the younger members of the company, who, having "fallen in" to fill up the ranks which time and death have decimated, are striving nobly to uphold the name and fame of the Continentals. Under the command of a gallant gentleman and excellent executive officer, the new Continentals have guarded and kept ever fresh the laurels won by their predecessors, adding an exceptional record of their own, both military and civic. Upon all patriotic occasions the *veterans* appear and march with the company. Our veteran companies are the pride and glory of New

Orleans. Citizens never tire of viewing the beautiful uniform and the martial step of the Continental Guards. And who can look upon Captain Pierce, bearing his trusty sword, keeping step equally well, whether he wears a finely-formed cork leg or stumps along on his favorite wooden one,—his bearing as proud as the proudest, his heroic soul looking gloriously forth from its undimmed windows,—and fail to remember proudly the young lieutenant who fell under the enemy's gun at Chickamauga? Or who can listen unmoved to the music of the cannon which so often woke the morning echoes upon the bloodiest battle-field of the war? A parade of the Washington Artillery is, indeed, a glorious and inspiriting sight. Here they come, gayly caparisoned, perfect in every detail of military equipment, led by elegant officers who may well ride proudly, for each is a true soldier and a hero. Scarcely less distinguished, save for the plainer uniform, are the rank and file that follow. Can these be the same men whom history delights to honor,—the heroes of a hundred battle-fields,—both in the army of Virginia and Tennessee, who, stripped to the waist, blackened with powder and smoke, bloody with streaming wounds, still stood to their guns, and, in answer to the enemy, thundered forth their defiant motto, " *Come and take us!*" And now—who more peaceful, who more public-spirited, who more kind in word and deed? Of the Virginia detachment I knew little except their splendid record. From the fifth company I frequently received patients during my service with the Army of Tennessee, for, like their comrades of Virginia, they seemed to be in every battle, and in the thick of it. In fact, New Orleans and the whole State of Louisiana, like every city and State in the South, are peopled with veterans and heroes. In comparatively few cases have military

organizations been kept up. Other duties engross the
late Confederates, of whom it may be truly said their
record of citizenship is as excellent as their war record.
If to any reader it occurs that I seem to be doing particular justice to New Orleans troops, I will say, let the
feeling which arises in your own breast regarding your
"very own" plead *for me.* Remember that my husband
was one of the famous Dreux Battalion, and afterwards
of Gibson's Brigade, also that Louisianians were exiles,
and that love of our home, with sorrow and indignation
on account of her humiliation and chains, drew us very
close together. But aside from this natural feeling
there was no shadow of difference in my ministration
or in the affection I bore towards all " my boys."

There was not a single Southern State unrepresented
among the bleeding victims of Chickamauga. From
that hardly-contested field, as from many others, a rich
harvest of glory has been reaped and garnered until
the treasure-houses of history are full to overflowing.
Glowing accounts of the splendid deeds of this or that
division, brigade, regiment, company, have immortalized
the names of—*their officers.* And what of the unfaltering *followers*, whose valor supported their brave leaders
and helped to *create* many a splendid record? Here lay
the shattered remnants, each ghastly wound telling its
own story of personal bravery. The fiery sons of
South Carolina, unsubdued by the perils they had
passed, unmindful of their gaping wounds, as ready
then to do and dare as when they threw down the
gauntlet of defiance and stood ready to defend the
sovereignty of their State. The men who followed
where the gallant Forrest led, "looking the warrior
in love with his work." The devoted patriots who
charged with Breckenridge. The tall, soldierly Tennesseeans, of whom their commander said, when asked

if he could take and hold a position of transcendent danger, "Give me my Tennesseeans, and *I'll take and hold anything;*" the determined, ever-ready Texans, who, under the immortal Terry, so distinguished themselves, and under other leaders in every battle of the war won undying laurels; North Carolinians, of whose courage in battle I needed no better proof than the pluck they invariably showed under the torture of fevered wounds or of the surgeon's knife; exiled Kentuckians, Arkansians, Georgians, Louisianians, Missourians, Marylanders, sternly resentful, and impatient of the wounds that kept them from the battle-field, because ever hoping to strike some blow that should sever a link in the chains which bound the homes they so loved; Alabamians, the number of whose regiments, as well as *their frequent consolidation,* spoke volumes for their splendid service; Georgians, who, having fought with desperate valor, now lay suffering and dying within the confines of their own State, yet unable to reach the loved ones who, unknowing what their fate might be, awaited with trembling hearts accounts of the battle, so slow in reaching them; Mississippians, of whom I have often heard it said, "their fighting and *staying qualities* were *magnificent.*" I then knew hundreds of instances of individual valor, of which my remembrance is now so dim that I dare not give names or dates. I am proud, however, to record the names of four soldiers belonging to the Seventeenth Mississippi Regiment: J. Wm. Flynn,* then a mere lad, but whose record will compare with the brightest; Samuel Frank, quartermaster; Maurice Bernhiem, quartermaster-sergeant, and Auerbach, the drummer of the regiment. I was proudly told by a member of Company G, Seventeenth Missis-

---

* Mr. Flynn is now pastor in charge of a Presbyterian Church in New Orleans, and is as faithful a soldier of the cross as once of the lost cause.

sippi, that Sam Frank, although excelling in every duty
of his position, was exceeding brave, often earnestly
asking permission to lead the skirmishers, and would
shoulder a musket sooner than stay out of the fight.
Maurice Bernhiem, quartermaster-sergeant, was also
brave as the bravest. Whenever it was possible he also
would join the ranks and fight as desperately as any
soldier. Both men were exempt from field-service.
Auerbach, the drummer of the Seventeenth, was also a
model soldier, always at his post. On the longest
marches, in the fiercest battles, whatever signal the
commanding officer wished to have transmitted by means
of the drum, night or day, amid the smoke of battle or
the dust of the march, Auerbach was always on hand.
The members of the Seventeenth declared that they
could never forget the figure of the small Jewish drummer, his little cap shining out here and there amid the
thick smoke and under a rattling fire. Before taking
leave of this splendid regiment, I will give an incident
of the battle of Knoxville, also related to me by one of
its members.

By some mismanagement, Longstreet's corps had no
scaling-ladders, and had to cut their way up the wall of
the entrenchment by bayonets, digging out step after
step under a shower of hot water, stones, shot, axes, etc.
Some of the men actually got to the top, and, reaching
over, dragged the enemy over the walls. General Hum-
phrey's brigade had practically taken the fort. Their
flag was flying from the walls, about a hundred men
having reached the top, where the color-bearer had
planted his flag, when the staff was shot off about an
inch above his hand. The men were so mad at losing
the flag, that they seized the shells with fuses burning
and hurled them back upon the enemy. Some of the
members of this gallant regiment were among the hun-

dreds equally brave who, after the battle of Chickamauga, became my patients. Scattered all through the
wards were dozens of Irishmen, whose awful wounds
scarcely sufficed to keep them in bed, so impatient were
they of restraint, and especially of inactivity,—so eager
to be at the front. Ever since the war I have kept in
my heart a place sacred to these generous exiles, who,
in the very earliest days of the Confederacy, flocked by
thousands to her standard, *wearing the gray as if it had
been the green*, giving in defence of the land of their
adoption the might of stalwart arms, unfaltering courage,
and the earnest devotion of hearts glad thus to give
expression to the love of liberty and hatred of oppression
which filled them. As Confederate soldiers they made
records unsurpassed by any, but they never forgot that
they were Irishmen, and bound to keep up the name
and fame of Old Ireland. So, company after company,
composing many regiments, appeared on fields of glory
bearing names dear to every Irish heart,—names which
they meant to immortalize, *and did.*

That I should be permitted to serve all these heroes,
to live among them, to minister to them, seemed to me
a blessing beyond estimation. Strange to say, although
my toil increased and the horror deepened, my health
did not suffer. After days and nights of immeasurable
fatigue, a few hours of sleep would quite restore me,
and I dared to believe that the supporting rod and staff
was given of God.

It now became very difficult to obtain food either
suitable or sufficient. The beef was horrible. Upon
two occasions rations of mule meat were issued, and
eaten with the only sauce which could have rendered
it possible to swallow the rank, coarse-grained meat,—
i.e., the ravenous hunger of wounded and convalescent
men. Meal was musty, flour impossible to be procured.

All the more delicate food began to fail utterly. A few weeks after the battle, Dr. S. M. Bemiss was ordered to Newnan, Georgia, to arrange for the removal of the hospital "post." We were, therefore, expecting a change of location, but quite unprepared for the suddenness of the order, or the haste and confusion that ensued. The *upsetness* was so complete that it almost seemed to me an actual fulfilment of a mysterious prophecy or warning often uttered by old negroes to terrorize children into good behavior: "Better mind out dar: fust thing *you* knows you ain't gwine ter know nuffin'." Everything seemed to be going on at once. The ambulance-train, with a few baggage-cars attached, was even then at the depot. A hoarse, stifled whistle apprised us of the fact, and seemed to hurry our preparation. Dr. McAllister was *everywhere*, superintending the removal with the energy natural to him. In the court-house all was confusion. Boxes were hastily filled with bedding, clothing, etc., thrown in helter-skelter, hastily nailed up, and as hastily carted down to the train. Sick and awfully wounded men were hurriedly placed upon stretchers, and their bearers formed an endless procession to the rough cars (some of them lately used to transport cattle, and dreadfully filthy). Here they were placed upon straw mattresses, or plain straw, as it happened. No provisions were to be had except sides of rusty bacon and cold corn-bread. These were shovelled into carts and transferred to the floor of the cars in the same manner. There was no time to cook anything, and the chances were whether we would get off at all or not. Procuring a large caldron, I dumped into it remnants of the day's dinner,—a little soup, a few vegetables, and some mule meat. The stoves had all been taken down, but there was a little cold cornmeal coffee, some tea, and a small quantity of milk. This I put into buckets; then,

10

importuning the surgeon in charge until he was glad to get rid of me by assigning me a cart, I mounted into it with my provisions and jolted off to the cars, where hundreds of tortured, groaning men were lying. There I met Dr. Gore (for both hospitals were to be moved on the same train), who helped me to hide my treasures and to administer some weak milk punch to the sufferers. Meanwhile, the pine-wood fires kindled in the streets all around the hospitals made the town look as though it was on fire, and threw its weird light upon masses of soldiery,—cavalry, infantry, artillery,—moving in endless numbers through the town, shaking the very earth with the tramp of men and horses and the heavy rumble of wheels. The men were silent, and looked jaded and ghastly in the lurid light. Some had bloody rags tied about head and hands, their breasts were bare, the panting breath could be heard plainly, their eyes shone fiercely through the grime of powder and smoke. They had been fighting, and were now retreating; still they marched in solid column, nor broke ranks, nor lost step. The faces of the officers were grave and troubled; none seemed to observe our frantic haste, but all to look forward with unseeing eyes. I did so long to have them rest and refresh themselves. During the whole of that eventful night my cheeks were wet, my heart aching sadly. Before daylight we were off. Railroads at that time were very defective and very rough. Ah, how terrible was the suffering of those wounded men as they were jolted and shaken from side to side! for haste was necessary to escape the enemy. About noon the train came to a full stop, nor moved again for many, many hours,—hours fraught with intense suffering to the sick and wounded, as well as to all who shared the hardships of that journey. It was reported that the enemy were passing either to the right or left, I do not

remember which. Not a wheel must move, not a column of smoke arise; so, with the engine fires extin-
guished, the train stood motionless in the midst of a
barren pine forest. The small supply of cooked food
was soon exhausted, the ladies on the train assisting
to feed the wounded soldiers. All were parched with
thirst. The only water to be procured lay in ruts and
ditches by the roadside, and was filthy and fetid. So
the day passed. All through the night every one was
on the alert, listening intently for sounds that might
mean danger. No lights, no roadside fires could be
allowed; but the moon shone brightly, and by its light
the surgeons moved about among the suffering men,
whose groans, united with the plaintive sigh of the chill
wind through the pine forest, served to make night dismal indeed. In the intervals of attending upon the sick
we slept as we could, leaning up against boxes, tilted
back in chairs against the side of the car, or lying down,
with anything we could get for pillows. Some of the
surgeons and attendants bivouacked under the trees in
spite of the cold. In the morning we were hungry
enough to eat the stale corn-bread, and tried to like it,
but even of that there was very little, for the wounded
men were ravenous. Drs. Gore and Yates set themselves to whittle some "army-forks," or forked sticks,
and, cutting the bacon in thin slices, made little fires
which they carefully covered with large pans to keep
the smoke from arising. By these they toasted slices of
bacon. Ah, how delicious was the odor, how excellent
the taste! Several hands were set at this work, but it
was necessarily very slow. I remained among my own
patients, while my servant climbed in and out of the
car, bringing as much meat as she could get, which I
distributed while she returned for more. The wounded
men were clamorous for it, crying out, "Give it to us

raw ; we can't wait." This we were soon compelled to do, as it was feared the smoke might escape and betray us. I cannot now recollect by what means we received the welcome order to move on, but it came at last, and on the morning of the third day we reached Newnan, Georgia, where, after a few days' bustle and confusion, we were pleasantly settled and had fallen into the old routine, Dr. Bemiss having arranged not only for excellent quarters but for fresh supplies of rations and hospital stores.

CHAPTER V.

Just here Memory lays a restraining hand upon my own. Turning to meet her gaze, it pleads with me to linger a while in this sweet and pleasant spot, peopled with familiar forms, and kindly faces, well-beloved in the past, fondly greeted once again. Ah, how closely our little band clung together, how enduring were the ties that bound us! Ignoring the shadow, seeking always to stand in the sunshine, we welcomed with yet unshaken faith the heavenly guest who stood in our midst, turning upon us almost for the last time an unclouded face, and eyes undimmed by doubt or pain,—the angel of Hope.

The ladies of Newnan were truly loyal, and in spite of the fact that the whole town was converted into hospitals, and every eligible place filled with sick, murmured not, but strove in every way to add to their comfort. I wish I could place every one before my readers to receive the meed of praise she so richly deserves; only a few, *very few*, names now occur to me. The hospitable mansion of Judge Ray was a complete rendezvous for convalescent soldiers; also the homes of Mrs. McKinstry and Mrs. Morgan. The latter was one of the most beautiful women I ever saw. Dr. Gore used to say, "She is just *plum pretty*." She was a perfect blonde, with a small head "running over" with short, golden curls. The Misses Ray were brunettes, very handsome and stately. Their brothers were in the army. Judge Ray never allowed his daughters to visit the hospitals, but atoned for that by unbounded hospitality. Mrs.

McKinstry was a constant visitor to the hospitals, and had her house full of sick soldiers. Only one church in the town was left vacant in which to hold services. Rev. R. A. Holland, then a young, enthusiastic Methodist minister, and a chaplain in the army, remained for some time in Newnan, holding meetings which were largely attended. Dr. Holland was long after the war converted to the Episcopal faith, and called to Trinity Church, New Orleans. The bishops and ministers of the Protestant Episcopal Church also held frequent services, and often Catholic priests came among the sick, who greatly valued their holy ministration. Through the kindness of a friend, an ownerless piano found in one of the stores was moved to my room, and, although not a good one, contributed largely to the pleasure of the soldiers, also serving for sacred music when needed. Mr. Blandner's lute, my piano, and Mrs. Gamble's soprano voice, joined to that of a Confederate tenor or bass, or my own contralto, made delicious music. Concerts, tableaux, plays, etc., were also given for the benefit of refugees or to raise money to send boxes to the front: at all these I assisted, but had no time for rehearsals, etc. I could only run over and sing my song or songs and then run back to my patients. Some money was realized, but the entertainments were never a great financial success, because all soldiers were invited guests. Still, some good was always accomplished. These amusements were greatly encouraged by physicians and others, as safety-valves to relieve the high-pressure of excitement, uncertainty, and dread which were characteristic of the time. I was always counted in, but seldom, *very* seldom, accepted an invitation, for it seemed to me like unfaithfulness to the memory of the gallant dead, and a mockery of the suffering in our midst. I could not rid myself of this feeling, and can truly say that during those fateful years, from the time when in Richmond the "starvation parties" were organized, until the end, I never found a suitable time to dance or a time to laugh or a time to make merry.

My own special kitchen (an immense wareroom at the back of the store, which was used for a distributing-room) was in Newnan well fitted up. A cavernous fireplace, well supplied with big pots, little pots, bake-ovens, and stew-pans, was supplemented by a cooking-stove of good size. A large brick oven was built in the yard close by, and two professional bakers, with their assistants, were kept busy baking for the whole post. There happened to be a back entrance to this kitchen, and although the convalescents were not allowed inside, many were the interviews held at said door upon subjects of vital importance to the poor fellows who had walked far into the country to obtain coveted dainties which they wanted to have cooked "like my folks at home fix it up." They were never refused, and sometimes a dozen different "messes" were set off to await claimants,— potato-pones, cracklin bread, apple-pies, blackberry-pies, squirrels, birds, and often *chickens.* For a long time the amount of chickens brought in by "the boys" puzzled me. They had little or no money, and chickens were always high-priced. I had often noticed that the men in the wards were busy preparing *fish-hooks,* and yet, though they often "went fishing," they brought no fish to be cooked. One day the mystery was fully solved. An irate old lady called upon Dr. McAllister, holding at the end of a string a fine, large chicken, and vociferously proclaiming her wrongs. "I *knowed* I'd ketch 'em: I *knowed* it. Jes' look a-here," and she drew up the chicken, opened its mouth, and showed the butt of a fish-hook it had swallowed. Upon further examination, it was found that the hook had been baited with a kernel of corn. "I've been noticin' a powerful disturbance among my fowls, an' every onct in while one of 'em would go over the fence like litenin' and I couldn't see what went with it. This mornin' I jes' sot down under the fence an' watched, and the fust thing I seed was a line flyin' over the fence right peert, an' as soon as it struck the ground the chickens all went for it, an' this yer fool chicken up and swallered it. Now, I'm a lone woman, an' my chickens an' my truck-patch is my livin', and *I ain't gwine to stan' no sich!*" The convalescents, attracted by the shrill, angry voice, gathered around. Their innocent surprise, and the wonder with which they examined the baited fish-hook and *sympathized with the old lady,* almost upset the gravity of the "sturgeons," as the old body called the doctors.

There was one dry-goods store still kept open in New-nan, but few ladies had the inclination or the means to go shopping. The cotton lying idle all over the South was then to a certain extent utilized. Everything the men wore was dyed and woven at home: pants were either butternut, blue, or light purple, occasionally light yellow; shirts, coarse, but snowy white, or what would now be called *cream.* Everybody knitted socks. Ladies, negro women, girls, and even little boys, learned to knit. Each tried to get ahead as to number and quality. Ladies' stockings were also knitted of all grades from stout and thick to gossamer or open-work, etc. Home-spun dresses were proudly worn, and it became a matter of constant experiment and great pride to improve the quality and vary colors. Warp and woof were finely spun, and beautiful combinations of colors ventured upon, although older heads eschewed them, and in con-sequence complacently wore their clean, smoothly-ironed gray, "pepper-and-salt," or brown homespuns long after the gayer ones had been faded by sun or water and had to be "dipped." Hats and bonnets of all sorts and sizes were made of straw or palmetto, and trimmed with the same. Most of them bore cockades of bright red and white (the "red, white, and red"), fashioned of strips knitted to resemble ribbons. Some used emblems denoting the State or city of the wearer, others a small Confederate battle-flag. Young faces framed in these pretty hats, or looking out from under a broad-brim, appeared doubly bewitching. Ladies worked early and late, first upon the fabric, and then upon beautifully-stitched homespun shirts, intended as gifts to favorite heroes returning to the front. During the winter nights the light of pine-knot fires had sufficed, but now Confederate candles were used. It did seem as if the bees were Southern sympathizers, and more faithfully than usual "improved each shining hour." The wax thus obtained was melted in large kettles, and yards of rags torn into strips and sewn together, then twisted to the size of lamp-wicks, were dipped into the liquid wax, cooled, and dipped again and again until of the right size. These yards of waxed rags were wound around a corncob or a bottle, then clipped, leaving about two yards "closely wound" to each candle. One end was left loose to light, and—here you have the recipe for Confederate candles.

When I came through the lines I was refused permission to bring any baggage; therefore my supply of clothing was exceedingly small. I had, however, some gold concealed about my person, and fortunately procured with it a plain wardrobe. This I had carefully treasured, but now it was rapidly diminishing. At least I must have *one* new dress. It was bought,—a simple calico, and not of extra quality. The cost was *three hundred dollars!* With the exception of a plain muslin bought the following summer for three hundred and fifty dollars, it was my only indulgence in the extravagance of dress during the whole war. Two pretty gray homespuns made in Alabama were my standbys.

A good-sized store had been assigned to me as a linen room and office. The linen room, standing upon the street, was very large, and shelved all around, a counter on one side, and otherwise furnished with splint chairs and boxes to sit upon. My sanctum lay behind it, and here my sick and convalescent boys came frequently, and dearly loved to come, to rest upon the lounge or upon my rocking-chair, to read, to eat nice little lunches, and often to write letters. The front room was the rendezvous of the surgeons. In the morning they came to consult me about diet-lists or to talk to each other. In the evening the promenade of the ladies generally ended here, the surgeons always came, and I am proud to say that a circle composed of more cultivated, refined gentlemen and ladies could not be found than those who met in the rough linen-room of the Buckner Hospital. Dr. McAllister often looked in, but only for a few moments. He was devoted to his business as surgeon in charge of a large hospital. The multifarious duties of the position occupied him exclusively. He was a superb executive officer: nothing escaped his keen observation. No wrong remained unredressed, no recreant found an instant's toleration. He was ever restless, and not at all given to the amenities of life or to social intercourse, but fond of spending his leisure moments at his own temporary home, which a devoted wife made to him a paradise. His manners to strangers were very stiff; his friendship, once gained, was earnest and unchangeable. Dr. Gamble, surgeon of the post, was an urbane, kindly gentleman. Business claimed his entire time also, and he was seldom seen outside of his office. The ladies of our little circle have been already mentioned, as well as most of the surgeons. Dr. Bemiss, of all others, was a general favorite. We did not see much of him, as he was a very busy man; but at least once a day he would find his way to the rendezvous, often looking in at the window as he "halted" outside for a little chat. Invariably the whole party brightened up at his coming. He was so genial, so witty, so sympathetic, so entirely *en rapport* with everybody. A casual occurrence, a little discussion involving, perhaps, a cunning attempt to enlist him on one side or the other, would prove the key to unlock a fund of anecdotes, repartee, *bon-mots*, and, best of all, *word-pictures*, for here Dr. Bemiss excelled every one I ever knew. My own relations with him were very pleasant, for he was my adviser and helper in using properly the Louisiana and Alabama funds. The friendship between Drs. Bemiss and Gore seemed almost like that of Damon and Pythias. I think that Dr. Bemiss was first surgeon in charge of the "Bragg," but when a larger field was assigned to him Dr. Gore succeeded, Dr. Bemiss still retaining in some way the position of superior officer. Both these men were eminent surgeons and physicians, possessing in a remarkable degree the subtle comprehension and sympathy which is so valuable a quality in a physician. The tie that bound these two embraced a third, apparently as incongruous as possible, —Dr. Benjamin Wible, also of Louisville, a former partner of Dr. Bemiss. Diogenes we used to call him, and he did his best to deserve the name.

His countenance was forbidding, except when lighted up by a smile, which was only upon rare occasions. He was intolerant of what he called "stuff and nonsense," and had a way of disconcerting people by *grunting* whenever anything like sentimentality or *gush* was uttered in his presence.

When he first came, his stern, dictatorial manner,

together with the persistent coldness which resisted all
attempts to be friendly and sociable, hurt and offended
me; but he was so different when among the sick, so
gentle, so benignant beside the bedsides of suffering men,
that I soon learned to know and appreciate the royal
heart which at other times he managed to conceal under
,a rough and forbidding exterior.

Dr. Archer, of Maryland, was as complete a contrast
as could be imagined. A poet of no mean order, in-
dulging in all the idiosyncrasies of a poet, he was yet
a man of great nerve and an excellent surgeon. Always
dressed with *careful* negligence, his hands beautifully
white, his beard unshorn, his auburn hair floating over
his uniformed shoulders in long ringlets, soft in speech,
so very deferential to ladies as to seem almost lover-
like, he was, nevertheless, very manly. Quite a cavalier
one could look up to and respect. At first I thought
him effeminate, and did not like him, but his tender ways
with my sick boys, the efficacy of his prescriptions, and
his careful orders as to diet quite won me over. Our
friendship lasted until the end of my service in the
Buckner Hospital, since which I have never seen him.
Another complete contrast to Diogenes was Dr. Conway, of Virginia, our *Chesterfield*. His perfect manners
and courtly observance of the smallest requirements of
good breeding and etiquette made us feel quite as if we
were lord and ladies. Dr. Conway had a way of con-
veying subtle indefinable flattery which was very elevating to one's self-esteem. Others enjoyed it in full, but
often, just as our Chesterfield had interviewed *me*, infus-
ing even into the homely subject of diet-lists much that
was calculated to puff up my vanity, in would stalk
Diogenes, who never failed to bring me to a realizing
sense of the hollowness of it all. Dr. Hughes was a
venerable and excellent gentleman, who constituted him-

self my mentor.· He never failed to drop in every day, being always ready to smooth tangled threads for me. He was forever protesting against the habit I had contracted in Richmond, and never afterwards relinquished, of remaining late by the bedside of dying patients, or going to the wards whenever summoned at night. He would say,."Daughter, it is not *right*, it is not *safe;* not only do you risk contagion by breathing the foul air of the wards at night, but some of these soldiers are mighty rough and might not always justify your confidence in them." But I would not listen. My firm belief in the honor of "my boys" and in their true and chivalrous devotion towards myself caused me to trust them utterly at all times and places. I can truly say that *never* during the whole four years of the war was that trust disturbed by even the roughest man of them all, although I was often placed in very trying circumstances, many times being entirely dependent upon their protection and care, *which never failed me.* So I used to set at naught the well-meant counsels of my kindly old friend, to laugh at his lugubrious countenance and the portentous shaking of his silvery head. We remained firm friends, however, and, though my dear old mentor has long since passed away, I still revere his memory. Dr. Yates was an ideal Texan, brave, determined, plain, and straightforward, either a warm, true friend or an uncompromising enemy. He wished to be at the front, and was never satisfied with hospital duties. Mrs. Yates was a favorite with all. Dr. Jackson, of Alabama, in charge of the officers' quarters, performed some miracles in the way of surgical operation. He was a great favorite with his patients, who complained bitterly because they were so often deprived of his services for a time, when his skilful surgery was needed at the front. Besides these were Drs. Devine, Ruell, Estell,

Baruch, Frost, Carmichael, Welford, and Griffith, none of whom I knew particularly well.

    *   *   *   *   *   *   *

Meantime, the wounded of several battles had filled and crowded the wards. As before, every train came in freighted with human misery. In the Buckner Hospital alone there were nearly a thousand beds, tenanted by every conceivable form of suffering.

An ambulance-train arrived one night, bringing an unusually large number of sick and wounded men, whose piteous moans filled the air as they were brought up the hill on "stretchers" or alighted at the door of the hospital from ambulances, which, jolting over the rough, country road, had tortured them inexpressibly.

Occasionally a scream of agony would arise, but more frequently suppressed groans bespoke strong men's suffering manfully borne. In the ward where those badly wounded were placed, there was so much to be done, that morning found the work unfinished.

It was, therefore, later than usual when I found time to pay my usual morning visits to other wards.

Upon entering Ward No. 4, my attention was attracted by a new patient, who lay propped up on one of the bunks near a window. He was a mere lad (perhaps twenty). His eyes, as they met mine, expressed so plainly a sense of captivity and extreme dislike of it that I felt very sorry for him. He had been dressed in a clean hospital shirt, but one shoulder and arm was bare and bandaged, for he was wounded in the left shoulder,—a slight wound, but sufficient to occasion severe pain and fever.

At first I did not approach him, but his eyes followed me as I paused by each bed to ascertain the needs of the sick and to bestow particular care in many cases.

At last I stood by his side, and, placing my hand upon his head, spoke to him. He moved uneasily, seemingly trying to repress the quivering of his lip and the tears that, nevertheless, would come. Not wishing to notice his emotion just then, I called the nurse, and, by way of diversion, gave a few trifling directions, then passed on to another ward.

Returning later, bringing some cooling drink and a bottle of Confederate bay-water (vinegar), I gave him to drink and proceeded to sponge off his head and hands. He submitted, as it seemed at first, unwillingly, but just as I turned to leave him he suddenly seized my hand, kissed it, and laid his burning cheek upon it. From that moment I was eagerly welcomed by him whenever I appeared among the sick.

When he began to mend and was allowed to talk freely, I learned his name, Charley Percy, that he was a native of Bayou Sara, Louisiana, and a member of the fifth company of Washington Artillery, Captain Slocomb commanding. He had been wounded at Resaca. I grew to love him dearly. As soon as he was permitted to leave his bed he became averse to remaining in the ward, and most of his waking hours were spent in the little room which was specially allotted to me. Whenever I returned after my rounds among the sick it was a certainty that the glad, bright presence awaited me, and that many little plans for my rest and comfort would make the rough place homelike.

He became to me like a dear young brother, devoted and ever-thoughtful. The matron's room at the hospital was called very often " Soldiers' Rest," and sometimes " The Promised Land," because many soldiers came there every day, and those newly convalescent made it a goal which they aspired to reach as soon as permitted.

This habit gave me an opportunity to use properly what might have been sent in boxes which arrived frequently from different quarters, filled with a variety of goodies, but in quantities entirely insufficient to supply all the soldiers. A sangaree or any other delicacy, taken while resting after a walk which taxed the weakened energies to the utmost, or a meal served outside the fevered air of the wards, did more to build up the strength than any amount of medicine could have done. As there never was, by any chance, a supply of these things for one thousand men (the usual number assigned to Buckner Hospital), delicacies (already becoming scarce) were served only to the very sick or to convalescents.

It was beautiful to see how young Percy delighted to assist in waiting on these visitors to " The Soldiers' Rest," —how his sprightliness pleased and amused them. His own great embarrassment seemed to be that he had lost all his clothes at the time he was wounded, so was compelled to wear the unbleached shirts with blue cottonade collars and cuffs, which were supplied to all patients, numbered to correspond with the bunks. These he called State's prison uniform. One day, however, Dr. Fenner from New Orleans, Louisiana, paid a visit to Buckner Hospital (then located at Newnan, Georgia), leaving with me two large boxes of clothing and stores for the Louisiana soldiers. Percy assisted to unpack these boxes, soon finding himself amply provided with underclothing and a nice jacket and pants of gray, also a new blanket. He was pleased, but not yet quite satisfied, for the jacket was simply gray. He wanted it trimmed with red.

It chanced that there was in one of the boxes a piece of red flannel. With this I trimmed the suit under his careful supervision. I can never forget how happy he was to get into this suit, or how he danced around me, pretending to go through the artillery drill, and to load and fire at imaginary Yankees.

Later, his cap was retrimmed, the letters and artillery badge furbished up, and one beautiful day was made sad and gloomy to his friends and myself by the departure of this brave, dear boy, to rejoin his command.

Eager, bright, full of fire and ardor, the young soldier went to meet his doom. He reached the front (where the company to which he belonged was always to be found) shortly before the battle of Peach-tree Creek, and here, his bright young face turned to the foe, his eager hands serving his gun to the last, he met a soldier's death.

Alas! poor Percy, his fate seemed hard; yet, while sincerely grieving, I remembered with some degree of comfort the fact that so he had wished to die,—" Upon the field of glory."

There came to the hospital at the same time with young Percy an intimate friend and comrade of his, whose name and the circumstances of his death were preserved in a diary kept by me, but which, with all my papers, fell into the hands of the enemy subsequently. This poor fellow had pneumonia, which soon developed into typhoid. He was delirious when brought in and never regained consciousness. Vainly I strove to soothe him, stroking back the long, straight hair, black as a raven's wing, vainly trying to close the magnificent black eyes, which forever stared into space, while the plaintive voice repeated ceaselessly, " *Viens à moi, oh, ma mère,*" and thus he moaned and moaned until at last the white eyelids drooped beneath the gaze of Death, and the finger of eternal silence was laid upon the fevered lips.

Of course Percy was not told how his friend died until long afterward, when his questions could no longer be

11*

evaded.　He was deeply moved, crying out, "*I* don't want to die like that.　If I must die during this war, I hope I shall be instantly killed upon the battle-field."　This wish was granted.

He sleeps in a soldier's grave.　In the light of eternity the sad mystery which still shadows the hearts of those who live to mourn the holy cause—loved and lost—exists no more for him.

Besides the "Buckner," there were the "Bragg" and two more hospitals, the names of which I have forgotten, one presided over by two gentle ladies,—Mrs. Harrison and Mrs. ——, of Florida,—whose devotion and self-sacrifice, as well as their lovely Christian character and perfect manners, made them well-beloved by everybody at the post.　Mrs. Harrison was a zealous Episcopalian.　Through her influence and correspondence frequent services were held in Newnan.　We several times enjoyed the ministrations of Bishops Quintard, Beckwith, and Wilmer.　The large number of wounded men, and the fearful character of their wounds, made skill and devotion on the part of the surgeons of the greatest importance.　These conditions were well fulfilled, and aided by the healthy locality "and" (during the first few months) "the excellent possibilities open to our foragers," many a poor fellow struggled back to comparative health.　I was particularly fortunate while in Newnan in having at my command supplies of clothing and money from both Louisiana and Alabama.　This, with the aid of my own wages, which, although I had refused to receive them, had accumulated and been placed to my account, and which I now drew, gave me excellent facilities for providing comforts, not only for the sick, but for the braves at the front, whose rations were growing "small by degrees and beautifully less."　Upon two occasions I received visits from the venerable

Dr Fenner, of Louisiana, and his colleague, Mr. Collins. Each time they left money and clothing, giving me large discretionary powers, although specifying that, as the money was supplied by Louisianians, the soldiers from that State should be first considered. Through Mr. Peter Hamilton, of Mobile, Alabama, I also received boxes of clothing and delicacies, and, upon two occasions, six hundred dollars in money, with the request, "Of course, help our boys *first*, but in *any case* where sufferings or need exist, use your own judgment." As there were hundreds entirely cut off from home, actually suffering from want of clothing, sometimes needing a little good wine or extra food, I found many occasions where it seemed to me right to use this discretionary power, especially during visits to the front, which I was called upon to make about this time, first to my husband and his comrades in Kingston and Dalton, later to Macon to look up some Louisiana and Alabama soldiers, and lastly to Atlanta, where my husband and many other friends lay in the trenches. (Of these experiences more hereafter.)

Mrs. Harrison, Mrs. Gamble, myself, and one or two others were the only Episcopalians among the ladies of the Post, but the services were attended by soldiers, both officers and privates. Mrs. Gamble, of course, led the choir. We could always find bassos and tenors. I sang alto. The music was really good. The death of Bishop Polk was a great grief to everybody, especially to the faithful few among us who revered him as a minister of The Church. Even while saying to ourselves and to each other " God knows best," we could not at once stifle the bitterness of grief, for it seemed as if a mighty bulwark had been swept away. I had known Bishop Polk as a faithful and loving shepherd of souls, feeding his flock in green pastures, tenderly leading the weary and grief-stricken ones beside the waters of comfort. But when the peaceful fold was invaded, when threatening howls were arising on every side,—casting aside for a time the garb of a shepherd, he sallied forth, using valorously his trusty sword, opposing to the advance of the foe his own faithful breast, never faltering until slain by the horrid fangs which greedily fastened themselves deep in his heart. As I have already mentioned, I made during the winter and spring several visits to the front. At one time my husband, a member of Fenner's Louisiana Battery, was with his command in winter quarters at Kingston, whither I went to pay a visit and to inquire after the needs of the "boys." My little son (who had by this time joined me at Newnan) accompanied me. Kingston was at this time a bleak, dismal-looking place. I stopped at a large, barn-like hotel, from the gallery of which, while sitting with visitors from camp, I witnessed an arrival of Georgia militia, whose disembarkation from a train in front of the hotel was met by a noisy demonstration. They were a strange-looking set of men, but had "store clothes," warm wraps, sometimes tall hats, in all cases *good ones.* This, with the air of superiority they affected, was enough to provoke the fun-loving propensities of the ragged, rough-looking veterans who had collected to watch for the arrival of the train. As the shaking, rickety cars passed out of sight, these raw troops walked up to the hotel and there strode up and down, assuming supreme indifference to the storm of raillery which assailed them. Of course my sympathies were with the veterans, and I laughed heartily at their pranks. One of the first to set the ball in motion was a tall, athletic-looking soldier clad in jeans pants, with a faded red stripe adorning one leg only, ragged shoes tied up with twine strings, and a flannel shirt which undoubtedly had been washed by the

Confederate military process (*i.e.*, tied by a string to a
bush on the bank of a stream, allowed to lie in the water
awhile, then stirred about with a stick or beat upon a
rock, and hung up to drip and dry upon the nearest
bush or tied to the swaying limb of a tree). "A shocking bad hat" of the slouch order completed his costume.
Approaching a tall specimen of "melish," who wore a new
homespun suit of "butternut jeans," a gorgeous cravat,
etc., the soldier opened his arms and cried out in intense
accents, "*Let* me kiss him for his mother!" Another
was desired to "come out of that hat." A big veteran,
laying his hand on the shoulder of a small, scared-looking,
little victim, and wiping his own eyes upon his old hat,
whined out, "I *say*, buddy, you didn't bring along no
sugar-teats, did you? I'm got a powerful hankerin'
atter some." An innocent-looking soldier would stop
suddenly before one of the new-comers neatly dressed,
peer closely at his shirt-front, renewing the scrutiny
again and again with increasing earnestness, then, striking an attitude, would cry out, "*Biled*, by Jove!" One,
with a stiff, thick, new overcoat, was met with the anxious inquiry, "Have you got plenty of *stuffing* in that
coat, about *here*" (with a hand spread over stomach
and heart), "because the Yankee bullets is mighty pene-
trating." Each new joke was hailed with shouts of
laughter and ear-piercing rebel yells, but at last the
"melish" was marched off and the frolic ended.

I received two invitations for the following day, one
to dine with the officers of Fenner's Louisiana Battery,
and one, which I accepted, from the soldiers of my husband's mess. About twelve o'clock the next morning
an ambulance stood before the door of the hotel. From
it descended a spruce-looking colored driver, who remarked, as he threw the reins over the mule's back,
"Don't nobody go foolin' wid dat da mule ontwill I comes

i

back. I jes gwine to step ober to de store yander 'bout
some biziness fur de cap'n. Dat mule he feel mity gaily
dis mornin'. Look like he jes tryin' hisseff when he fin'
nuffin' behin' him but dis amperlants (ambulance) stid ob
dem hebby guns." Off he went, leaving the mule standing without being tied, and looking an incarnation of
mischief. The road to camp was newly cleared and full
of stumps and ruts. As I stood upon the upper gallery
awaiting the return of our Jehu, our little boy, taking advantage of the extra fondness inspired in the heart of his
father by long absence, clamored to be lifted into the ambulance. This wish was gratified, his father intending to
take the reins and mount to the driver's seat, but before he
could do so the mule started off at headlong speed, with
Georgie's scared face looking out at the back, and perhaps
a dozen men and boys in hot pursuit. The mule went on
to camp, creating great alarm there. The child in some
miraculous manner rolled out at the back of the ambulance, and was picked up unhurt. This accident delayed matters a little, but in due time we arrived at the
village of log-huts, called "Camp," and, having paid
our respects to the officers, repaired to the hut of my
husband's mess. The dinner was already cooking outside. Inside on a rough shelf were piles of shining tin-
cups and plates, newly polished. The lower bunk had
been filled with new, *pine* straw, and made as soft as
possible by piling upon it all the blankets of the mess.
This formed the chair of state. Upon it were placed,
first, myself (the centre figure), on one side my husband, exempt from duty for the day, on the other my
little boy, who, far from appreciating the intended
honor, immediately "squirmed" down, and ran off on a
tour of investigation through the camp. The mess consisted of six men including my husband, of whom the
youngest was Lionel C. Levy, Jr., a mere boy, but a

splendid soldier, full of fun and nerve and dash. Then
there was my husband's bosom friend, J. Hollingsworth,
or Uncle Jake, as he was called by everybody. Of the
industrial pursuits of the mess, he was the leading spirit,
indeed, in every way his resources were unbounded. His
patience, carefulness, and pains-taking truly achieved
wonderful results in contriving and carrying into execution plans for the comfort of the mess. He always
carried an extra haversack, which contained everything
that could be thought of to meet contingencies or repair
the neglect of other people. He was a devoted patriot
and a contented, uncomplaining soldier; never sick,
always on duty, a thorough gentleman, kindly in im-
pulses and acts, but——well, yes, there was one spot upon
this sun,—he was a confirmed bachelor. He could face
the hottest fire upon the battle-field, but a party of
ladies—*never* with his own consent. Upon the day in
question, however, I was not only an invited guest, but
the wife of his messmate and friend. So, overcoming
his diffidence, he made himself very agreeable, and
meeting several times afterward during the war, under
circumstances which made pleasant intercourse just as
imperative, we became fast friends, and have remained
so to this day. John Sharkey, Miles Sharkey, and one
more, whose name I have forgotten, comprised, with
those mentioned above, the entire mess. The dinner
was excellent, better than many a more elegant and
plentiful repast of which I have partaken since the war.
All the rations of beef and pork were combined to make
a fricassee *à la camp*, the very small rations of flour being
mixed with the cornmeal to make a large, round loaf
of "stuff." These delectable dishes were both cooked
in bake-ovens outside the cabin. From cross-sticks,
arranged gypsy-fashion, swung an iron pot, in which
was prepared the cornmeal coffee, which, with "long

sweetening" (molasses) and without milk, composed the meal. In this well-arranged mess the work was so divided that each man had his day to cut all the wood, bring all the water, cook, wash dishes, and keep the cabin in order. So, on this occasion there was no confusion. All was accomplished with precision. In due time a piece of board was placed before me with my rations arranged upon it in a bright tin plate, my coffee being served in a gorgeous mug, which, I strongly suspect, had been borrowed for the occasion, having once been a shaving-mug. Dinner over, Lieutenant Cluverius called to escort me through the camp, and at the officers' quarters I met many old acquaintances. Upon inquiry, I found the boys in camp contented and entirely unwilling to receive any benefit from the fund placed in my hands. They had taken the chances of a soldier's life, and were quite willing to abide by them.

The terrible bumping which I had experienced while riding to camp, in the ambulance drawn by the "gaily mule," disinclined me for another ride. So, just at sunset, my husband and I, with our boy and one or two friends, walked through the piny woods to the hotel, whence I returned next day to Newnan. This was during the winter. Later, I made a second trip, this time to Macon, having been called upon to supply money to the family of an old soldier (deceased) who wanted to reach home. Wishing to investigate in person, I went to Macon. On the morning of my return, while passing through one of the hospitals, I met at the bedside of a Louisiana soldier a member of Fenner's Battery, John Augustin, of New Orleans. At the depot we met again, and the gentleman very kindly took charge of me. I was going to Newnan, he returning to camp. Delightful conversation beguiled the way. Among other subjects, poets and poetry were discussed

I told him of Dr. Archer, and a beautiful "Ode to Hygeia" composed by him, parts of which I remembered and repeated. Gradually I discovered that Mr. Augustin had an unfinished manuscript of his own with him, entitled "Doubt," and at last persuaded him to let me read it. Finding me interested, he yielded to my earnest request,—that he would send me all his poems in manuscript. In due time they came, and with them a dedication to myself, so gracefully conceived, so beautifully expressed, that I may be pardoned for inserting it here.

"L'ENVOI.

"TO MRS. FANNIE A. BEERS.

"To you, though known but yesterday, I trust
    These winged thoughts of mine.
Be not, I pray, too critically just,
    Rather be mercy thine!

"Nor think on reading my despairing rhymes
    That I am prone to sigh.
Poets, like children, weep and laugh at times,
    Without scarce knowing why!

"Thoughts tend to heaven, mine are weak and faint.
    Please help them up for me;
The sick and wounded bless you as a saint,
    In this my patron be;

"And as the sun when shining it appears
    On dripping rain awhile,
Make a bright rainbow of my fancy's tears
    With your condoling smile.
"KINGSTON February 23, 1864."

At the front, desultory fighting was always going on. Our army under General Johnston acting on the defensive, although retreating, contesting every step of the way, and from intrenched position, doing great

12

damage to the enemy. As the spring fairly opened,
our troops became more actively engaged. From the
skirmishes came to us many wounded. In May, the
battle of New Hope Church was fought. General Johnston, in his "Narrative," speaks of this as "the *affair* at
New Hope." Judging from my own knowledge of the
number of wounded who were sent to the rear, and
the desperate character of their wounds, I should say
it was a *very terrible* "affair." A great many officers
were wounded and all our wards were full. There
came to me some special friends from Fenner's Louisiana Battery, which was heavily engaged, losing several
men and nearly all the horses. Lieutenant Wat. Tyler
Cluverius, while standing on the top of the breastworks and turning towards his men to wave his sword,
was shot through both shoulders, a very painful wound,
but which the gallant young soldier made light of, pretending to be deeply mortified because "he had been
shot in the back." Although an exceptional soldier, he
was a most troublesome patient, because his strong
desire to return to his command made him restless and
dissatisfied, greatly retarding his recovery. Indeed,
he would not remain in bed or in his ward. A more
splendid-looking officer I never saw. Better still, under his jacket of gray there beat a heart instinct with
every virtue which belongs by nature to a Virginia
gentleman. With the ladies of the "post" he became a
prime favorite. So kind and attentive were they that
I gave myself little thought concerning him. He was
off and away in a wonderfully short time, for duty lay
at the front and the strongest attractions could not out-
weigh its claims.

W. T. Vaudry, also of Fenner's Louisiana Battery, was
by his own request sent to me. His wound was as painful as any that can be imagined. He had been struck

full in the pit of the stomach by a spent ball, and was completely doubled up. He had been left on the field for dead, and for some time it was feared that fatal internal injuries had been received. From the nature of the wound, a full examination could not be made at first. Speedy relief was quite impossible. Even the loss of a limb or the most severe flesh-wound would have caused less intense agony. Courage and endurance equally distinguish the true soldier: the one distinction was his already, the other he now nobly won during days of exquisite torture. I little thought as I bent over him day after day, bathing the fevered brow, meeting with sorrowful sympathy the eyes dim with anguish, that in this suffering *boy* I beheld one of the future deliverers of an outraged and oppressed people. The officers' ward was delightfully situated on the corner of the main street. Its many windows commanded a pleasant view of a beautiful shaded square in the midst of which stood the brick court-house (now filled with sick, and pertaining to the Bragg Hospital). The windows on the side street gave a view far up the street, becoming a post of observation for the gallant young officers within, who invariably arranged themselves here "*for inspection,*" at the usual hour for the ladies' promenade, looking as became interesting invalids, returning with becoming languor the glances of bright eyes in which shone the pity which we are told is "akin to love." Later these knights being permitted to join in the promenade, made the very most of their helplessness, enjoying hugely the necessary ministrations so simply and kindly given. Among these officers were two whose condition excited my most profound sympathy as well as required special care. Both were exiles; both badly wounded. One, indeed, bore a wound so terrible that even though I looked upon it every day, I could never behold it without a shudder. From a little above the knee to the toes the mechanism of the leg was entirely exposed, except upon the heel, which always rested in a suspensory bandage lifted above the level of the bed upon which he rested. Every particle of the flesh had sloughed off, and the leg began to heal not "by first intention" but by unhealthy granulations like excrescences. These had constantly to be removed, either by the use of nitric acid (I believe) or by the knife. As may be imagined, it was horribly painful, *and there was no chloroform.* Day after day I was sent for, and stood by, while this terrible thing was going on, wiping the sweat from the face that, though pale as death, never quivered. Save an occasional groan, deep and suppressed, there was no "fuss."

Does it seem to you that this was exceptional, dear reader? Ah! no; in the wards outside, where lay hundreds of *private soldiers,* without the pride of rank to sustain them, only their simple, noble manhood, I daily witnessed such scenes. The courage and daring of our soldiers have won full appreciation from the whole world. Of their patient endurance, I was for four years a constant witness, and I declare that it was sublime beyond conception. I cannot remember the name of the heroic officer whose wound I have described. I remember, however, that Dr. Jackson treated it successfully, and that in the desperate days, towards the close of the war, the wounded man was again at his post. I know not whether he fell in battle or if he still lives bearing that horrible scar. Captain Weller, of Louisville, Kentucky, was also an inmate of the same ward. My remembrance of him is that he also was badly wounded. I also recollect that he was a great favorite with his comrades in the ward, who spoke enthusiastically of his "record." He was never gay like the others, but self-contained and reticent, and frequently **grave** and sad, as became an exile from "the old Kentucky home." My cares were at this time of constant skirmishing, greatly increased by anxiety for my husband. He had at the battle of New Hope Church, while carrying ammunition from the caisson to the gun, received a slight wound in the left foot, but did not consider it of sufficient importance to cause him to leave his command. Later, however, he succumbed to dysentery, and after the battle of Jonesboro', although having served his gun to the last, he was utterly overcome, and fell by the road-side. The last ambulance picked him up, and he was sent to Newnan, as all supposed, to die. Had I not been in a position to give him every advantage and excellent nursing he must have died. Even with this, the disease was only arrested, not cured, and for years after the war still clung about him. Under Providence, his life was saved at that time. This one blessing seemed to me a full recompense for all I had hitherto encountered, and a thorough justification of my persistence in the course I marked out for myself at the beginning of the war. Various "*affairs*" continued to employ the soldiers at the front; in all of these our losses were *comparatively* small. I never saw the soldiers in better spirits. There was little if any "shirking." As soon as—almost before—they were recovered they cheerfully reported for duty. The "expediency" of Johnston's retreat was freely discussed. All seemed to feel that the enemy was being drawn away from his base of supplies into a strange country, where he would be trapped at last, and to feel sure that it was "all right." "Let old Joe alone, *he* knows what he is about," and on every hand expressions of strong affection and thorough confidence. The army was certainly far from being "demoralized," as General Hood must have discovered, when, immediately afterward, on the 22d of July, and later at Franklin, they withstood so magnificently the shock of battle, and at the word of command hurled themselves again and again against the enemy, rushing dauntlessly onward to meet overwhelming numbers and certain death. On the 18th of July, the news reached us that General Johnston had been relieved from command, and that General Hood had succeeded him. I knew nothing of the relative merits of the two commanders, and had no means of judging but by the effect upon the soldiers by whom I was then surrounded. The whole post seemed as if stricken by some terrible calamity. Convalescents walked about with lagging steps and gloomy faces. In every ward lay men who wept bitterly or groaned aloud or, covering their faces, refused to speak or eat. From that hour the buoyant, hopeful spirit seemed to die out. I do not think anything was ever the same again. For, when after the awful sacrifice of human life which followed the inauguration of the new policy, the decimated army *still* were forced to retreat, the shadow of doom began to creep slowly upon the land. The anchor of *my* soul was my unbounded confidence in President Davis; while he was at the helm I felt secure of ultimate success, and bore present ills and disappointments patiently, *never doubting.* Meantime, disquieting rumors were flying about, railroad communication was cut off here and there, and with it mail facilities. Of course the Confederate leaders were apprised of the movements of the Federals, but at the hospital post we were constantly on the *qui vive.* Large numbers of convalescents were daily returning to the front, among them Lieutenant Cluverius, Mr. Vaudry, and Captain Weller.

Rumors of the approach of the Federal forces under McCook had for days disquieted our minds. The little town of Newnan and immediately surrounding country was already full of refugees. Every day brought more. Besides, the presence of hundreds of sick and wounded, in the hospitals which had been established there, rendered the prospect of an advance of the enemy by no means a pleasant one. But, as far as the hospitals were concerned, the surgeons in charge must await orders from headquarters. As long as none were received, we felt comparatively safe.

One night, however, a regiment of Roddy's Confederate Cavalry quietly rode in, taking possession of the railroad depot at the foot of the hill, and otherwise mysteriously disposing of themselves in the same neighborhood. The following morning opened bright and lovely, bringing to the anxious watchers of the night before that sense of security which always comes with the light. All business was resumed as usual. I had finished my early rounds, fed my special cases, and was just entering the distributing-room to send breakfast to the wards, when a volley of musketry, quickly followed by another and another, startled the morning air. Quickly an excited crowd collected and rushed to the top of the hill commanding a view of the depot and railroad track. I ran with the rest. "*The Yankees! the Yankees!*" was the cry. The firing continued for a few moments, then ceased. When the smoke cleared away, our own troops could be seen drawn up on the railroad and on the depot platform. The hill on the opposite side seemed to swarm with Yankees. Evidently they had expected to surprise the town, but, finding themselves opposed by a force whose numbers they were unable to estimate, they hastily retreated up the hill. By that time a crowd of impetuous boys had armed themselves and were running down the hill on our side to join the Confederates. Few men followed (of the citizens), for those who were able had already joined the army.

Those who remained were fully occupied in attending to the women and children.

It was evident that the fight was only delayed. An attack might be expected at any moment. An exodus from the town at once began.

Already refugees from all parts of the adjacent country had begun to pour into and pass through, in endless procession and every conceivable and inconceivable style of conveyance, drawn by horses, mules, oxen, and even by a single steer or *cow*. Most of these were women and boys, though the faces of young children appeared here and there,—as it were, "thrown in" among the "plunder,"—looking pitifully weary and frightened, yet not so heart-broken as the anxious women who knew not where their journey was to end. Nor had they "where to lay their heads," some of them having left behind only the smoking ruins of a home, which, though "ever so lowly," was "the sweetest spot on earth" to them. McCook, by his unparalleled cruelty, had made his name a horror.

The citizens simply stampeded, "nor stood upon the order of their going." There was no time for deliberation. They could not move goods or chattels, only a few articles of clothing; no room for trunks and boxes. Every carriage, wagon, and cart was loaded down with human freight; every saddle-horse was in demand. All the negroes from the hospital as well as those belonging to the citizens were removed at once to a safe distance. These poor creatures were as much frightened as anybody and as glad to get away. Droves of cattle and sheep were driven out on the run, lowing and bleating their indignant remonstrance.

While the citizens were thus occupied, the surgeons in charge of hospitals were not less busy, though far more collected and methodical. Dr. McAllister, of the

"Buckner," and Dr. S. M. Bemiss, of the "Bragg," were both brave, cool, *executive* men. Their self-possession, their firm, steady grasp of the reins of authority simplified matters greatly. Only those unable to bear arms were left in the wards. Convalescents would have resented and probably disobeyed an order to remain. Not only were they actuated by the brave spirit of Southern soldiers, but they preferred anything to remaining to be captured,—better far death than the horrors of a Northern prison. So all quietly presented themselves, and, with assistant-surgeons, druggists, and hospital attendants, were armed, officered, and marched off to recruit the regiment before mentioned.

The ladies, wives of officers, attendants, etc., were more difficult to manage, for dread of the "Yankees," combined with the pain of parting with their husbands or friends, who would soon go into battle, distracted them. Fabulous prices were offered for means of conveyance. As fast as one was procured it was filled and crowded. At last, all were sent off except one two-horse buggy, which Dr. McAllister had held for his wife and myself, and which was driven by his own negro boy, Sam. Meantime, I had visited all the wards, for some of the patients were very near death, and all were in a state of great and injurious excitement. I did not for a moment pretend to withstand their entreaties that I would remain with them, having already decided to do so. Their helplessness appealed so strongly to my sympathies that I found it impossible to resist. Besides, I had an idea and a hope that even in the event of the town being taken I might prevail with the enemy to ameliorate their condition as prisoners. So I promised, and quietly passed from ward to ward announcing my determination, trying to speak cheerfully. Excitement, so great that it produced outward calm, enabled me to resist the angry remonstrances of the surgeon and the tearful entreaties of Mrs. McAllister, who was nearly beside herself with apprehension. At last everybody was gone; intense quiet succeeded the scene of confusion. I was *alone,—left in charge.* A crushing sense of responsibility fell upon my heart. The alarm had been first given about eight o'clock in the morning. By three the same afternoon soldiers, citizens, *all* had disappeared.

Only a few men who, by reason of wounds too recently healed or from other causes, were unable to march or to fight had been left to act as nurses.

I sat down upon the steps of my office to think it over and to gather strength for all I had to do. On either side of me were two-story stores which had been converted into wards, where the sickest patients were generally placed, that I might have easy access to them. Suddenly, from one of the upper wards, I heard a hoarse cry, as if some one had essayed to give the rebel yell. Following it a confused murmur of voices. Running hastily up-stairs, I met at the door of the ward a ghastly figure, clad all in white (the hospital shirt and drawers), but with a military cap on his head. It was one of my fever patients who had been lying at death's door for days. The excitement of the morning having brought on an access of fever with delirium, he had arisen from his bed, put on his cap, and started, yelling, "*to join the boys !*" Weak as I had supposed him to be, his strength almost over-mastered my own. I could hardly prevent him from going down the stairs. The only man in the ward able to assist me at all was minus an arm and just recovering after amputation. I was afraid his wound might possibly begin to bleed, besides, I knew that any *man's* interference would excite the patient still more. Relying upon the kindly, chivalrous feeling which my presence always seemed to inspire in my patients, I promised to get his gun for him if he would go back and put on his clothes, and, placing my arm around the already tottering and swaying figure, by soothing and coaxing got him back to the bed. A sinking spell followed, from which he never rallied. In a lower ward another death occurred, due also to sudden excitement.

Fearful of the effect that a knowledge of this would have upon other patients, I resorted to deception, declaring that the dead men were better and asleep, covering them, excluding light from windows near them, and even pretending at intervals to administer medicines.

And now came another trial, from which I shrank fearfully, but which must be borne.

In the " wounded wards," and in tents outside where men having gangrene were isolated, horrible sights awaited me,—sights which I trembled to look upon,— fearful wounds which had, so far, been attended to only by the surgeons.

These wounds were now dry, and the men were groaning with pain. Minute directions having been left with me, I must nerve myself to uncover the dreadful places, wash them, and apply fresh cloths. In the cases of gangrene, poultices of yeast and charcoal, or some other preparation left by the surgeons.

Entering Ward No. 3, where there were many badly-wounded men, I began my work upon a boy of perhaps nineteen years, belonging to a North Carolina regiment, who had one-half of his face shot away.

My readers may imagine the dreadful character of the wounds in this ward, when I relate that a day or two after a terrible battle at the front, when dozens of wounded were brought in, so badly were they mangled and so busy were the surgeons, that I was permitted to dress this boy's face unaided. *Then* it was bad enough, but neither so unsightly nor so painful as *now* that inflammation had supervened. The poor boy tried not to flinch. His one bright eye looked gratefully up at me. After I had finished, he wrote upon the paper which was always at his hand, "You didn't hurt me like them doctors. Don't let the Yankees get me, I want to have another chance at *them* when I get well." Having succeeded so well, I " took heart of grace," and felt little trepidation afterward. But—oh! the horror of it. An Arkansas soldier lay gasping out his life, a piece of shell having carried away a large portion of his breast, leaving the lungs exposed to view. No hope, save to alleviate his pain by applying cloths wet with cold water. Another, from Tennessee, had lost a part of his thigh, —and so on. The amputations were my greatest dread, lest I might displace bandages and set an artery bleeding. So I dared not remove the cloths, but used an instrument invented by one of our surgeons, as may be imagined, of primitive construction, but which, wetting the tender wounds gradually by a sort of spray, gave great relief. Of course, fresh cloths were a constant necessity for suppurating wounds, but for those nearly healed, or simply inflamed, the spray was invaluable. The tents were the last visited, and by the time I had finished the rounds, it was time to make some arrangements for the patients' supper, for wounded men are always hungry.

I remember gratefully to this day the comfort and moral support I received during this trying ordeal from a South Carolina soldier, who even then knew that his own hours were numbered, and was looking death in the face with a calm resignation and courage which was simply sublime. He had been shot in the spine, and from the waist down was completely paralyzed. After he had been wounded, some one unintentionally having laid him down too near a fire, his feet were burned in a shocking manner. He was one of the handsomest men I ever saw, and, even in his present condition, of commanding presence and of unusual intelligence. I strive in vain to recall his name, but memory in this as in many other cases of patients to whom I was particularly attracted will present their faces only. Calling me to his bedside he spoke kindly and cheerfully, praising my efforts, encouraging me to go on, drawing upon his store of general knowledge for expedients to meet the most trying cases.

Everything that Dr. McAllister did was well and completely done. He was kind-hearted, generous, ready to do or sacrifice anything for the real good of his patients; but his rules once laid down became immutable laws, not to be transgressed by any. His constant supervision and enforcement of rules affected every department of the hospital. In my own, I had only to report a dereliction of duty, and the fate of the culprit was sealed. If a woman, I had orders to discharge her; if a man, the next train bore him to his regiment or to the office of the medical director, upon whose tender mercies no wrong-doer could rely.

Consequently, I had only to go to my well-ordered kitchen to find ready the food which it had been my first care to have prepared in view of the (as I hoped) temporary absence of the cooks. The departing men had all taken marching rations with them, but there was still plenty of food on hand. A bakery was attached to the Buckner. We also owned several cows. In the bakery was plenty of corn-bread and some loaves of flour-bread, although flour was even then becoming scarce.

The cows, with full udders, stood lowing at the bars

G   *k*   13

of the pen. Among the doubts and fears that had assailed me, the idea that I might have trouble with these cows never occurred to my mind. During my childhood my mother had owned several. I had often seen them milked. One had only to seize the teats firmly, pull quietly downward, and two streams of rich milk would follow. Oh, yes! I could do that easily. But when I arrived at the pen, a tin bucket in one hand, a milking-stool in the other, and letting down the bars, crept inside, the cows eyed me with evident distrust and even shook their horns in a menacing manner which quite alarmed me. However, I marched up to the one which appeared the mildest-looking, and sitting down by her side, seized two of the teats, fully expecting to hear the musical sound of two white streamlets as they fell upon the bottom of the tin bucket. *Not a drop could I get.* My caressing words and gentle remonstrances had not the slightest effect. If it is possible for an animal to feel and show contempt, it was revealed in the gaze that cow cast upon me as she turned her head to observe my manœuvres. I had heard that some cows have a bad habit of holding back their milk. Perhaps this was one of them. I would try another. Removing the stool to the side of another meek-looking animal, I essayed to milk *her*. But she switched her tail in my face, lifting a menacing, horrid hoof. "*Soh, bossy!*" cried I. "Pretty, *pretty* cow that makes pleasant milk to soak my bread." In another moment I was seated flat upon the ground, while my pretty, pretty cow capered wildly among the rest, so agitating them that, thinking discretion the better part of valor, I hastily climbed over the fence at the point nearest to me and returned to the kitchen.

What should I do now? Perhaps one of the decrepit nurses left in the ward knew how to milk. But no, they did not, except one poor, limping rheumatic who could only use one hand. Just then a feeble-looking patient from the Bragg Hospital came tottering along. He also knew how to milk, and they both volunteered to try. Much to my surprise and delight, the cows *now* behaved beautifully, perhaps owing to the fact that, obeying the injunctions of my two recruits, I provided each with a bundle of fodder to distract their attention during the milking process. There was more milk than I could possibly use, as nearly all the convalescents were absent. So I set several pans of it away, little thinking how soon it would be needed.

By the time all had been fed, I felt very weary; but it was midnight before I found a minute's time to rest.

I had made frequent rounds through all the buildings of the hospital, each time finding some one who had need of me. At last, wearied out by the excitement of the day, the sick grew quiet and inclined to sleep. Released for a time, I sat down on the steps of my office to think and to listen: for I did not know anything of the whereabouts of the enemy. The town might have been surrendered. At any moment the Federal soldiers might appear. Just then, however, the streets were utterly deserted. The stillness was oppressive.

If I could only discover a friendly light in one of these deserted dwellings. Oh, for the sound of a kindly voice, the sight of a familiar face!

Doubtless there may have been some who had remained to protect their household gods, but they were women, and remained closely within doors.

Melancholy thoughts oppressed me. Through gathering tears I gazed at the pale moon, whose light seemed faded and wan. There came to me memories of the long-ago, when I had strayed among the orange-groves of my own dear home under a moonlight far more radiant, happy in loved companionship, listening with delight to the voices of the night, which murmured only of love and joy and hope, inhaling the perfume of a thousand flowers. To-night, as the south wind swept by in fitful gusts, it seemed to bear to my ears the sound of sorrow and mourning from homes and shrines where hope lay dead amid the ruined idols cast down and broken by that stern iconoclast—*War.*

As I sat thus, buried in thought, a distant sound broke the silence, sending a thrill of terror to my heart. It was the tramp of many horses rapidly approaching. "Alas! alas! the enemy had come upon us from the rear. Our brave defenders were surrounded and their retreat cut off."

I knew not what to expect, but anxiety for my patients banished fear. Seizing a light-wood torch, I ran up the road, hoping to interview the officers at the head of the column and to intercede for my sick, perhaps to prevent intrusion into the wards. To my almost wild delight, the torch-light revealed the dear old gray uniforms. It was a portion of Wheeler's Cavalry sent to reinforce Roddy, whose meagre forces, aided by the volunteers from Newnan, had held the Federals in check until now, but were anxiously expecting this reinforcement.

The men had ridden far and fast. They now came to a halt in front of the hospital, but had not time to dismount, hungry and thirsty though they were. The regimental servants, however, came in search of water with dozens of canteens hung around them, rattling in such a manner as to show that they were quite empty. For the next half-hour, I believe, I had almost the strength of Samson. Rushing to the bakery, I loaded baskets with bread and handed them up to the soldier-boys to be passed along until emptied. I then poured all the milk I had into a large bucket, added a dipper, and, threading in and out among the horses, ladled out dipperfuls until it was all gone. I then distributed about four buckets of water in the same way. My excitement was so great that not a sensation of fear or of fatigue assailed me. Horses to the right of me, horses to the left of me, horses in front of me, snorted and pawed; but God gave strength and courage: I was not afraid.

A comparatively small number had been supplied, when a courier from Roddy's command rode up to hasten the reinforcements. At once the whole column was put in motion. As the last rider disappeared, and the tramping of the horses died away in the distance, a sense of weariness and exhaustion so overpowered me that I could have slept where I stood. So thorough was my confidence in the brave men who were sure to repel the invaders that all sense of danger passed away.

My own sleeping-room was in a house situated at the foot of the hill. I could have gone there and slept securely, but dared not leave my charges. Sinking upon the rough lounge in my office, intending only to rest, I fell fast asleep. I was awakened by one of the nurses, who had come to say that I was needed by a patient whom he believed to be dying, and who lay in a ward on the other side of the square.

As we passed out into the street, another beautiful morning was dawning. Upon entering Ward No. 9, we found most of the patients asleep. But in one corner, between two windows which let in the fast-increasing light, lay an elderly man, calmly breathing his life away. The morning breeze stirred the thin gray hair upon his hollow temples, rustling the leaves of the Bible which lay upon his pillow. Stooping over him to feel the fluttering pulse, and to wipe the clammy sweat from brow and hands, I saw that he was indeed

13*

dying, a victim of that dreadful scourge that decimated the ranks of the Confederate armies more surely than many battles,—dysentery,—which, if not cured in the earlier stages, resulted too surely, as now, in consumption of the bowels.

He was a Kentuckian, cut off from home and friends, and dying among strangers. An almost imperceptible glance indicated that he wished me to take up his Bible. The fast-stiffening lips whispered, " *Read.*" I read to him the Fourteenth Chapter of St. John, stopping frequently to note if the faint breathing yet continued. Each time he would move the cold fingers in a way that evidently meant " *go on.*" After I had finished the reading, he whispered, so faintly that I could just catch the words, " *Rock of Ages,*" and I softly sang the beautiful hymn.

Two years before I could not have done this so calmly. At first every death among my patients seemed to me like a personal bereavement. Trying to read or to sing by the bedsides of the dying, uncontrollable tears and sobs would choke my voice. As I looked my last upon dead faces, I would turn away shuddering and sobbing, for a time unfit for duty. *Now,* my voice did not once fail or falter. Calmly I watched the dying patient, and saw (as I had seen a hundred times before) the gray shadow of death steal over the shrunken face, to be replaced at the last by a light so beautiful that I could well believe it came shining through " the gates ajar."

It was sunrise when I again emerged from Ward No. 9. Hastening to my room, I quickly bathed and re-dressed, returning to my office in half an hour, refreshed and ready for duty.

The necessity for breakfast sufficient to feed the hungry patients recalled to me the improvidence of my action in giving away so much bread the night before. It had gone a very little way toward supplying the needs of so large a body of soldiers, and now my own needed it.

There was no quartermaster, no one to issue fresh rations. Again I had the cows milked, gathered up all the corn-bread that was left, with some hard-tack, and with the aid of the few decrepit nurses before mentioned made a fire, and warmed up the soup and soup-meat which had been prepared for the convalescent table the day before, but was not consumed. My patients, comprehending the situation, made the best of it. But the distribution was a tedious business, as many of the patients had to be fed by myself.

I had hardly begun when some of the men declared they "heard guns." I could not then detect the sound, but soon it grew louder and more sustained, and then we *knew* a battle was in progress. For hours the fight went on. We awaited the result in painful suspense. At last the ambulances came in, bringing some of the surgeons and some wounded men, returning immediately for others. At the same time the hospital steward with his attendants and several of our nurses arrived, also the linen-master, the chief cook, and the baker. With them came orders to prepare wards for a large number of wounded, both Confederate *and Federal.* Presently a cloud of dust appeared up the road, and a detail of Confederate cavalry rode into town, bringing eight hundred Federal prisoners, who were consigned to a large cotton warehouse, situated almost midway between the hospital and the railroad depot.

My terrible anxiety, suspense, and heavy responsibility was now at an end, but days and nights of nursing lay before all who were connected with either the Buckner or Bragg Hospitals. Additional buildings were at once seized and converted into wards for the reception of the wounded of both armies. The hospital

attendants, though weary, hungry, and some of them
terribly dirty from the combined effect of perspiration,
dust, and gunpowder, at once resumed their duties.
The quartermaster reopened his office, requisitions were
made and filled, and the work of the different departments was once more put in regular operation.

I was busy in one of the wards, when a messenger
drove up, and a note was handed me from Dr. McAllister,—" Some of our men too badly wounded to be moved
right away. Come out at once. Bring cordials and
brandy,—soup, if you have it,—also fill the enclosed
requisition at the drug-store. Lose no time."

The battle-field was not three miles away. I was
soon tearing along the road at breakneck speed. At an
improvised field-hospital I met the doctor, who vainly
tried to prepare me for the horrid spectacle I was about
to witness.

From the hospital-tent distressing groans and screams
came forth. The surgeons, both Confederate and Federal, were busy, with coats off, sleeves rolled up, shirt-
fronts and hands bloody. But *our* work lay not
here.

Dr. McAllister silently handed me two canteens of
water, which I threw over my shoulder, receiving also
a bottle of peach brandy. We then turned into a
ploughed field, thickly strewn with men and horses,
many stone dead, some struggling in the agonies of
death. The plaintive cries and awful struggles of the
horses first impressed me. They were shot in every
conceivable manner, showing shattered heads, broken
and bleeding limbs, and protruding entrails. They
would not yield quietly to death, but continually raised
their heads or struggled half-way to their feet, uttering
cries of pain, while their distorted eyes seemed to reveal
their suffering and implore relief. I saw a soldier shoot

one of these poor animals, and felt truly glad to know
that his agony was at an end.

The dead lay around us on every side, singly and in
groups and *piles;* men and horses, ·in some cases, apparently inextricably mingled. Some lay as if peacefully sleeping; others, with open eyes, seemed to glare
at any who bent above them. Two men lay as they
had died, the "Blue" and the "Gray," clasped in a fierce
embrace. What had passed between them could never
be known; but one. was shot in the head, the throat of
the other was partly torn away. It was awful to feel
the conviction that unquenched hatred had embittered
the last moments of each. They seemed mere youths,
and I thought sadly of the mothers, whose hearts would
throb with equal anguish in a Northern and a Southern
home. In a corner of the field, ·supported by a pile of
broken fence-rails, a soldier sat apparently beckoning to
us. On approaching him we discovered that he was
quite dead, although he sat upright, with open eyes and
extended arm.

Several badly wounded men had been laid under the
shade of some bushes a little farther on; our mission
lay here. The portion of the field we crossed to reach
this spot was in many places slippery with blood. The
edge of my dress was red, my feet were wet with it. As
we drew near the suffering men, piteous glances met our
own. "Water! water!" was the cry.

Dr. McAllister had previously discovered in one of
these the son of an old friend, and although he was apparently wounded unto death, he hoped, when the ambulances returned with the stretchers sent for, to move
him into town to the hospital. He now proceeded with
the aid of the instruments, bandages, lint, etc., I had
brought to prepare him for removal. Meantime, taking
from my pocket a small feeding-cup, which I always

carried for use in the wards, I mixed some brandy and water, and, kneeling by one of the poor fellows who seemed worse than the others, tried to raise his head. But he was already dying. As soon as he was moved the blood ran in a little stream from his mouth. Wiping it off, I put the cup to his lips, but he could not swallow, and reluctantly I left him to die. He wore the blue uniform and stripes of a Federal sergeant of cavalry, and had a German face. The next seemed anxious for water, and drank eagerly. This one, a man of middle age, was later transferred to our wards, but died from blood-poisoning. He was badly wounded in the side. A third could only talk with his large, sad eyes, but made me clearly understand his desire for water. As I passed my arm under his head the red blood saturated my sleeve and spread in a moment over a part of my dress. So we went on, giving water, brandy, or soup; sometimes successful in reviving the patient, sometimes able only to whisper a few words of comfort to the dying. There were many more left, and Dr. McAllister never for a moment intermitted his efforts to save them. Later came more help, surgeons, and attendants with stretchers, etc. Soon all were moved who could bear it.

Duty now recalled me to my patients at the hospital.

My hands and dress and feet were bloody, and I felt sick with horror.

As I was recrossing the battle-field accompanied by Dr. Welford, of Virginia, the same terrible scenes were presented to the view. The ground was littered with the accoutrements of soldiers,—carbines, pistols, canteens, haversacks, etc. Two cannon lay overturned, near one of which lay a dead Federal soldier still grasping the rammer. Beneath the still struggling horses lay human forms just as they had fallen. Probably they had been dead ere they reached the ground, but I felt a shuddering dread lest perhaps some lingering spark of life had been crushed out by the rolling animals.

We had nearly reached the road when our attention was arrested by stifled cries and groans proceeding from a little log cabin which had been nearly demolished during the fight. Entering, we found it empty, but still the piteous cries continued. Soon the doctor discovered a pair of human legs hanging down the chimney, but with all his pulling could not dislodge the man, who was fast wedged and only cried out the louder.

"Stop your infernal noise," said the doctor, "and try to help yourself while I pull." By this time others had entered the cabin, and their united effort at length succeeded in dislodging from the chimney,—not a negro, but a white man, whose blue eyes, glassy with terror, shone through the soot which had begrimed his face. He had climbed up the chimney to escape the storm of shot, and had so wedged himself in that to release himself unaided was impossible. Irrepressible laughter greeted his appearance, and I—I am bitterly ashamed to say—fell into a fit of most violent hysterical laughter and weeping. Dr. Welford hurried me into the buggy, which was near at hand, and drove rapidly to town, refusing to stop at the hospital, landing me at my room, where some ladies who came from I know not where kindly helped me to bed. Under the influence of a sedative I soon fell into a deep sleep, awakening at daylight to find my own servant (who had returned with other negroes during the night) standing at my bedside. The surgeons had sent a little of the precious *real coffee*, of which there was only one sack left. Upon awakening, I was to be at once served with a cup. A warm bath followed. By six o'clock I was once more at the hospital, ready for duty, after two days and nights, during which, it seemed to me, I had lived for years.

Even at this early hour, Buckner hospital presented a scene of great activity. Some of the surgeons had remained all night on duty, and were still busy; while others, having snatched a few hours of sleep, were now preparing for their trying work.

In almost every ward lay a few wounded Federals, but, all the spare beds having been filled, a long, low, brick building, on the corner opposite the drug-store, once used as a cotton-pickery, was fitted up as comfortably as the limited hospital-supplies at our command would allow for the Federals exclusively, and they were permitted to have the attendance of their own surgeons, although ours always responded readily, if needed.

These Federal surgeons appeared to me to be very indifferent to the comfort of their patients, and to avoid all unnecessary trouble. They were tardy in beginning their work the morning after the battle, and, when they were ready, coolly sent in *requisitions* for *chloroform*, which, having been (contrary to the dictates of humanity and to the customs of civilized nations) long since declared by their government "contraband of war," was almost unattainable, and used by our Confederate surgeons only in extreme cases. In all minor, and in some severe, operations the surgeons relied upon the manly fortitude of the patients, and, *God bless our brave boys*, they bore this cruel test with a courage fully as worthy to be recorded as the most brilliant action on the battle-field.

On the morning in question, as I made my early rounds, there met me everywhere ghastly reminders of the battle,—men shot and disfigured in every conceivable manner. Many, fresh from the hands of the surgeons, exhausted by suffering, looked as if already

Death had claimed them for his own. Attendants were constantly bearing into different wards fresh victims from the operating-rooms, where the bloody work would still go on for hours. These must have immediate attention,—must be closely watched and strongly nourished. This was *my* blessed privilege; and, thanks to the humane and excellent policy adopted by General Johnston, and continued by General Hood,—both of whom looked well to the *ways of quartermasters* and *commissaries*,—the means to provide for the sick and wounded were always at hand,—at least, up to the time of which I write.

Some of my favorite patients, whom, previous to this battle, I had nursed into convalescence, were now thrown back upon beds of pain. In one corner I found a boy whom I had nursed and fed through days and nights of suffering from typhoid fever. His name was Willie Hutson, and he belonged to the —— Mississippi Regiment. Two days ago he had been as bright as a lark, and pleading to be sent to the front. Now he lay, shot through the breast, so near death that he did not know me. As I bent over him with tearful eyes, a hand placed upon my arm caused me to turn. There stood Dr. Gore, his kind face full of sympathy, but greatly troubled, at his side a Federal surgeon in full uniform. Dr. Gore said, "This is one of my old chums, and——" But I cried out, "Oh, doctor! I *cannot*,— look" (indicating with my hand first Willie, then the entire ward)! Passing swiftly out, I fled to my office and locked myself in, shedding hot tears of indignation. The dreadful work of the invaders had been before my eyes all the morning. I felt as if I could have nothing to do with them, and did not wish to see one of them again. They had not only murdered my poor boy Willie, but dozens of dearer friends. They were even

14

now running riot in the home I loved. They were invaders!

I could *not* meet them,—could not nurse them.

It is painful thus to reveal the thoughts of my wicked, unchristian heart; but thus I reasoned and felt just then.

After a while a note from Dr. Gore was handed me. He said (in substance), " I know how bitterly you feel, but pray for strength to cast out evil spirits from your heart. Forget that the suffering men, thrown upon our kindness and forbearance, are *Yankees*. Remember only that they are God's creatures and helpless prisoners. They need you. Think the matter over, and do not disappoint me. Gore."

I do not believe that ever before or since have I fought so hard a battle. God helping me, I decided to do right. The short, sharp contest ended—I acted at once.

On my way to the Federal wards, I met more than one hospital-attendant carrying off a bloody leg or arm to bury it. I felt then, and saw no reason to alter my opinion afterwards, that some of their surgeons were far rougher and less merciful than ours ; and I do not believe they ever gave the poor, shattered fellows the benefit of a doubt. It was easier to amputate than to attend a tedious, troublesome recovery. So, off went legs and arms by the wholesale.

I had not been five minutes in the low, brick ward, where lay the most dangerously wounded Federals, when all animosity vanished and my woman's heart melted within me.

These were strangers and unwelcome, but far from home and friends, suffering, dying. The surgeon said to me, " Madam, one-half the attention you give to your own men will save life here."

The patients were all badly, many fatally, wounded.

c

They were silent, repellent, and evidently expectant of insult and abuse, but after a while received food and drink from my hands pleasantly, and I tried to be faithful in my ministrations.

I believe that most of the soldiers in this ward were from Iowa and Indiana.

One I remember particularly, a captain of cavalry, who was shot through the throat and had to receive nourishment by means of a rubber tube inserted for the purpose. A young man in a blue and yellow uniform—an aide or orderly—remained at his side day and night until he died. His eyes spoke to me eloquently of his gratitude, and once he wrote on a scrap of paper, "God bless you," and handed it to me. He lived about five days.

The mortality was very considerable in this ward. I grew to feel a deep interest in the poor fellows, and treasured last words or little mementoes as faithfully for their distant loved ones as I had always done for Confederates.

Among the personal belongings taken from me by raiders at Macon, Georgia, was a large chest, full of articles of this kind, which I intended to return to the friends of the owners whenever the opportunity offered.

In another ward were several renegade Kentuckians, who constantly excited my ire by noting and ridiculing deficiencies, calling my own dear boys "Old Jeff's ragamuffins," etc. One day Dr. Gore happened to be visiting this ward when these men began their usual teasing. Something caused me to eulogize Dr. Gore and all the Kentuckians who had sacrificed so much for "The Cause." One of these fellows then said, "Well, *I'm* a Kentuckian too, what have you got to say about *me?*" I replied, "I think you hold about the same relation to the true sons of Kentucky that Judas Iscariot bore to the beloved disciple who lay upon the bosom of our Saviour." Then walked out of the ward.

It was rather a spiteful repartee, I must confess, but was provoked by many ill-natured remarks previously made by this renegade, and had the good effect of putting an end to them.

We were comparatively safe once more,—for how long no one knew. I now became very anxious about the men in the trenches at Atlanta who were lying day after day, always under fire. Suffering from insufficient food, exposed to the scorching sun or equally pitiless rain, sometimes actually knee-deep in water for days. The bombardment was heavy and incessant, ceasing only for a while at sunset, when carts were hastily loaded with musty meat and poor corn-bread, driven out to the trenches, and the rations *dumped* there. Many of my friends were lying in these trenches, among them my husband. In addition to other ills, the defenders of Atlanta were in instant danger of death from shot or shell. I *could not bear it.* The desire to see my husband once more, and to carry some relief in the shape of provisions to himself and his comrades could not be quelled. Many things stood in the way of its accomplishment, for, upon giving a hint of my project to my friends at Newnan, a storm of protest broke upon my devoted head. Not one bade me God-speed, *everybody* declared I was crazy. "A *woman* to go to Atlanta under such circumstances; how utterly absurd, how mad." So I was obliged to resort to deception and subterfuge. My first step was to request leave of absence, that I might forage for provisions to be sent to the front by the first opportunity.

Dr. McAllister very kindly accorded me his permission, placing at my disposal an ambulance and a driver, advising me, however, not to follow the main road or the beaten track which had already been drained

by foragers, but to go deep into the piny woods. Said
he, "Only one of our foragers has ever been through
that region, and his reports were not very encouraging.
The people want to keep all they have got for home-
consumption, and greatly distrust 'hospital people,' but
if success is possible, *you* will succeed." In anticipa-
tion, this ride into deep, odorous pine woods seemed delightful. When the ambulance with its "captured"
mule drove up before my door, I gayly climbed into it,
and, waving merry adieux to half-disapproving friends
(among them Dr. Hughes, with his distressed face, and
Diogenes, who looked daggers at me), set off in high
glee. The ride along the pleasant road was lovely;
early birds sung sweetly; the dew, yet undisturbed,
glistened everywhere, the morning breeze blew freshly
in my face. As the sun began to assert his power, I
became eager to penetrate into the shady woods, and
at last, spying a grand aisle in "Nature's temple," bade
the driver enter it. For a while the result was most
enjoyable. The spicy aroma of the pines, the brilliant
vines climbing everywhere, the multitude of woodland
blossoms blooming in such quantities and variety as I
had never imagined, charmed my senses, and elevated
my spirit. Among these peaceful shades one might
almost forget the horror and carnage which desolated
the land. The driver was versed in wood-craft, and
called my attention to many beauties which would have
otherwise escaped me. But soon his whole attention
was required to guide the restive mule through a laby-
rinth of stumps and ruts and horrible muddy holes,
which he called " hog wallows ;" my own endeavors were
addressed to " holding on," and devising means to ease
the horrible joltings which racked me from head to foot.
After riding about two miles we came to a small clearing, and were informed that the road for ten miles was

l **14***

"tolerbal clar" and pretty thickly settled. So after par-
taking of an early country dinner, also obtaining a small
amount of eggs, chickens, etc., at exorbitant prices, we
resumed our ride. That expedition will never be forgotten by me. At its close, I felt that my powers of
diplomacy were quite equal to *any* emergency. Oh, the
sullen, sour-looking women that I sweetly smiled upon,
and flattered into good humor, praising their homes, the
cloth upon the loom, the truck-patch (often a mass of
weeds), the tow-headed babies (whom I caressed and
admired), never hinting at my object until the innocent victims offered of their own accord to "show me
round." At the spring-house I praised the new country
butter, which "looked so very good that I must have
a pound or two," and then skilfully leading the conversation to the subject of chickens and eggs, carelessly
displaying a few crisp Confederate bills, I at least became the happy possessor of a few dozens of eggs and
a chicken or two, at a price which only their destination
reconciled me to.

At one house, approached by a road so tortuous
and full of stumps that we were some time before
reaching it, I distinctly heard a dreadful squawking
among the fowls, but when we arrived at the gate,
not one was to be seen, and the mistress declared she
hadn't a "*one:* hadn't saw a chicken for a *coon's* age."
Pleading excessive fatigue, I begged the privilege of
resting within the cabin. An apparently unwilling
assent was given. In I walked, and, occupying one of
those splint chairs which so irresistibly invite one to
commit a breach of good manners by "tipping back," I
sat in the door-way, comfortably swaying backward
and forward. Every once in a while the faces of children, either black or white, would peer at me round
the corner of the house, then the sound of scampering

bare feet would betray their sudden flight. Suddenly I caught sight of a pair of bare, black feet protruding from under the bed. Presently an unmistakable squawk arose, instantly smothered, but followed by a fluttering of wings and a *chorus* of squawks. So upset was the lady of the house that she involuntarily called out, "*You Isrul!*" "Ma'am," came in a frightened voice from under the bed, then in whining tones, "I dun try to mek 'em hush up, but 'pears like Mass Debbel be on dey side, anyhow."

Further concealment being impossible, I said, "Come, you have the chickens ready caught, I'll give you your own price for them." She hesitated—and was lost, for producing from my pocket a small package of snuff, to which temptation she at once succumbed, I obtained in exchange six fine, fat chickens. As I was leaving she said, in an apologetic tone, "Well, I declah, I never knowed you was going to light, or I wouldn't have done sich a fool-trick."

Stopping at every house, meeting with varied success, we at last, just at night, arrived at a farm-house more orderly than any we had passed, where I was glad to discover the familiar face of an old lady who had sometimes brought buttermilk and eggs to the sick. At once recognizing me, she appeared delighted, and insisted upon my "lighting" and having my team put up until morning. This I was glad to do, for it was quite out of the question to start on my homeward journey that night. Greatly I enjoyed the hospitality so ungrudgingly given, the appetizing supper, the state bed in the best room, with its "sunrise" quilt of patch-work. Here was a Confederate household. The son was a soldier. His wife and his little children were living "with ma" at the old homestead. The evening was spent in talking of the late battle. Here these women were, living in the depths of the woods, consumed with anxiety, seldom hearing any news, yet quietly performing the monotonous round of duty with a patience which would have added lustre to the crown of a saint.

I talked until (wonderful to relate) my tongue was tired: my audience being the old, white-haired father, the mother, the wife, and the eager children, who were shy at first, but by degrees nestled closer, with bright eyes from which sleep seemed banished forever.

The next morning when, after a substantial breakfast, I was once more ready to start, every member of the family made some addition to my stores, notably, a few pounds of really good country butter. This was always highly prized by the soldiers. As a general thing, when the cows were fed upon cotton-seed the butter was white and "waxy," this was yellow and firm. The oldest girl brought me a pair of socks she had herself knitted; one of the little boys, six eggs laid by his own "dominiker," which he pointed out to me as she stalked about the yard proud of her mottled feathers and rosy comb.

Even the baby came toddling to the door saying, "Heah, heah," and holding out a snowy little kitten. The old gentleman, mounting his horse, offered to "ride a piece" with us. Thanks to his representations to the neighbors, I was able in a short time to turn my face homewards, having gathered an excellent supply of chickens, eggs, hams, home-made cordials, peach and apple brandy, and a few pairs of socks. The old farmer also showed us a way by which we could avoid a repetition of the tortures of yesterday, and rode beside the ambulance to the main road. I remember well how he looked, as he sat upon his old white mule, waiting to see the last of us. His hat, pushed back, showed a few locks of silvery hair; his coarse clothes and heavy, home-made boots were worn in a manner that betrayed the Southern gentleman.

The parting smile, still lingering upon his kindly face, could not conceal the "furrows of care," which had deepened with every year of the war. But, alas! I cannot recall his name, although I then thought I could never forget it.

Upon arriving at Newnan, I lost no time in preparing my boxes for the front. Everything was cooked; even the eggs were hard-boiled. There was sufficient to fill two large boxes. Having packed and shipped to the depot my treasures, I prepared for the final step without hesitation, although not without some doubt as to success in eluding the vigilance of my friends. Announcing my determination to see the boxes off, I—accompanied by my maid—walked down to the depot just before train-time. There was only one rickety old passenger-car attached to the train. This, as well as a long succession of box- and cattle-cars, were crowded with troops,—reinforcements to Atlanta. Taking advantage of the crowd, I, with Tempe, quietly stepped on board, escaping discovery until just as the train was leaving, when in rushed Dr. McAllister, who peremptorily ordered me off; but, being compelled to jump off himself, failed to arrest my departure. I was in high spirits. On the train were many soldiers whom I had nursed, and who cared for my comfort in every way possible under the circumstances. I was the only lady on the train, so they were thoughtful enough to stow themselves in the crowded boxes behind, that I might not be embarrassed by a large number in the passenger-car. At last, as we approached Atlanta, I heard the continuous and terrific noise of the bombardment. The whistle of the engine was a signal to the enemy, who at once began to shell the depot. I did not realize the danger yet, but just as the train "slowed up" heard a shrieking sound, and saw the soldiers begin to dodge.

Before I could think twice, an awful explosion followed;
the windows were all shivered, and the earth seemed to
me to be thrown in cart-loads into the car. Tempe
screamed loudly, and then began to pray. I was paralyzed with extreme terror, and *could* not scream. Before I could speak, another shell exploded overhead,
tearing off the corner of a brick store, causing again
a deafening racket. As we glided into the station, I
felt safer; but soon found out that every one around
me had business to attend to, and that I must rely
upon myself.

The shells still shrieked and exploded; the more
treacherous and dangerous solid shot continually demolished objects within our sight. For a few hours I
was so utterly demoralized that my only thought was
how to escape. It seemed to me *impossible* that any
body of soldiers could voluntarily expose themselves
to such horrible danger. I thought if *I* had been a
soldier I must have deserted from my first battle-field.
But at last I grew calmer; my courage returned, and,
urged by the necessity of finding shelter, I ventured
out. Not a place could I find. The houses were closed
and deserted, in many cases partly demolished by shot
or shell, or, having taken fire, charred, smoking, and
burnt to the ground.

All day frightened women and children cowered and
trembled and hungered and thirsted in their under-
ground places of refuge while the earth above them
shook with constant explosions. After a while I grew
quite bold, and decided to stow myself and my boxes
in the lower part of a house not far from the depot.
The upper story had been torn off by shells. I could
look through large holes in the ceiling up to the blue
sky. The next move was to find means of notifying my
husband and his friends of my arrival. I crept along

the streets back to the depot, Tempe creeping by my
side, holding fast to my dress. Then I found an officer
just going out to the trenches, and sent by him a pencilled note to Lieutenant Cluverius, thinking an officer
would be likely to receive a communication, when a
private might not. Soon after sunset, my husband
joined me, and soon after many friends. They were all
ragged, mud-stained, and altogether unlovely, but seemed
to me most desirable and welcome visitors.

One of my boxes being opened, I proceeded to do the
honors. My guests having eaten very heartily, filled
their haversacks, and, putting "*a sup*" in their canteens,
returned to camp to send out a fresh squad. The next
that came brought in extra haversacks and canteens
"for some of the boys who couldn't get off," and these
also were provided for.

With the last squad my husband was compelled to go
back to camp, as just then military rules were severe,
and very strictly enforced. I passed the night in an
old, broken arm-chair, Tempe lying at my feet, and
slept so soundly that I heard not a sound of shot or
shell. Very early next morning, however, we were
awakened by a terrible explosion near us, and directly
afterwards heard that within a hundred yards of our
place of refuge a shell had exploded, tearing away the
upper part of a house, killing a man and his three
children, who were sleeping in one of the rooms. This
made me very uneasy, and increased Tempe's terror to
such an extent that she became almost unmanageable.
During the next day I actually became accustomed to
the noise and danger, and "with a heart for any fate"
passed the day. At night my levee was larger than
before; among them I had the satisfaction of seeing
and supplying some Alabama, South Carolina, and
Tennessee soldiers. That night the bombardment was

terrific. Anxiety for my husband, combined with a shuddering terror, made sleep impossible.

The next morning, my husband having obtained a few hours' leave of absence, joined me in my shattered retreat. The day was darkened by the agony of parting. It seemed to me *impossible* to leave him under such circumstances, and really required more courage than to face the shot and shell. But I could easily see that anxiety for me interfered with his duty as a soldier, so—we must part. On the same evening I returned to Newnan, where my friends were so overjoyed at my safe return that they forbore to upbraid. Soon afterward the battle of Jonesboro' again filled our wards with shattered wrecks. As I have already stated, my husband then came for the first time to claim my care. Before he was quite able to return to duty, the post was ordered to Fort Valley, Georgia, a pleasant and very hospitable town, where new and excellent hospital buildings had been erected. From here Mr. Beers returned to his command. The day of his departure was marked by hours of intense anguish which I yet shudder to recall. The train which stopped at the hospital camp to take up men returning to the front was crowded with soldiers,—reinforcements. I had scarcely recovered from the fit of bitter weeping which followed the parting, when, noticing an unusual commotion outside, I went to the door to discover the cause. Men were running up the railroad track in the direction taken by the train which had just left. A crowd had collected near the surgeon's office, in the midst of which stood an almost breathless messenger. His tidings seemed to have the effect of sending off succeeding groups of men in the direction taken by those I had first seen running up the road. Among them I discovered several surgeons. Something was wrong. Wild with apprehension, I sped over to the office, and there learned that the train of cars loaded and crowded with soldiers had been thrown down a steep embankment, about three miles up the road, and that many lives were lost. Waiting for nothing, I ran bareheaded and frantic up the track, for more than a mile never stopping, then hearing the slow approach of an engine, sunk down by the side of the track to await its coming. Soon the engine appeared, drawing very slowly a few platform- and baggage-cars loaded with groaning, shrieking men, carrying, also, many silent forms which would never again feel pain or sorrow. The surgeons upon the first car upon descrying me crouching by the roadside, halted the train and lifted me upon the last car, where, among the " slightly hurt," I found my husband, terribly bruised and shaken, but in no danger. Arrived at camp, where tents had been hastily pitched, the wounded and dying were laid out side by side in some of the largest, while others received the dead. The sights and sounds were awful in the extreme. At first I could not muster courage (shaken as I had been) to go among them. But it was necessary for purposes of identification, so I examined every one, dying and dead, feeling that *certainty*, however dreadful, might be better borne by loving hearts than prolonged suspense.

Among these dreadful scenes came a minister of God, whose youthful face, pale and horror-stricken, yet all alight with heavenly pity and love, I can never forget. Tenderly he bent above these dying men, his trembling lips touched by divine inspiration, whispering words precious to parting souls. Unshrinkingly he performed his mission to those who yet lived, then, passing among the dead, lovingly composed and prepared for decent burial the mutilated bodies. One burial-service served

H   15

for all; this was as tenderly rendered as if each unfortunate had been dear to himself.

This young clergyman was Rev. —— Green, of Columbia, S. C., a near relative of the eminent divine and inspired patriot, Dr. B. M. Palmer, now of New Orleans.

Few patients were sent to Fort Valley. Upon recovering from the effects of the railroad accident, my husband again left for his command. Growing dissatisfied, I applied to Dr. Stout for a position nearer the front. Not receiving a satisfactory reply, went to Macon, where for a few weeks I remained at one of the hospitals, but still felt that I was losing time, and doing very little good. In November I was offered a position in a tent-hospital near the front, which I eagerly accepted, little dreaming (God help me!) of the hardship and disappointment which awaited me.

CHAPTER VI.

OMEGA.

The detention of the railroad-train belated us, and when we (I and my servant) were left at a small station in Mississippi, night had fallen. The light from a little fire of pine knots, built on the ground outside, while illuminating the rough depot and platform, left the country beyond in deeper darkness. It was bitterly cold. The driver of the ambulance informed me, we had "quite a piece to ride yet." A moment later, Dr. Beatty rode up on horseback, welcomed me pleasantly, waiting to see me safely stowed away in the ambulance. The ride to camp was dismal. I continued to shiver with cold; my heart grew heavy as lead, and yearned sadly for a sight of the pleasant faces, the sound of the kindly voices, to which I had been so long accustomed. At last a turn in the road brought us in sight of the numberless fires of a large camp. It was a bright scene, though far from gay. The few men who crouched by the fires were not roistering, rollicking soldiers, but pale shadows, holding their thin hands over the blaze which scorched their faces, while their thinly-covered backs were exposed to a cold so intense that it congealed the sap in the farthest end of the log on which they sat. Driving in among these, up an "avenue" bordered on either side by rows of white tents, the ambulance drew up at last before the door of my "quarters,"—a rough cabin built of logs. Through the open door streamed the cheery light of a wood-fire, upon which pine knots had been freshly thrown.

171

A bunk at one side, made of puncheons, and filled with pine straw, over which comforts and army-blankets had been thrown, hard pillows stuffed with straw, having coarse, unbleached cases, a roughly-made table before the fire, a lot of boxes marked "Q. M.," etc., to serve as seats, and you have my cabin in its entirety.

Drawing my box up close to the fire, I sat down, Tempe, in the mean while, stirring the coals and arranging the burning ends of the pine in true country style.

Presently my supper was brought in,—corn-bread, cornmeal coffee, a piece of musty fried salt meat, heavy brown sugar, and no milk. I was, however, hungry, and ate with a relish. Tempe went off to some region unknown for *the* supper, returning unsatisfied and highly disgusted with the "hog-wittles" which had been offered to her. Soon Dr. Beatty called, bringing with him Mrs. Dr. ——, a cheery little body, who, with her husband, occupied a room under the same roof as myself, a sort of hall open at both ends dividing us.

We had some conversation regarding the number of sick and the provisions for their comfort. On the whole, the evening passed more cheerfully than I had expected. My sleep that night was dreamless. I did not even feel the cold, although Tempe declared she was " dun froze stiff."

Very early I was astir, gazing from the door of my cabin at my new sphere of labor.

Snow had fallen during the night, and still came down steadily. The path was hidden, the camp-fires appeared as through a mist. A confused, steady sound of chopping echoed through the woods. I heard mysterious words, dimly saw figures moving about the fires. Everything looked unpromising,—dismal. Chilled to the heart, I turned back to my only comfort, the splendid fire Tempe had built. My breakfast was exactly as supper had been, and was brought by the cook, a detailed soldier, who looked as if he ought to have been at the front. He apologized for the scanty rations, promising some beef for dinner.

Soon Dr. Beatty, accompanied by two assistant-surgeons, appeared to escort me to the tents. I went gladly, for I was anxious to begin my work. What I saw during that hour of inspection convinced me, not only that my services were needed, but that my work must be begun and carried on under almost insurmountable difficulties and disadvantages. I found no comforts, no hospital stores, insufficient nourishment, a scarcity of blankets and comforts, even of pillows. Of the small number of the latter few had cases; all were soiled. The sick men had spit over them and the bed-clothes, which could not be changed because there were no more. As I have said, there were no comforts. The patients looked as if they did not expect any, and seemed sullen and discontented. The tents were not new, nor were they all good. They seemed to me without number. Passing in and out among them, I felt bewildered and doubtful whether I should ever learn to know one from another, or to find my patients. Part of the camp was set apart for convalescents. Here were dozens of Irishmen. They were so maimed and shattered that every one should have been entitled to a discharge, but the poor fellows had no homes to go to, and were quite unable to provide for themselves. There were the remnants of companies, regiments, and brigades, many of them Louisianians, and from other States outside the Confederate lines. Had there been any fighting to do, they would still have "taken a hand," maimed as they were. The monotony of hos-

15*

pital camp-life made them restless; the rules they found irksome, and constantly evaded; they growled, complained, were always "in hot water," and almost unmanageable.

The first time I passed among them they eyed me askance, seeming, I feared, to resent the presence of a woman. But I made it my daily custom to visit their part of the camp, standing by their camp-fires to listen to their "yarns," or to relate some of my own experiences, trying to make their hardships seem less, listening to their complaints, meaning in earnest to speak to Dr. Beatty regarding palpable wrongs. This I did not fail to do, and whenever the doctor's sense of justice was aroused, he promptly acted on the right side. I do not wish to convey to my readers the idea that there were men always sullen and disagreeable. Far from it, they were a jolly set of men when in a good humor, and, like all Irishmen, full of wit and humor. After I became known to them their gentle, courteous treatment of me never varied. They were very fond of playing cards, but whenever I appeared upon one of the avenues, every card would disappear. Not one ever failed to salute me, often adding a "God bless you, ma'am, may the heavens be your bed," etc. Disliking to interfere with their only amusement, I let them know that I did not dislike to see them playing cards. At this they were very pleased, saying, "Sure, it's no harrum; it's not gambling we are; divil a cint have *we* to win or lose." One day I stopped to look on a moment at a game of euchre. One of the players had lost an arm (close to the shoulder). Said he, "Sure, ma'am, it's bating the b'ys intirely, I am." I did not understand, so he explained, with a comic leer at the others,—"Sure, haven't I always the '*lone hand*' on thim?" At once I recalled a similar remark made by an Irish soldier lying in the hospital at Newnan, who had just lost one of his legs; when I condoled with him, he looked up brightly, and, pointing at his remaining foot, explained, " Niver mind, this feller *will go it alone and make it.*"

Among the surgeons in camp was one who had highly offended these convalescents by retiring to his cabin, *pulling the latch-string inside* and remaining deaf to all calls and appeals from outside. Mutterings of discontent were heard for a while, but at last as there was no further mention of the matter, I believed it was ended.

About this time the actions of the convalescents began to appear mysterious: they remained in their tents or absented themselves, as I supposed, upon foraging expeditions. Frequently, I found them working upon cowhorns, making ornaments as I thought (at this business Confederate soldiers were very expert). One day I caught sight of a large pile of horns and bones just brought in, but still thought nothing of it. Shortly, however, a small deputation from the convalescent camp appeared at the door of my cabin just as I was eating my dinner: all saluted; the spokesman then explained that the " b'ys" were prepared to give the obnoxious surgeon a " siranade" that same night. They had been working for weeks to produce the instruments of torture which were then all ready. " We don't mane to scare *ye*, ma'am, and if it'll be displazin' to ye, sure we'll give it up." I told them that I did not want to know about it, and was sorry they had told me, but I would not be frightened at any noise I might hear in the night. " All right, ma'am," said the spokesman, winking at the others to show that he comprehended. The party then withdrew. About midnight such a startling racket suddenly broke the stillness that in spite of my previous knowledge, I *was* frightened. Horns of all grades of sound, from deep and hoarse to shrill, tin cups and pans clashed together or beaten with bones, yells, whistling, and in short every conceivable and inconceivable noise.

After the first blast, utter stillness; the startled officers, meanwhile, listening to discover the source of the unearthly noise, then, as if Bedlam had broken loose, the concert began once more. It was concentrated around the cabin of the surgeon so disliked. As the quarters of the officers were somewhat removed from the hospital proper, and very near my own, I got the full benefit of the noise. I cannot now say why the racket was not put a stop to. Perhaps because the serenaders numbered over one hundred and the surgeons despaired of restoring order. At all events, during the whole night we were allowed to sink into slumber, to be aroused again and again by the same hideous burst of sound. I only remember that the next day the horns, etc., were collected and carried away from camp, while the offenders were refused permission to leave their quarters for a while.

In the sick camp there lay over two hundred sick and wounded men, faithfully attended and prescribed for by the physicians, but lacking every comfort. Dr. Beatty was worried about the sick, but under the circumstances what could he do? Soon after occurred the terrible battle of Franklin, when our tents were again filled with wounded men. These men were unlike any I have ever nursed. Their shattered forms sufficiently attested courage and devotion to duty, but the enthusiasm and pride which had hitherto seemed to me so grand and noble when lighting up the tortured faces of wounded soldiers, appearing like a reflection of great glory, I now missed. It seemed as if they were yet revengeful and unsatisfied; their countenances not yet relaxed from the tension of the fierce struggle, their eyes yet gleaming with the fires of battle. The tales they told made me shudder: Of men, maddened by the horrible butchery going on around them, mounting the horrible barricade (trampling out in many instances the little sparks of life which might have been rekindled), only to add their own bodies to the horrid pile, and to be trampled in their turn by comrades who sought to avenge them; of soldiers on both sides, grappling hand to hand, tearing open each other's wound, drenched with each other's blood, *dying* locked in a fierce embrace. It turns me sick even now when I remember the terrible things I then heard, the awful wounds I then saw. During the whole period of my service, I never had a harder task than when striving to pour oil upon these troubled waters, to soothe and reconcile these men who talked incessantly of "sacrifice" and useless butchery. This was particularly the case with General Clebourne's men, who so loved their gallant leader that, at his death, revenge had almost replaced patriotism in their hearts.

I do not consider myself competent, nor do I wish to criticise the generals who led our armies and who, since the war, have, with few exceptions, labored assiduously to throw the blame of failure upon each other. I have read their books with feelings of intense sorrow and regret,—looking for a reproduction of the glories of the past,—finding whole pages of recrimination and full of "all uncharitableness." For my own part, I retain an unchanged, unchangeable respect and reverence for *all* alike, *believing each to have been a pure and honest patriot, who, try as he might, could not surmount the difficulties which each one in turn encountered.*

A brave, *vindictive* foe, whose superiority in numbers, in arms, and equipment, and, more than all, *rations*, they could maintain indefinitely. And to oppose them, an utterly inadequate force, whose bravery and unparalleled endurance held out to the end, although hunger gnawed at their vitals, disease and death daily decimated

m

their ranks, intense anxiety for dear ones exposed to dangers, privations, all the horrors which everywhere attended the presence of the invaders, torturing them every hour.

While yielding to none in my appreciation of the gallant General Hood, there is one page in his book which always arouses my indignation and which I can never reconcile with what *I know* of the history of the Army of Tennessee, from the time General Hood took command to the surrender. Truly, they were far from being like "dumb driven cattle," for *every man* was "*a hero* in the strife.*" It seems to me that the memory of the battle of Franklin alone should have returned to General Hood to "give him pause" before he gave to the public the page referred to:

(Extract.)

"My failure on the 20th and the 22d to bring about a general pitched battle arose from the unfortunate policy pursued from Dalton to Atlanta, and which had wrought 'such' demoralization amid rank and file as to render the men unreliable in battle. I cannot give a more forcible, though homely, exemplification of the morale of the troops at that period than *by comparing the Army to a team* which has been allowed to balk at every hill, one portion will make strenuous efforts to advance, whilst the other will refuse to move, and thus paralyze the exertions of the first. Moreover, it will work fault-lessly one day and *stall* the next. No reliance can be placed upon it at any stated time. Thus it was with the army when ordered into a general engagement, one corps strugged nobly, whilst the neighboring corps frus-trated its efforts by simple inactivity; and whilst the entire Army might fight desperately one day, it would fail in action the following day. Stewart's gallant attack on the 20th was neutralized by Hardee's inertness on the right; and the failure in the battle of the 22d is to be attributed also to the effect of the 'timid defensive' policy of this officer, who, although a brave and gallant soldier, neglected to obey orders, and swung away, totally independent of the main body of the Army."

Time softens and alleviates all troubles, and this was no exception. But the winter was a very gloomy one: my heart was constantly oppressed by witnessing suffering I could not relieve, needs which could not be met. The efforts of the foragers, combined with my own purchases from country wagons (although Dr. Beatty was liberal in his orders, and I spent every cent I could get), were utterly insufficient, although the officers of this camp-hospital were self-denying, and *all* luxuries were reserved for the sick. I hit upon an expedient to vary the rations a little, which found favor with the whole camp. The beef was simply atrocious. I had it cut into slices, let it lie in salt with a sprinkling of vinegar for a day, then hung the pieces up the chimneys until it was smoked. I first tried it in my own cabin, found it an improvement, and so had a quantity prepared for the hungry wounded. And so these dark days sped on, bringing, in due time,

THE LAST CONFEDERATE CHRISTMAS.

I will here subjoin an article originally written for the *Southern Bivouac*, which will give my readers an idea of how the Christmas-tide was spent.

For some time previous I had been revolving in my mind various plans for the celebration of Christmas by making some addition to the diet of the sick and wounded soldiers then under my charge. But, plan as I would, the stubborn facts in the case rose up to confront me, and I failed to see just how to accomplish my wishes. We were then located at Lauderdale Springs, Mississippi. I, with my servant, Tempe, occupied one room of a small, double house, built of rough-hewn logs, and raised a few feet from the ground; a sort of hall, open at both ends, separated my room from one on the opposite side occupied by Dr. —— and his wife. All around, as far as one could see, amid the white snow and with lofty pine-trees towering above them, extended the hospital-tents, and in these lay the sick, the wounded, the dying. Hospital-supplies were scarce, our rations of the plainest articles, which, during the first years of the war, were considered absolute necessaries, had become priceless luxuries. Eggs, butter, chickens came in such small quantities that they must be reserved for the very sick. The cheerfulness, self-denial, and fellow-feeling shown by those who were even partly convalescent, seemed to me to be scarcely less admirable than the bravery which had distinguished them on the battle-field. But this is a digression: let me hasten to relate how I was helped to a decision as to Christmas "goodies." One morning, going early to visit some wounded soldiers who had come in during the night, I found in one tent a new-comer, lying in one of the bunks, his head and face bandaged and bloody. By his side sat his comrade,—wounded also, but less severely,—trying to soften for the other some corn-bread, which he was soaking and beating with a stick in a tin cup of cold water. He explained that the soldier with the bandaged head had been shot in the mouth, and could take only soft food. I said, "Don't give him that. I will bring him some mush and milk, or some chicken soup." He set down the cup, looked at me with queer, half-shut eyes, then remarked, "Yer ga-assin' now, ain't ye?"

Having finally convinced him that I was not, I re-

tired for a moment to send the nurse for some food.
When it came, and while I was slowly putting spoonfuls of broth into the poor, shattered mouth of his
friend, he stood looking on complacently, though with
his lip quivering. I said to him, "Now, what would
you like?" After a moment's hesitation he replied,
"Well, lady, I've been sort of hankerin' after a sweet-
potato pone, but I s'pose ye couldn't noways get that?"
"There," thought I, "that's just what I *will* get and
give them all for Christmas dinner."

Hastening to interview the surgeon in charge, I easily
obtained permission to go on the next day among the
farmers to collect materials for my feast. An ambulance was placed at my disposal.

My foraging expedition was tolerably successful, and
I returned next evening with a quantity of sweet potatoes, several dozen eggs, and some country butter. Driving directly to the door of my cabin, I had my treasures
securely placed within; for, although holding my sol-
dier-friends in high estimation, I agreed with the driver
of the ambulance,—"Them 'taturs has to be taken in
out of the cold." My neighbor's wife, Mrs. Dr. ——, entered heartily into my plans for the morrow, promising
her assistance. My night-round of visits to the sick
having been completed, I was soon seated by my own
fireside, watching the operation of making and baking a
corn hoecake, which, with some smoked beef of my own
preparation and a cup of corn-coffee, made my supper on
this Christmas eve. It was so bitterly cold that I did
not undress; but, wrapping a blanket around me, lay
down on my bunk. Tempe also rolled herself up, and
lay down before the fire. In order to explain what followed, I must here say that the boards of my floor were
only laid, not fastened, as nails were not to be had. I was
awakened from "the first sweet sleep of night" by an un-

16

earthly yell from Tempe, who sprang unceremoniously upon my bunk, grasping me tightly, and crying, "O Lord, Miss ——, yearthquate dun cum!" Sitting up, I was horrified to see the boards of the floor rising and falling with a terrible noise. A moment later I realized the situation. A party of hogs had organized a raid, having for its object my precious potatoes. A sure-enough "yearthquate" would have been less appalling to me, as I have always been mortally afraid of hogs. Just then one of the invaders managed to knock aside a board and get his head in full view. I shivered with terror, but Tempe now grasped the state of the case, and, being "to the manner born," leaped forward to execute dire vengeance on the unfortunate hog. Seizing a burning stick from the fire, she rushed upon the intruder, who had gotten wedged so that advance or retreat was alike impossible. Her angry cries, and the piercing squeals of the hog, roused all in the vicinity. Help soon came, our enemies were routed, quiet was restored. My pones were a great success. All who were allowed by their surgeons partook of them. I had two immense pans full brought to my cabin, where those who were able brought their plates and cups, receiving a generous quantity of the pone and a cup of sweet milk.

But these struggles and hardships were nothing in comparison to what was now to befall us. The constant fighting and daily-increasing number of wounded at the front required the presence of experienced surgeons. After the battle of Franklin some of ours were sent up. In one or two instances those who replaced them were young and inexperienced. They were permitted to attend the convalescents and light cases. One morning, I was aroused very early by a nurse who begged me to go to one of the convalescents who had been calling for me all night.

Arrived at the tent, which at that hour was rather
dark, I lifted the flap to enter, but was arrested by a
piteous cry from the patient, who lay facing the entrance.
" For God's sake keep out that light," said he, " it hurts
my eyes." The nurse said, " It's measles he has, ma'am."
So I concluded the pained eyes were not unusual.

Approaching the bunk, and taking the patient's hand,
I found he had a raging fever. But when I placed my
hand upon his forehead, and felt the dreadful pustules
thickly covering it, my heart almost ceased to beat. An
unreasoning terror overpowered me; my impulse was to
flee at once from that infected tent. But I must not
give any alarm, so I simply said to the nurse, " I will
go to Dr. Beatty for some medicine; let no one enter
this tent until I come back." Dr. Beatty was not yet
out of his cabin, but receiving my urgent message, soon
appeared. I said, " Doctor, in tent No. — there is a
very sick man; can we look at the books and learn
what diagnosis his surgeon has made ?" We went
to the office, found the patient's name and number:
diagnosis,—*Measles.* I then said, " Dr. Beatty, it is not
measles, but, I fear, smallpox." At once, the doctor
strode off, followed closely by myself. As before, the
tent was dark. " Lift those flaps high," said the surgeon.
It was done, and there lay before us a veritable case of
smallpox.

Dr. Beatty's entire calmness and self-possession quite
restored my own. Said he, " I must have time to consult my surgeons, to determine what is to be done.
Meanwhile, retire to your cabin. You will hear from
me when matters are arranged."

The next few hours were for me fraught with fearful
anxiety and uncertainty,—yes, *uncertainty*,—for (to my
shame, let it be recorded) I actually debated in my own
mind whether or not to desert these unfortunate boys of

mine, who could not themselves escape the threatened danger.

God helping me, I was able to resist this terrible temptation. I had, I reasoned, been already exposed as much as was possible, having attended the sick man for days before. Having dedicated myself to the *Holy Cause*, for better or worse, I could not desert it even when put to *this* trying test. So, when Dr. Beatty came to say that in a few hours quarantine would be established and rigidly enforced, offering me transportation that I might at once go on with the large party who were leaving, I simply announced my determination to remain, but asked that Tempe might be sent to her owners in Alabama, as I dared not risk keeping her.

The poor fellow who had been first seized died that night, and afterward many unfortunates were buried beneath the snow-laden pines. Some of the nurses fell sick; from morning until night, after, far into the night, my presence was required in those fever-haunted tents.

When not on duty, the loneliness of my cabin was almost insupportable. Sometimes I longed to flee away from the dismal monotony. Often I sat upon my door-step almost ready to scream loudly enough to drown the sad music of the pines. Since the war I have seen a little poem by John Esten Cooke, which always reminds me of the time when the band in the pines brought such sadness to my own heart:

"THE BAND IN THE PINES.

" Oh, band in the pine-wood cease!
　Cease with your splendid call;
　The living are brave and noble,
　　But the dead were bravest of all!

" They throng to the martial summons,
　To the loud, triumphant strain;

And the dear bright eyes of long-dead friends
    Come to the heart again.

" They come with the ringing bugle
    And the deep drum's mellow roar,
Till the soul is faint with longing
    For the hands we clasp no more !

" Oh, band in the pine-wood cease
    Or the heart will melt in tears,
For the gallant eyes and the smiling lips
    And the voices of old years !"

When, at last, we were released from durance vile,
the Confederate army had retreated. Of course, the
hospitals must follow it. By this time my health was
completely broken down. The rigors of the winter,
the incessant toil, the hard rations had done their work
well. I was no longer fit to nurse the sick. In February I left the camp, intending to go for a while wherever
help was needed, relying upon a change to recuperate
my exhausted energies.

But from that time there was so much irregularity as
far as hospital organization was concerned that one
scarcely knew how best to serve the sick. Besides,
the presence of a lady had become embarrassing to the
surgeons in charge of hospitals, who, while receiving
orders one day which were likely to be countermanded
the next, often having to send their stores, nurses,
etc., to one place while they awaited orders in another,
could find no time to provide quarters and sustenance
for a lady. As an illustration of this state of things, I
will here give an extract from a letter addressed to me
after the war by Dr. McAllister, of the " Buckner Hospital."

" I was ordered late in November to Gainesville, Alabama; before reaching that place, my orders were

16*

changed to Macon; in February to Auburn, Alabama; thence to the woods to organize a tent hospital. No sick were sent there, and I had nothing to do but to build. Put up eighty large tents, built octagon homes, with rounded tops, and flag-poles on the top of each. Everything looked gloomy, but I kept on as if I expected to remain there always. Just as I had everything completed, received orders to move to Charlotte, North Carolina. When I got to Columbus, Georgia, was ordered to send on my stores with my negroes and women-servants, in charge of a faithful man, while I and my detailed men were to remain in the city during its investment, and as long as the struggle lasted, but at last to save myself, and join my stores in Macon, Georgia. Remained during the fight, while the city fell, and all my detailed men were captured; rode out of the city by the light of the burning buildings, and my road was lighted for twelve or fifteen miles by the burning city; borrowed horses about twelve at night, caught the last retreating train, put my servants Noel and Sam on it; rode on with my true friend Dr. Yates. Found the servants at Genoa Station, a distance of thirty-five miles, next morning at sunrise, thence to Macon; next night found my wife on the same crowded box-car; left her with Mrs. Yates, Mrs. Calan, and another lady from Columbus. Some of my stores had been sent to Atlanta, and some had been sent to Macon; then the railroad was cut between Macon and Atlanta; I had either to remain at Macon and be captured, or take the only road that was clear to Fort Valley, which I did, leaving my wife and Mrs. Yates at Dr. Green's. Yates, myself, Sam, and Noel took to the woods, and there remained about ten days, living as best we could. Then there was a flag of truce, and we came into Fort Valley. Thousands of Yankee cavalry were there in camps; all the railroads cut so we could not leave. One night we stole from the Yankees two good mules, borrowed a wagon, and took our wives across the country until we could strike one end of the Atlanta road, of which the Yankees had not got possession; went on into the city of Atlanta, where I met Dr. Stout, who told me the game was up, that my stores were some of them at Congress Station, some hundred miles away on the Augusta road, and for me to go on there and surrender to the first Yankee who commanded me to do so. Great heaven! what a shock to me! I would rather have died than to have heard it. I went down the road and found my stores, but did not have the honor of surrendering to the Yankees. A mob, constituted of women, children, and renegade Confederate soldiers, and with some negroes, charged my encampment and took everything except my wife, and trunks, and Mrs. Yates, and her trunks, which we saved by putting them into a wagon and driving for our lives out of the back alley of the town. At last we came to Atlanta, where we parted with Dr. and Mrs. Yates. My wife and I travelled to Marion in an old wagon, leaving the poor negroes scattered about in the woods. I only had time to tell them to go where they came from, to their former owners. After a tedious journey, having to beg my bread, I arrived at home (Marion, Alabama) about the first of May, 1865."

The same irregularities existed everywhere; my state of health forbade me to follow these erratic movements: indeed, I was utterly broken down and therefore made my way, not without great difficulty and many detentions, to Alabama, where my little boy had preceded me. Even then, we never dreamed of surrender, nor did the sad news reach us until many days after it had taken place. We were utterly incredulous, we could not, would not believe it. Meanwhile, the state of things described in one of the articles contained in another part of this book, designed for children (Sally's ride) culminated in the long-dreaded *Raid.*

Why the raiders had recrossed the river, returning to Selma, and leaving undisturbed (alas! only for a time) the elegant plantation-homes which lay all along their route, remained a mystery. It was certain that a detachment of them had been seen and reported by our own scouts, who at that time were in the saddle day and night " watching their motions;" the negroes also declared, " Dey was dare, *suah,* 'case we dun *seed* 'em." All able-bodied men had long ago gone to the front. The " home-guard," who were doing their best to keep watch and ward over helpless women and children, were only boys, full of ardor and courage, but too young to join the army, or men who from age or disability were also ineligible. These knew every inch of ground, every hiding-place for many miles. At every plantation they were expected and welcome, whenever they could find an opportunity to dash in, dismount, report the state of matters outside, and hastily swallow the "snack" always kept ready and set before them without loss of time, quite as a matter of course.

The news brought by these scouts, far from quieting apprehension, tended to increase and deepen it. The old man who, time out of mind, had managed the little ferry fifteen miles away, had been shot for refusing to ferry over some Federal soldiers. The bright light so anxiously watched one dark night proved to have been a fire, which had consumed the dwelling, gin-house, stables, etc., of a widowed cousin. Her cows had been slaughtered, her horses stolen, her garden and " truck-patch" ploughed all over in the search for hidden silver. Other and even more hideous tales (alas! too true) appalled the hearts and tried the courage of the women, who yet must never give up *trying* to protect the interests confided to them, must *seem* to hold the reins of power when really they were at the mercy of the negroes, who (to their credit be it spoken) behaved under these trying circumstances extremely well, in some cases showing the most affectionate solicitude and sympathy. They could not, however, in all cases be trusted to withstand the bribes sure to be offered for information as to hiding-places of valuables. So, little by little, silver and jewelry were made up into small packages to be disposed of secretly.

For several days all were on the *qui vive*. The fearful suspense, dread, and anguish of that time will never be forgotten by those who shared those anxious vigils; from earliest light until nightfall, restless feet traversed the house and yard, anxious eyes watched every possible approach,—the road, the woods, the plantation. At night, not one of the " white folks" thought of undressing; the very last of a bag of real coffee, which had been treasured like gold, was now brought out. During the day, the usual sweet-potato coffee was served. In the cool April nights, a cheerful fire always blazed in the open fireplace of the parlor, by it was set a pot of very strong coffee, upon which the ladies relied to keep them awake. One at a time would doze in her chair or upon the sofa, while the others kept watch, walking from window to window, listening at the fast-locked door, starting at every sound. Occasionally the dogs would bark furiously: " There they are!" cried everybody, and rising to their feet, with bated breath and wildly-beating hearts, they would listen until convinced that their four-footed friends had given a false alarm. Those of the women-servants who had no husbands begged every night to sleep "in de house." They were terrified. Their mattresses strewed the floors, and it really seemed as if they were a kind of protection, although they always fell asleep and snored so loudly as to drive the ladies, who wanted to listen for outside sounds, to the verge of distraction. Some one would occasionally interrupt the noise by administering to each in turn a good shake or insisting upon a change of position, but at best the lull was temporary. Soon one of the sleepers would give a suppressed snort, to be immediately joined by one after another, until the unearthly chorus once more swelled to rack the quivering nerves of the listeners.

Sometimes a peculiar tapping announced the presence outside of the master of the house. Creeping softly to the window of an empty room, the wife would receive assurances of present safety. She would then hand out valuable packages of silver or jewelry to be hidden far in the woods in places unknown to any but the owner, who marked the way to the buried treasure by "blazing" certain trees. Many valuables were hidden in this way and recovered after the war. The feeble condition of Colonel —— added tenfold to the anxiety of his family, for, although he persisted in doing his duty, it was certain that continual exposure and fatigue might at any time prove fatal. Insidious disease was even then gnawing at his vitals; but, Spartan-like, he folded above the dreadful agony the robe of manly courage and dignity, which hid it from even those who knew him best. Amid all the darkness and sorrow his pleasant smile cheered, his commanding presence inspired respect and confidence. From the windows of his soul shone the steady light of the patriotism that hopeth all things, believeth all things, endureth all things. It was not God's will that he should go forth to battle, but with a kindly heart and generous hand he helped the soldiers to do their duty by caring for their "loved ones at home."

Meanwhile the noble wife proved a helpmate indeed. A true type of Southern women. Not a duty was neglected. She looked well to the ways of her household and the well-being of the negroes committed to her care. The spinning and weaving of cloth for the almost naked soldiers in the field went on; the quarters were visited, the sick were cared for. The calm, steady voice read to the old, precious promises, or instructed the young negroes as to the way of truth. So day after day passed, the same anxious dread chilling all hearts, added fear always recurring as the darkness came with its terrible possibilities.

April had come, bringing a greater profusion of flowers, painting the face of nature with lovelier hues. No one knew why the neighborhood had thus far escaped being "raided." One evening the scouts (not one alone, but several) reported, "Not a Yankee on this side the river. Gone off on a raid miles on the other side." Colonel —— came in later confirming the report. He was persuaded to remain for one night's rest, and immediately retired to his room. About dusk two men in the disguise (it is *now* believed) of Confederate soldiers—ragged, worn, *barefooted*, and hungry—came stealing in, apparently fearful of being discovered and taken prisoners. No one suspected them. They were warmly welcomed. A supper of broiled ham, milk, eggs, corn-muffins, and real coffee was set before them. They were afterwards shown to a comfortable cabin in the yard,—"the boys' room,"—provided with every comfort, a servant to wait on them, and left to repose. These also having assured the ladies that "the Yanks" had gone off on a raid on the other side, it was deemed safe to take advantage of such an opportunity to go regularly to bed and rest, in preparation for whatever might befall afterwards. By ten o'clock everybody was sound asleep. About midnight one of the ladies, hearing a slight noise, arose and looked out the window. Old Whitey was walking about the yard, nibbling the grass. Knowing he was never allowed in the yard, she simply supposed that one of the servants had left open the quarter-gate. Not another sound save the mule's step broke the stillness of the night. Strange to say, the dogs were nowhere to be seen, nor did they bark at the mule. Wondering a little at this circumstance, the lady was about to lie down again, when simultaneously every door of the house was assailed with the butts of guns with a terrific noise. At the same time many hoarse voices yelled, "Open these doors, d—— y——! Open up, here, or we'll burn the house over your heads!" Everybody at once realized the situation. In that fearful moment strength and courage seemed to come as from above. The servants, sleeping upon the floor, began to scream, but were instantly silenced. The ladies, slipping on dressing-gowns, but never stopping to put on shoes or stockings, quietly opened the doors. Instantly the whole house swarmed with Federal soldiers. Their first act was to capture Colonel —— and drag him outside the house, giving him no time to put on any clothes save his pants and night-shirt. The raiders then proceeded to ransack the house. Every room, every closet, every trunk, box, drawer, was rifled. Two men went to the sideboard, quietly gathering up the few silver spoons, forks, ladles, etc., not hidden, wrapped them up and put them in their pockets. Others stripped off the pillow- and bolster-cases, stuffing them with clothing, pictures, etc., tied them together, and placed them ready to be slung over the backs of their horses. Bayonets were thrust through portraits; the sofas, beds, and lounges were pierced in search of concealed valuables; bureau-drawers were emptied, then pitched out of the doors or windows; the panels of locked *armoires* were broken or kicked to pieces to get at the contents; even the linen sheets were dragged off the beds and thrust into already full sacks and bags. Meanwhile, bonfires had been kindled in the yard. By the light the swarming demons carried on their destructive work outside. Around the pans of delicious milk in the dairy men reached over each others' heads to fill their tin cups. Buttermilk, clabber, fresh butter, disappeared in an instant. In the basement the officers were feasting on ham, etc. The smoke-house was left bare. Sugar, meal, flour, rice, were emptied into the yard, and stamped or shuffled into the dust. Axes or the butts of guns were employed to literally smash everything. Ham, shoulder-meat, etc., were tossed into wagons. Cows were driven off, and, oh, the beautiful horses, the *pride* and pets of their owners, were *led*, snorting and frightened, into the road, where the saddles of the cavalry-horses were put upon their shivering backs preparatory to being mounted and ridden away by their new masters.

With perfect calmness the ladies watched the havoc and desolation which was being wrought in their beloved home, among their household treasures. To one of them had been given, some time previous, a sacred trust, a watch which before the war had been presented to a minister by his congregation. When dying in one of the Confederate hospitals he had given it to Mrs. ——, begging that, if possible, it might be sent to his wife in Arkansas. This watch had been concealed upon the tester of a bed, and so far had escaped discovery. But one of the servants having given information regarding it, suddenly two soldiers dragged Mrs. —— into her own room, where they believed it was concealed. She positively refused to give it up. Throwing off the mattress, the men held a match to the feather-bed beneath, saying, "*Here* goes your d——d old house, then." Had the house been her own she might still have resisted, but as she was only a guest, and had been sheltered and most kindly treated, the watch was given up. The ruffians then insisted upon searching her, and in trying to force a ring from her finger, bruised and hurt the tender flesh. Even the negro cabins were searched. In several instances small sums of money which had been saved up were taken. Many threats to burn up "the whole business" were made, but, for some unknown reason, not carried into effect. Just at dawn the raiders mounted their horses and rode away, recrossing the river to Selma with their prisoners. As they rode through the "quarters," the negro men joined them on mules, horses, or on foot. Among the prisoners rode Colonel —— upon an old, worn-out horse, without saddle or bridle. By his side, guarding him and mounted upon the colonel's magnificent riding-horse, fully accoutred, was a negro man belonging to a neighboring plantation, who had guided the Federals to "ole ——'s place." Just behind, upon a sorry mule, escorted by a mixture of negroes and Yankees riding his own fine horses, came Colonel M——, his head erect, his eyes blazing scornfully, glancing from side to side, or drawing a sharp, hard breath between his clinched teeth as he overheard some ribald jest. His house and gin-house had been burned, his fields laid waste; he had left his young daughters without protection and without shelter. What the ladies felt as they saw this sad cavalcade pass out of sight may not be told. Morning dawned upon a scene of desolation, sickening in the extreme,—ruin, waste, wreck everywhere. The house emptied of everything valuable, floors filthy with the prints of muddy feet, the garden ruined, furniture battered and spoiled. Outside, broken barrels, boxes, etc., strewed the earth; lard, sugar, flour, meal were mingled together and with the sandy soil; streams of molasses ran down from broken casks; guns which had belonged to the family were broken and splintered and lay where they had been hurled; fences were broken down. Had there been any stock left, there was nothing to keep them out of garden or yard. Only old Whitey was left, however, and he walked gingerly about sniffing at the cumbered ground, looking as surprised as he was able. The carriage and buggy had been drawn out, the curtains and cushions cut and *smeared thoroughly with molasses and lard*. Breakfast-time arrived, but no Ruthy came up from the quarter; no smoke curled upward from the kitchen-chimney; a more hopeless, dismal party could not well be imagined than the three women who walked from room to room among the *débris*, neither noticing or caring for the losses, only intensely anxious regarding the helpless prisoner, who was surely suffering, but whom they could not hope to relieve. As the day wore on, some of the women from the quarters ventured near, bringing some coarse food which had been cooked in their own cabins; they would not, however, go inside the house, " Mass Yankee tole us we gwine ter get kill ef we wait on you all." Towards evening Mrs. —— walked down to the "quarter." Not a man was to be seen. The women were evidently frightened and uncertain as to how far the power of "Mass Yankee" extended. Their mistress had been a kind friend, and their habitual obedience and respect for her could not at once be overcome, but the threats and promises of the Federals had disturbed and unsettled them. Aunt Sophy was an old servant who had nursed Mrs. ——'s mother. For years she had been an invalid, kindly nursed and cared for by her master and mistress, receiving her meals from the family table, and having always some of the younger servants detailed to wait on her. Passing by her cottage now, Mrs. —— was astonished to see it empty. "Where is Sophy? what has happened to her?" "Oh, she dun gone to Selma." "That is impossible; why, she has not walked even as far as the house for months." "Well, she dun gone, shuah; she make Elsie hitch up ole Whitey in de cart and dribe her ober. One genplum he gwine gib her a mule for her own sef and forty acres ob groun'; so she dun gon' ter see 'bout hit." "Did any one else go?" "Oh, yes, mistis, Uncle Albert and Aunt Alice dey go too, and dey want we all to go 'long, but I's gwine ter wait untwill sees what Jack got ter say, 'cause I ain't gwine *nowha* dragging all dem chillum along untwill I knows for sartin whar I's gwine ter stop." Sick at heart, the lady turned away, slowly returning to the desolated house. Her occupation was gone; order and system could not be restored. There was nothing before the anxious woman but to watch and wait for news. On the second day one of the negro men returned, bringing a tale almost too horrible for belief,—Colonel M——, whose defiant bearing had incensed his captors more and more, had been shot down for refusing to obey orders. "Master was well, but looked mighty bad." The man also brought the first news of the surrender, a rumor which all refused to believe, although even the possibility filled all breasts with terrible forebodings. *Could* it be true? No! a thousand times no! And yet, —oh, the dread, the anguish of waiting to know.

The bright sunlight, the waving trees, the joyous notes of the feathered songsters seemed a mockery. Their stricken hearts cried out to all the beautiful things of nature,—

> "How can ye bloom so fresh and fair?
> How can ye sing, ye little birds, and I so weary, fu' o' care?"

Towards evening on the third day of suspense the master returned fresh from the prison, weary, ragged, dirty, and utterly woe-begone, for he had been set at liberty only to learn that liberty was but an empty sound. Sadly he confirmed the story of the surrender. The kindly eyes still strove to cheer, but their happy light was forever quenched. The firm lip quivered not as he told to the sorrowing women the woful tale, but the iron had entered his soul and rankled there until its fatal work was accomplished. Ah, many a noble spirit shrunk appalled from the "frowning Providence" which then and long afterwards *utterly* hid the face of a merciful and loving Father. And yet, as mother Nature with tender hands and loving care soon effaces all traces of havoc and desolation, creating new beauties in lovely profusion to cover even the saddest ruins, so it is wisely ordered that time shall bring healing to wounded hearts. The women who on that April evening long ago grieved so bitterly over the news of the surrender have since known deep sorrow, have wept over many graves. But, like all the women of the South, they have taken up the burden of life bravely, and, God helping them, will not falter or fail until He shall release them.

By and by, the men and boys of the family, from distant Appomattox, from the Army of Tennessee, came straggling home. All had walked interminable miles,— all were equally ragged, dirty, foot-sore, weary, dejected, despairing. They had done their best and had failed. Their labor was ended.

All over the land lay the ruins of once happy homes. As men gazed upon them, and thought of the past and *the future,* the apathy of despair crept over them; life seemed a burden too heavy to be borne; they longed to lay it down forever. For a time, men who had faced death again and again while struggling for *freedom,*

17*

could not find courage to look upon the desolation of the land, or to face the dread future. Closing their weary eyes, they slept until the clanking of chains awakened them.

Despotic power wrung the already bleeding, tortured heart of the South, until crying aloud, she held out to her sons her fettered hands. And then, fully aroused, hearing the piteous cries, the rattle of chains, seeing the beloved face, full of woe, conscious of every bitter, burning tear (which as it fell, seemed to sear their own hearts), struggling to reach, to succor her, they found *themselves* bound and powerless to save.

Alas, dear friends, that the pathway which opened so brightly, which seemed to lead to heights of superlative glory, should have ended beside the grave of hope. Oh, was it not hard to believe that " whatever is is right?" To kneel submissively in this valley of humiliation, and lift our streaming eyes to the heavens, that seemed of brass, to the Father who, it then appeared, had forgotten to be merciful. The glory which even then was apparent to the outside world, could not penetrate the clouds which hung above us.

The land was yet red with blood that had been poured out *in vain.* From once happy homes came wails of grief and despair.

Even the embers were dead upon the hearths around which loved ones should never more gather.

And since hope is dead, and naught can avail to change the decrees of Fate, let me close this record of mingled glory and gloom, for here must be written,—

OMEGA.

CHAPTER VII.

CONFEDERATE WOMEN.

No historian can faithfully recount the story of the war and leave untouched the record made by Southern women. Their patriotism was not the outcome of mere sentiment, but a pure steady flame which from the beginning of the war to the end burned brightly upon the altars of sacrifice, which they set up all over the land. "The power behind the throne" never ceased to be felt. Its spirit pervaded every breast of the living barricades which opposed the invaders, nerved every arm to battle for the right, inspired valorous deeds which dazzled the world. From quiet homes far from the maddening strife, where faithful women toiled and spun, facing and grappling with difficulties, even dangers, never complained of, came bright, cheery letters, unshadowed by the clouds which often hung dense and dark over their daily pathway but glowing with unshaken faith, undaunted patriotism, lofty courage, and more than all pride in the exceptional bravery which *they always took for granted.* Men must not fail to come up to the standard set up in simple faith by mothers, wives, daughters, and, as all the world knows, *they did not.*

It was my daily business during the war to read and answer letters to sick soldiers. Almost all were such as I have described. A few, alas! were far different. As I read them and watched the agony they caused, I understood why some men became deserters, and absolutely revered the manliness and patriotism which resisted a temptation so terrible.

It seemed once that I could never forget the contents of letters which particularly impressed me, but am sorry I have done so and cannot reproduce them here. *One* I can *never* forget. A tall, splendid Missouri soldier came into my office one morning, his face convulsed with grief. Handing me a letter, he sank into a chair, burying his face in his hands and sobbing pitifully. A letter had been somehow conveyed to him from his sister-in-law announcing that his wife was dying of consumption. Appended to the letter (which was sad enough) were a few lines written by the trembling hand of the dying one. "Darling, do not let any thoughts of me come between you and your duty to our country. I have longed to see you once more, to die with my head upon your breast; but that is past,—I am calm and happy. We have long known that this parting must be; perhaps when my soul is free I may be nearer you. If possible, my spirit will be with you wherever you are."

I can only recall these few lines. A volume could not convey more strongly the spirit of Southern women, strong even in death. I could only offer the stricken soldier the little comfort human sympathy can give, but my tears flowed plentifully as he told me of his wife and his home.

He was, as I afterwards learned, killed at the battle of Franklin. I thought almost with pleasure of the happy reunion which I felt sure must have followed.

How often I have marshalled into the hospital wards mothers and wives, who for the sake of some absent loved one had come from homes many miles away, to bring some offering to the sick. Timid, yet earnest women, poorly dressed, with sunbrowned faces and rough hands, yet bearing in their hearts the very essence of loving-kindness towards the poor fellows upon whose pale faces and ghastly wounds they looked with "round-eyed wonder" and pity. After a while they would gain courage to approach some soldier whom they found "sort o' favored" their own, to whom they ventured to offer some dainty, would stroke the wasted hand, smooth the hair, or hold to the fevered lips a drink of buttermilk or a piece of delicious fruit. Ah, *how many* times I have watched such scenes! To the warmly-expressed thanks of the beneficiaries they would simply answer, " That is nothing; 'mebbe' somebody will do as much *for mine* when he needs it."

About seven miles from Ringgold, Georgia, lived an old couple, Mr. and Mrs. Russell, who, although ardently loving *the cause*, were too old and feeble to *serve* it otherwise than by their unceasing prayers, and by giving freely of their substance to sustain the patients at the hospitals then established at Ringgold. Their daughter, " Miss Phemie," a beautiful young girl, was never weary of conferring benefits upon the Southern soldiers; every day she rode in, never minding even heavy storms, and often riding upon a wagon because it would hold a larger supply of vegetables, etc. Many a soldier was taken to the homestead to be cared for. Those who could not go from under medical or surgical treatment were often treated to little rides. Her devotion to the soldiers I can never forget.

Among the sick and wounded who were sent to the hospital at Newnan were many Georgians whose homes were within twenty-five or thirty miles.

After the fight at Missionary Ridge, two boys, brothers, were brought in. One was threatened with pneumonia; the other, a lad of sixteen, had his right arm shattered from the shoulder down. At his earnest request his mother was sent for; the necessary amputation being deferred awhile, because he begged so hard that the surgeon should await her arrival. She had to ride all the way on a wagon drawn by a steer (oh, mothers, can you not imagine the agony which attended that lengthened journey?), and she was so long detained that I had to take her place at her boy's side while the operation was performed. The boy rapidly sunk,—when his mother came was past speaking, and could only express with his dying eyes his great love for her. Kneeling beside him, she watched intently, but without a tear or a sob, the dear life fast ebbing away. The expression of that mother's face no one who saw it can ever forget.

When all was over, I led her to my own room, where she asked to be left alone for a while. At last, in answer to the sobbing appeals of her remaining son, she opened the door. He threw himself into her arms, crying out, "Buddie's gone, but you're got me, ma, and I'll never leave you again. I'll help you take Buddie home, and I'll stay with you and help you work the farm."

The mother gently and tenderly held him off a little way, looking with burning eyes into his face; her own was pale as death, but not a sob or tear yet. Quietly she said, "No, my son, your place is not by me; I can get along as I have done; you are needed yonder (at the front); *go* and avenge your brother; he did his duty to the last; don't disgrace him and me. Come, son, don't cry any more; you're mother's man, you know."

That same night that mother started *alone* back to her home, bearing the coffined body of her youngest son, parting bravely from the elder, whose sorrow was overwhelming. Just before leaving, she took me aside and said, "My boy is no coward, but he loved his Buddie, and is grieving for him; try to comfort him, won't you?"

I did try, but during the whole night he paced with restless feet up and down my office. At daylight I sat watching his uneasy slumber.

A few weeks later a young wife came by train to visit her husband, who lay very ill of fever, bringing with her a lovely blue-eyed baby girl about two years old.

I found a room for her at a house near the hospital, and she was allowed to nurse her husband. When he was nearly ready to report for duty, a fearful accident happened by which the baby nearly lost her life, and was awfully disfigured. At the house where the young wife boarded there was a ferocious bull-dog, which was generally kept chained until it showed such evident fondness for the babe that he was sometimes allowed to lie upon the gallery beside it while it slept, and the little one on awakening would crawl all over the dog, who patiently submitted, and would affectionately lick her face.

One day, however, when the family were all assembled upon the gallery, the dog suddenly sprung upon the little girl, fastening his dreadful fangs in one side of her face. Everybody was stricken with horror. Nothing availed to make the beast loosen his hold, until suddenly he withdrew his teeth from the child's face and fastened them once more in her shoulder. At last, as no other alternative presented itself, some one placed a pistol to his ear and killed him. The baby on being released still breathed, but was so torn and disfigured that the sight turned strong men sick.

The father fell in a swoon; the young mother, pale and shaking as with an ague, yet held her mutilated babe through all the examination and the surgical operations which followed. For two weeks it seemed as if the child must die, but she did not, and soon, unconscious of her disfigurement, began to play and smile. All pitied the unfortunate father when, after some time allowed him through sympathy with his misfortune, it became necessary for him to return to the front. He had borne an excellent record, but now broke down utterly, declaring he *could not* leave his child. The young wife, putting down with a strong hand her own sorrow, actually set herself to rouse her husband to a sense of duty, and succeeded; I was present at the depot when the brave, girlish wife waved to the soldier a smiling farewell, and afterwards witnessed her vain efforts to suppress the short, sharp screams of agony which had been kept under as long as her husband needed to be upheld, but which after his departure convulsed her at intervals for hours.

There are two women against whom, during and since the war, I held and still hold a grudge. One was of that class of women who undervalue and strive to undo all the good done by others; who hold opinions and views which they absolutely insist upon carrying out regardless of consequences.

During the whole four years of the war I was annoyed by these would-be directresses of hospitals. They would intrude themselves into my wards, where they hesitated not to air their superior knowledge of all sickness, to inspire discomfort and distrust in the patients by expressive gestures, revealing extreme surprise at the modes of treatment, and by lugubrious shakes of the head their idea of the inevitably fatal result. While the kindly women, who, though already overburdened, would take from the wards of the hospital enough of convalescents or sick men to crowd their own homes, often thereby saving lives,—always doing good,— these prowling women would manage to convey their sense of the dreadful condition of hitherto well-satisfied patients without ever suggesting a remedy. In one of the large churches used for sick-wards in Newnan lay a young man from Maryland, who had suffered the amputation of an arm. The wound had been carefully bandaged, the arteries taken up, etc., but as inflammation supervened the pain became almost unbearable, the poor fellow moaned unceasingly. One night two old women visited the ward. Afterward, upon making my last round, I found the young man above mentioned so quiet that I did not disturb him. It so happened that Dr. Merriweather, of Alabama, was in Newnan, in close attendance upon his young son, who had received a most peculiar and apparently fatal wound. He was shot through the liver. The wound, at all times excessively painful, exuded bile. Whenever Dr. Merriweather wanted an hour's rest I took my place at the bedside of the lad. Interest in the case took me very frequently to the ward. Just before bedtime, therefore, I returned to the side of young Merriweather to let his father off for a while. Inquiring of the nurse as to the patient who had been so restive, I learned that he had neither moved nor spoken. Feeling uneasy, I walked over to the corner where he lay. At once I heard a drip, drip, drip, and, calling for a light, soon discovered that the bed and floor were bloody. Dr. Yates was called at once, but too late. That dreadful meddler, the old woman visitor, had actually dared to loosen the bandages, and the poor victim, feeling only relief, had sunk tranquilly to his death.

The other was a heartless girl, who has, I feel sure, by this time made a selfish, unloving wife to some poor man. Her lover, after the battle of Franklin, was brought to the tent hospital, having lost a leg and being wounded in the face. He confided to me the fact of his engagement to " one of the prettiest and *peartest* girls in 'Massissip,'" and begged me to write her of his condition, and, said the poor fellow, " If she don't care about sticking to a fellow murdered up like I am, I reckon I'll have to let her off" (this with a sigh). Then, with a brighter look, "Maybe she'll stick, anyhow." How he watched for the answer to that letter! His restlessness was pitiful to see. I tried to help him by reading to him and by relating to him instances of women who only loved more because the object of their affection had been unfortunate. Among other things, I told him of the noble English girl who wrote to her mangled lover that she still loved and would marry him " if there was enough of his body left to contain his soul." Afterward I felt sorry that I had encouraged him to hope, for it was my misfortune to read to him a very cold letter from his lady-love, who declined to marry " a *cripple*." She wanted a husband who could support her, and as some man who lived near was " mighty fond of her company and could give her a good home," she reckoned she would take his offer under consideration.

For a few days my poor young friend was inconsolable; but one morning I found him singing. " I've been thinking over that matter," said he, " and I reckon I've had a lucky escape. That trifling girl would never have made me a good, faithful wife." From that day he seemed to have recovered his cheerfulness. I have never forgiven that faithless girl.

All over the South, wherever "pain and anguish wrung the brow" of their defenders, women became " ministering angels."

Even those who had been bereft of their own suppressed their tears, stifled the cry of bleeding hearts, and, by unwearied attention to living sufferers, strove to honor their dead. Self-abnegation was, during the war, a word of meaning intense and real. Its spirit had its dwelling-place in the souls of faithful women, looked out from the bright eyes of young girls, whose tender feet were newly set in a thorny pathway, as well as from the pale, stricken faces of those whose hearts the thorn had pierced.

Among the tender and true women with whom I have corresponded since the war is the mother of Colonel Robadeaux Wheat, the noble Louisianian who fell at Gaines's Mill. I have several of her letters by me, written in the tremulous hand of one who had passed her seventy-ninth birthday, but glowing with love for the *cause*, and fondest pride in the sons who died in its defence. It is touching to see how she clings to and cherishes the record, given by his companions in arms, of "Robadeux's" last hours on earth, when, in the early morning, before going forth to battle, his heart seemed to return to the simple faith of his boyhood, and, gathering his subordinate officers around him in his tent, he read reverently the service of prayer which committed himself and them to the protection of the God of battles. Mrs. Wheat's letters are, I think, among the most beautiful and touching I ever read, yet sprightly and interesting. Believing that all my readers will feel an interest in the mother of glorious "Bob Wheat," I will here transcribe a small portion. In one letter she says,—

"I am, thank God, in excellent health for one aged seventy-eight. My husband was born in this city (Washington, D. C.) in *the year one, he says.*

"We shall soon celebrate the fifty-ninth anniversary of our marriage, and he is deeply engaged upon some 'post-nuptial lines' for me."

In another,—

"I want to send you a sword and flag for the Exposition. How I wish I could *take* it to New Orleans, where I lived many years when my husband was rector

of St. Paul's Church! You know, our second son, I. T
Wheat, was Secretary of the Secession Committee when
Louisiana seceded, also Secretary of the Legislature.
He was killed at Shiloh at the same hour as General
Sydney Johnston, and is buried in Nashville. We are
hoping to have the dear brother's monument in Holly-
wood, Richmond, where both beloved ones shall rest in
the same grave." . . . . In conclusion, "Our love and
blessings rest ever on yourself and all friends of our
hero sons. Truly yours, in Christian fellowship,

"Selima Wheat."

Here is the record of another mother, who is to this
day proud of the splendid record made by her sons, and
devoted in the memory of *the cause.*

At the commencement of the war there lived in
Sharon, Mississippi, Mr. and Mrs. O'Leary, surrounded
by a family of five stalwart sons. Mrs. Catharine
O'Leary was a fond and loving mother, but also an
unfaltering patriot, and her heart was fired with love
for the cause of Southern liberty. Therefore, when her
brave sons, one after the other, went forth to battle for
the right, she bade them God-speed. "Be true to your
God and your country," said this noble woman, "and
never disgrace your mother by flinching from duty."

Her youngest and, perhaps, dearest was at that time
only fifteen. For a while she felt that his place was
by her side; but in 1863, when he was barely seventeen, she no longer tried to restrain him. Her trembling
hands, having arrayed the last beloved boy for the sacrifice, rested in blessings on *his* head ere he went forth.
Repressing the agony which swelled her heart, she
calmly bade him, also, "Do your whole duty. If you
must die, let it be with your face to the foe." And so
went forth James A. O'Leary, at the tender age of seven-

teen, full of ardor and hope. He was at once assigned to courier duty under General Loring. On the 28th of July, 1864, at the battle of Atlanta, he was shot through the hip, the bullet remaining in the wound, causing intense suffering, until 1870, when it was extracted, and the wound healed for the first time. Notwithstanding this wound, he insisted upon returning to his command, which, in the mean time, had joined Wood's regiment of cavalry. This was in 1865, and so wounded he served three months, surrendering with General Wirt Adams at Gainesville. A short but very glorious record. This young hero is now residing in Shreveport, Louisiana, is a successful physician, and an honored member of the veteran association of that city,—Dr. James A. O'Leary.

Of his brothers, the oldest, Ignatius S. O'Leary, served throughout the war, and is now a prominent druggist of Vicksburg, Mississippi.

Dr. Richard O'Leary, surgeon P. A. C. S., now practises medicine in Vicksburg.

Cornelius O'Leary, badly wounded at the battle of Fredericksburg, lay on the field for hours with the legions of friend and foe alternately charging over him. After a long illness he recovered, and is now a planter near Sharon, Mississippi.

John Pearce O'Leary was killed in the battle of the Wilderness.

Mrs. O'Leary still lives in Sharon. The old fire is unquenched.

There are two names of patriotic women which will always awaken in every Southern heart profound veneration, and imperishable love and gratitude,—women who devoted themselves so entirely, so continuously to the soldiers of the Confederacy as to obliterate self, unconsciously winning for themselves the while a name and fame which history will proudly record.

Their names—written in many hearts, fondly cherished in the homes of veterans whose children are taught to revere them—are Mrs. Buck Morris and Mrs. L. M. Caldwell. Mrs. Morris was by birth a Kentuckian, but at the beginning of the war resided with her husband, a prominent and wealthy lawyer, in Chicago, Illinois.

Her sympathies, always Southern, became strongly enlisted upon the side of the unfortunate prisoners at Camp Douglas. Both Judge Morris and his wife were deeply implicated in the plot to release these men. Their home in Chicago was a place of secret rendezvous for Southerners who, in the interest of these prisoners, were secretly visiting Chicago.

By some means constant communication with the prisoners was established, and if they still suffered horribly, hope revived among them for a while, and her blessed presence lightened their burdens. Mrs. Morris well knew that by implicating herself in the plot she was placing herself and husband in a position to suffer in their own persons and property in case of failure. Death would be the most probable consequence. Yet she risked it all. To use her own words, copied from a letter which I received from her shortly before her death, "I *did* help my suffering, starving countrymen, who were subjected to the horrors of Camp Douglas. I loved them with all the sympathy and pride of a mother, and I did spend upon them every dollar of my own money and as much of my husband's as I could *get* by fair means or foul in my hands.

"At the close of the war we found ourselves broken in health and fortune, but my husband had still enough left for our support; but the great Chicago fire swept our all away.

"Should my health improve, I wish to make an effort to send you a fuller account, and to add my small morsel of praise to the gallantry and patient endurance of the most bitter and maddening trials that men were ever called upon to endure.

"One unselfish action I would like to have recorded of a member of J. H. Morgan's command, the same to which my dear friend Colonel B. F. Forman belonged, and he can tell you how proud all Kentucky was of her brave boys. This is what I wish to write, because I like to have every noble deed recorded. After my good brother, Ex-Governor Blackman (who has administered medicine whenever I needed it), removed to Tennessee, and I felt the attack coming on from which I have so long and so severely suffered, I applied to Dr. R. Wilson Thompson for medical advice, and, receiving it, put my hand in my pocket. He said, almost sternly, 'No, no, Mrs. Morris, do not attempt that; you cannot do it,' and, rising abruptly, left the house. Returning the second day, he said, 'I fear you did not understand me, Mrs. Morris: I feel as every Confederate soldier feels, or ought to feel,—that he could never do enough for *you; we* could never receive pay from *you* for anything.' And so for the last five months he, although like many of our brave boys has had many hardships to endure, and his constitution shattered, has come through snow and sleet night and day to minister to the relief of an old woman who only did her duty to him and his people twenty long years ago. How few remember to be grateful so long! Present my best love to my old friend B. F. Forman. I remain always your friend and well-wisher,

"Mrs. Mary B. Morris.

"Spring Station, Kentucky."

From one of the many Louisiana soldiers who received, at the hands of Mrs. Caldwell, the tender care and excellent nursing which doubtless saved his life, I have received a description of the "Refuge," which, during three years of the war, was opened to Louisiana soldiers; not to officers, although a few personal friends of Mr. and Mrs. Caldwell were there by special invitation; but it was understood that none but private soldiers were expected without an invitation, while all privates were welcomed as to a home.

"The 'Refuge,' the residence of John E. Caldwell during the war, was situated in Amherst County, Virginia, about three and a half miles from Lynchburg. The residence was of peculiar build, having more the appearance of the Queen Anne style of architecture than any else, and was probably the only house in that section of country where the constructor had diverged from the accepted style for a country residence, hence, even in its isolated situation, it was known far and wide. The estate comprised an area of about eight hundred acres, and was cultivated in wheat, corn, etc. The route to it from Lynchburg lay, for about a mile and a half, along the north side of the James River, from which the road turned at almost right angles toward the north, over an undulating country, and through a long lane, which was part of the farm.

"The house stood about fifty yards from the road, and presented a rather picturesque appearance, the lawn being surrounded by a fence, outside of which and in front of the house a circular lawn had been laid out, around which was the carriage drive.

"There were four rooms on the ground floor of the house, and two in the main building up-stairs, and two additional rooms which had been added, but were so situated that an accurate description would be hard to give, and perhaps harder to understand after giving.

"The house faced nearly east, and had a porch up- and down-stairs, and on the north side a gallery. There were the usual out-houses, and a feature of the place was the spring, which was situated at the foot of the hill upon which the house stood. Water was supplied from this spring by means of a ram-pump with pipes. Around the spring was a growth of very fine walnut- and chestnut-trees, which made it a very cool retreat during the warm days of summer. A large orchard of apples, plums, and peaches was immediately in the rear of the residence. Between the farm and the road which led from Lynchburg to Amherst Court-House, a distance of about two miles, was a thick growth of woods, consisting principally of chestnut-trees.

" The whole face of the country consisted of hills and dales, and was rather rugged; the soil rather poor, probably having been exhausted by long cultivation. The nearest house was fully a mile distant, that section of country being but sparsely settled."

Their painful journey thitherward ended, just imagine what it must have been to these suffering men to arrive at such a haven of rest!—a "refuge" indeed. Think of the cool, breezy chambers, clean and white and fragrant, *like home,* of the tender ministry of that gentle woman, whose loving service was theirs to command, of the country food, of the cool, sparkling water from the spring under the oaks, held to fevered lips by ever-ready hands, while the favored patients drank at the same time draughts of sympathy from eyes whose kindly glances fell upon the humblest as upon their very own. The excellence and faithfulness of the nursing is fully proved by the fact that while three or four hundred patients were sent to this blessed "Refuge," no mortality occurred among the soldiers, the only death being that of a little son of Captain Laurence Nichols, who had fallen in battle at Gaines's Mill, and whose widow found in this lovely, hospitable home a temporary resting-place for the body of her gallant husband, and shelter for herself and child, a lovely boy of three years, who was thence transferred to the arms of the Good Shepherd. Sad, indeed, were the hearts of the little band of women gathered at the "Refuge."

The trials of the bereaved wife and mother were indeed sore and hard to be borne, but she could go to the graves of her dead and there pray for faith to look upward, where she knew her treasures were safe for time and for eternity. Under the same roof the wife of General Francis T. Nichols passed days and nights of agonizing suspense. Her husband was wounded and a prisoner. She knew he had suffered amputation of an arm, but could learn nothing more. *Rumors* were fearful enough to distress the young wife, whose trembling heart was filled with foreboding. Every few days reports that *seemed* true startled her,—he was *dead.* Alas! it might be true, for how could he live in the midst of enemies to whom his high spirit would not bend, wounded, suffering, deprived of the loving care for which he pined? Again, he had tried to escape in the garb of a peddler, and had been taken up as a spy (which no one who knew him believed). In that sad household Mrs. Caldwell's duties became onerous and multifarious enough to appall one less stout-hearted or less devoted to the cause. The inmates of the dwelling looked to her for sympathy, advice, nursing, and all kinds of attention, as well as for the comfort which could come only by superexcellent housekeeping. And all this was done, and *well* done, by one woman, inspired by supreme devotion to the *Confederate cause* and its defenders. Truly such a woman deserves to be immortalized, to live in history long after the hearts that now enshrine her image shall have ceased to beat.

Later, larger hospital accommodation having been

provided, it became difficult to obtain permission for private soldiers to leave the wards to which they had been assigned.

Mr. and Mrs. J. Edwards Caldwell then resolved to fill up the "Refuge" with their own friends among the officers, saying to each other, " We will do all the good we can, and will agree to sustain each other in any course without consulting." Very sick and very badly-wounded patients were now sent to Mrs. Caldwell. In fact, cases which were considered hopeless, but lingering, were despatched from the hospital to the "Refuge" to die, but not one of them did what was expected of him. The efforts of Mrs. Caldwell were blessed of God, and her patients, without exception, improved. One of these was Lawson Lewis Davis, of New Orleans, wounded at Frazier's Mills, near Richmond. He was suffering from a terrible wound, the cap of the shoulder having been removed. He suffered for a whole year before recovering. A still more remarkable case was that of Captain Charles Knowlton, Tenth Louisiana Regiment. He was wounded in the knee in November, 1863, and was at once invited to the "Refuge," but, having recession of the knee, was compelled to remain under surgical treatment until April, 1864, when he was sent to Mrs. Caldwell, and remained nine months more under her care. An order had been issued that in all such cases amputation should be performed, but Dr. Reid, of Richmond, his attendant surgeon, decided to attempt to save the limb, and was successful. Out of many cases of the kind, this was the only one recorded where amputation was avoided and the patient's life was saved.

Captain Knowlton now resides near Hopevilla, East Baton Rouge, Louisiana, is married, and has two children. Another desperate case was that of John McCormick, from whose leg nearly all the bones were removed, but who also recovered.

There were, besides, three men sick of fever and dysentery, desperately ill, considered hopeless when sent to the "Refuge," but who all recovered. This is certainly a remarkable record, and one to be proud of. Among the patients was that noble patriot, Colonel Alcibiades de Blanc, of St. Martin's Parish, Louisiana, of whom Lousianians proudly relate that he refused to be made a brigadier-general, saying he did not feel competent to fill such a position, and was content to serve his country as a private soldier, feeling that no position could be more honorable.

Of Company K, Eighth Louisiana, and Company H, Seventh Louisiana, nearly all the sick and wounded enjoyed, at one time or another during the war, the hospitalities of the "Refuge." General Hays was a personal friend and honored guest. Henry Weir Baker there recovered from typhoid fever. This gentleman was a member of Washington Artillery, a distinction which is enough of itself, without an added word of praise. He is now residing in New Orleans, a successful journalist, and has been untiring in his patriotic efforts to develop the splendid resources of Louisiana. Fred Washington, of New Orleans, was also saved to his country by the kindly attentions of Mrs. Caldwell. He also is an honored citizen of New Orleans, engaged as a journalist, and is one of the faithful few who *do not forget.*

He is an active member of the association A. N. Va., always "to the fore" when opportunities occur to honor the dead Confederates or to succor the living.

Of the hundreds who now live to remember with liveliest gratitude the "Refuge" they once found from the horrors and toils and pains of battle, and the gentle hostess who so unweariedly ministered to them, I can gather only a few names besides those already mentioned,—those of Lieutenant Brooks, Seventh Louisiana; Dr. Henry Larreux, —— ——; Lieutenant Henri Puisson, Tenth Louisiana.

Mr. and Mrs. Caldwell were New Orleans people. Their temporary home in Virginia was taken with the definite object in view of offering a "refuge" to sick and wounded Louisiana soldiers. She is, of course, proud of its "record" and her own, but simply says in her letter to me, "On opening the 'Refuge' (Mr. John Edwards Caldwell said to his wife) we will each do all we find to do, and all we *can* do, without consulting or telling each other what we do. And this we carried out."

While seeking materials for this sketch, I have interviewed several of the veterans who were in Virginia her guests and patients. I had but to mention her name to ask, "Do you know Mrs. Caldwell, of the 'Refuge?'" and forthwith the eyes of stern men grew misty, and an indescribable look brightened careworn faces, the look I know so well and have learned to think more beautiful than "any light that falls on land or sea." "*Know her!* Why, but for her I must have died." Thus to become of blessed memory is worth a lifetime of toil and self-devotion. And yet the *cause* and its defenders were worth it all, and more. As far as the wounded and sick soldiers are concerned, I am sure that Mrs. Caldwell, equally with myself and all others, who during the war were so blessed as to be permitted to minister to them, will be willing to declare that magnificent as were their brave deeds, their patient endurance seemed almost "the better part of valor."

There is one bright, shining record of a patriotic and tireless woman which remains undimmed when placed beside that of the most devoted of Confederate women: I refer to Mrs. Rose Rooney, of Company K, Fifteenth

K   19

Louisiana Regiment, who left New Orleans in June, 1861, and never deserted the "b'ys" for a day until the surrender.

She was no hanger-on about camp, but in everything but actual fighting was as useful as any of the boys she loved with all her big, warm, Irish heart, and served with the undaunted bravery which led her to risk the dangers of every battle-field where the regiment was engaged, unheeding the zip of the minies, the shock of shells, or the horrible havoc made by the solid shot, so that she might give timely succor to the wounded or comfort the dying. When in camp she looked after the comfort of the regiment, both sick and well, and many a one escaped being sent to the hospital because Rose attended to him so well. She managed by some means to keep on hand a stock of real coffee, paying at times thirty-five dollars per pound for it. The surrender almost broke her heart. Her defiant ways caused her to be taken prisoner. I will give in her own words an account of what followed.

"Sure, the Yankees took me prisoner along with the rest. The next day, when they were changing the camps to fix up for the wounded, I asked them what would they do with *me*. They tould me to 'go to the divil.' I tould them, 'I've been long enough in his company; I'd choose something better.' I then asked them where any Confederates lived. They tould me about three miles through the woods. On my way I met some Yankees. They asked me, 'What have you in that bag?' I said, 'Some rags of my own.' I had a lot of rags on the top, but six new dresses at the bottom; and sure I got off with them all. Then they asked me if I had any money. I said no; but in my stocking I had two hundred dollars in Confederate money. One of the Yankees, a poor divil of a private soldier, handed to me three twenty-five cents of Yankee money. I said to him, ' Sure, you must be an Irishman.' ' Yes,' said he. I then went on till I got to the house. Mrs. Crump and her sister were in the yard, and about twenty negro women—no men. I had not a bite for two days, nor any water, so I began to cry from weakness. Mrs. Crump said, ' Don't cry, you are among friends.' She then gave me plenty to eat,—hot hoe-cake and buttermilk. I stayed there fifteen days, superintending the cooking for the sick and wounded men. One-half of the house was full of Confederates, and the other of Yankees. They then brought us to Burkesville, where all the Yankees were gathered together. There was an ould doctor there, and he began to curse me, and to talk about all we had done to their prisoners. I tould him, ' And what have *you* to say to what you done to *our* poor fellows?' He tould me to shut up, *and sure I did.* They asked me fifty questions after, and I never opened me mouth. The next day was the day when all the Confederate flags came to Petersburg. I had some papers in my pocket that would have done harrum to some people, so I chewed them all up and ate them, but I wouldn't take the oath, and *I never did take it.* The flags were brought in on dirt-cars, and as they passed the Federal camps them Yankees would unfurl them and shake them about to show them. My journey from Burkesville to Petersburg was from eleven in the morning till eleven at night, and I sitting on my bundle all the way. The Yankee soldiers in the car were cursing me, and calling me a damn rebel, and more ugly talk. I said, ' Mabbe some of you has got a mother or wife ; if so, you'll show some respect for *me.*' Then they were quiet. I had to walk three miles to Captain Buckner's headquarters. The family were in a house near the battle-ground, but the door was shut, and I didn't know who was inside, and I couldn't see any light. I sat down on the porch, and thought I would have to stay there all night. After a while I saw a light coming from under the door, and so I knocked; when the door was opened and they saw who it was, they were all delighted to see me, because they were afraid I was dead. I wanted to go to Richmond, but would not go on a Yankee transportation. When the brigade came down, I cried me heart out because I was not let go on with them. I stayed three months with Mrs. Cloyd, and then Mayor Rawle sent me forty dollars and fifty more if I needed it, and that brought me home to New Orleans."

Mrs. Rooney is still cared for and cherished by the veterans of Louisiana. At the Soldiers' Home she holds the position of matron, and her little room is a shrine never neglected by visitors to "Camp Nichols."

Upon every occasion when the association of A. N. Va. appear as an association, Mrs. Rooney is with them, an honored and honorary member. Neatly dressed, her cap of the real Irish pattern surmounting her face, beaming with pride in " the *b'ys.*"

In fiery patriotism, unfaltering devotion, defiant courage the women of New Orleans had no rival, save the women of Baltimore. I know no other place where the fiery furnace was so hot, the martyrdom so general or so severe. In both instances the iron hand of despotism failed to crush or subdue.

Women continued to give aid and comfort to Confederate soldiers in hospital and prison, using every art they possessed to accomplish their ends. The sick were nursed and fed and comforted. Prisoners were assisted to escape, concealed until they could be spirited away, while their fair friends bravely faced and dared the consequences of discovery, never hesitating to avow their partisanship, crying, "If this be treason, make the most of it." A dozen arrests among these devotees did no good, for their name was legion. Every house was a nest of "treason;" for here dwelt the women whose best beloved were Confederate soldiers.

And when the end came, when the bravest soldiers returned, wretched and despairing, even weeping bitter tears within the faithful arms that sheltered them, the faces which bent above them still bravely smiled. Beloved voices whispered of encouragement and hope, patient hearts assumed burdens under which men fainted and failed.

From the root of patriotism, deeply buried in the hearts of Southern women, sprung a new and vigorous growth. Its tendrils overspread and concealed desolate places; the breath of its flowers filled all the land, stealing over the senses like an invigorating breeze.

"There is life in the old land yet," said men to each other. Let us cherish and develop it. And so, once more each lifted his heavy burden, and finding it unexpectedly lightened, turned to find at his side, no longer a helpless clinging form which should hamper his every step, but a true woman, strong in the love which defied discouragement, "with a heart for any fate," a *helpmeet*, indeed, who hereafter would allow no burden to remain unshared.

Thus faithful to the living, the women of the South never forgot their dead heroes. At first it was impossible to do more than to "keep green" their sacred graves, or to deposit thereon a few simple flowers, but the earliest rays of the sun of prosperity fell upon many a "storied urn and animated bust," raised by tireless love and self-sacrifice, to mark "the bivouac of the dead." In connection with one of these, erected by the ladies of New Orleans, in Greenwood Cemetery, I know an anecdote which has always seemed to me particularly beautiful and touching, as illustrative of an

19*

exquisite sentiment which could have had its birth only in the heart of a true and tender woman. After the removal of the bones of the Confederate soldiers, who had died in and about New Orleans, from their lowly graves to their last resting-place, under their grand and beautiful monument, many people repaired thither as to a shrine. Among them appeared one evening Mrs. H——, a sister of the gallant and ever-lamented Major Nelligan, of the First Louisiana. After viewing the monument, Mrs. H—— strolled over among the graves, and there came upon a few bones of Confederate soldiers, which had been accidentally left upon the ground.

They seemed to her so precious, so sacred, that they must have sepulchre; but how should she accomplish this end? Nothing that she had or could get, in short, nothing that had been used would do. Instantly she sought the first store where a piece of new linen could be bought; returning with it, she reverently laid the bones within it, and, without speaking a word to any one of her intentions, buried them in the garden at home, where they now lie.

I have not yet told all I know about Confederate women, nor even the half, nor is it needful that I should. While recounting their history to future generations, Fame will put by her brazen trumpet, yet sing their praises in tones so sweet and clear that all the world shall hear and wonder and admire.

CHAPTER VIII.

AN INCIDENT OF THE BATTLE OF THE WILDERNESS.

THESE facts were related to me by a Virginia soldier, and woven by me into a story for the *Southern Bivouac*.

On the night of May 11, 1864, Lee had withdrawn his forces from a salient point called the "Horseshoe," in consequence of a retrograde or flank movement of the enemy opposite that point. A battery of artillery, consisting of four companies, which was to have occupied that point, was removed some two miles back. At early dawn, word was brought that Grant's forces had again advanced, and the artillery was ordered to return with all speed. Faster and faster they advanced until they reached the top of the hill, in the very toe of the Horseshoe, to find themselves in the jaws of the enemy. It fell to the lot of a non-commissioned officer of Captain W. P. Carter's Battery to prepare the ammunition. He first cut the fuse for one second's time. After preparing several shells and receiving no word from his general he made ready several charges of canister, knowing the enemy to be close at hand. Still nobody came for the ammunition. He observed next that the drivers of the limber-chest had dismounted and left their horses, and the horses being without a driver, backed the wheels of the limber over the ammunition. To prevent damage, he seized the off-leader by the bridle, turning them back to a front position. While doing this, he distinctly heard the minie-balls crashing through the bones of the horses. They did not fall at once, however, and he had just gotten them to a front position, when a forcible blow upon the right shoulder, made by the enemy's color-bearer with the point of his staff, showed him that they were upon him. There was no time to say "good-morning," so he beat a hasty retreat around his limber, "*Sauve que peut.*" He had scarcely commenced to run when he felt a heavy blow about the middle of his back. His thought was, "Can that color-bearer have repeated his blow, or am I struck by a ball, which has deadened the sense of feeling?" There being no flow of blood, however, he concluded he was not much hurt. After a run of forty yards he came to the dry bed of a stream between two hills. Here he paused to reconnoitre. The morning fog and the smoke of battle obscured the view, except close to the ground. Crouching on all-fours, he peered below the cloud of smoke toward the crest of the hill where the battery was. He soon saw that the case was hopeless, and the battery in possession of the enemy. Looking to the left, he read in the anxious countenance of an aide-de-camp on horseback that matters at that point were in a desperate case. Running up the bed of the stream, he reached the shelter of the woods on his left. So far he had run parallel to the line of battle. When well in the woods, turning at right angles, it seemed that he had made his escape. Meeting just then with an officer of the battery (the only one who escaped) and several comrades, a brief consultation was held, suddenly cut short by a continuous roar of musketry in the rear and near the heel of the Horseshoe, showing that the party were in danger of being enclosed and cut off within the circle. The consultation was summarily ended, and flight again resumed. This time they ran well out of the Horseshoe and out of danger, stopping not until they met Lee's reinforcements going to the front. Here, from a point of safety, they could hear war holding high revelry in the bottom below. Now, for the first time the soldier took occasion to examine his knapsack. A minie-ball had entered the lower part, passing through sixteen folds of tent-cloth, many folds of a blanket, riddling several articles of underwear, and finally burying itself in a small Bible. Such was its force that not a leaf from Revelations to Genesis remained without impress of the ball, and half the leaves were actually penetrated.

Just at this time he was overjoyed to see his brother (about whom he had been painfully anxious) returning to the rear with a company of the Richmond Howitzers, who, having spent all their ammunition, came to replenish their chests. This young man had been color-bearer of the company, and when the battery first reached the hill, had turned to the woods on his left to tie his horse. Hearing a wild yell, which he supposed to be the battle-cry of the Confederates, he joined lustily in the shout and rushed forward bearing his colors. The fog and smoke concealing from him the true state of affairs, it was a terrible shock to see, suddenly, the enemy's color floating from the battery. Realizing for the first time that all was lost, he hastily lowered his flag between the chests of a caisson, and, tearing off the colors, thrust them into his bosom, throwing the staff away. He then ran into the woods and up the lines, where he came upon a company of the Richmond Howitzers, and served with them until their ammunition was exhausted.

A remarkable circumstance connected with the above incident was the fact that, during the confusion and haste following the order for the hasty march, the brothers lost sight of each other, and the elder (who bore the flag) was compelled to gallop to the front, leaving the tent-cloth and blankets, which usually were

p

included in the roll behind the saddle, to be carried in the other's knapsack. The first thought of the younger was impatience at the unusual burden he had to carry into battle, but reflection brought with it a feeling (perhaps a premonition), "It is all right and perhaps the means of saving my life." In less than half an hour it had proved indeed a blessing in disguise.

The owner of the Bible, then a youth of nineteen, now a minister of the Protestant Episcopal Church, cherishes the book and the minie-ball, not only as a memento of the war, but with feelings of deepest gratitude, which find appropriate expression in the consecration of his life to Him who "protected his head in the day of battle." It is his earnest hope that he may, by the blessing of God, so expound the teaching of that blessed Book as to make it a means of salvation to many souls.

CHAPTER IX.

FENNER'S LOUISIANA BATTERY.

DEAR friends, when you read the caption of this page in my book of "Memories," do not accuse me in your hearts of favoritism. Of all soldiers who wore the gray, only one was nearer than others to my heart. I took no special pride in one organization above others, save in the command to which my husband belonged. Surely this is quite natural.

Who does not remember the epidemic of blue cockades which broke out in New Orleans during the winter of 1860 and 1861, and raged violently throughout the whole city? The little blue cockade, with its pelican button in the centre and its two small streamers, was the distinguishing mark of the "Secessionist."

By none was it more universally and proudly worn than by the youth and young men, who, in April, 1861, discarded it with their citizen's dress and began "the wearing of the gray," which they have helped to make a garb of honor and a glory forever.

When the Dreaux Battalion embarked for Pensacola, it was with a definite purpose in view, and a certain conviction that they would at once meet and vanquish the enemy. Their prowess was to teach the Yankee a lesson and to settle matters inside of sixty days. They fully expected to fight, and were eager to begin. Day after day, night after night, they momentarily expected an assault upon Fort Pickens. But they did *not* expect to be set at the hard duty of digging and wheeling sand hour after hour, and throwing up intrenchments under a burning sun.

Then the irksomeness of being under military discipline, which at first was frequently infringed. For instance, a party of Orleans Cadets overstayed their leave of absence an hour or two; "upon our return we found ourselves locked up in the guard-house for four hours and a half."

Here is an account of one of the monotonous days, transcribed from a letter of one of the Orleans Cadets, a boy who had been used at home to take his coffee before rising, a late, comfortable breakfast, and to walk down-town at his leisure on the shady side of the street, clad in the cool, white linen suit then so universally worn: "We get up at five o'clock to attend roll-call; at 6.30 get our coffee and our breakfast, which consists of crackers and salt pork; at 7.30, back to our tents and pack our knapsack, rub our guns, and get ready for parade at nine o'clock.

"We are now drilling at light infantry tactics (Hardee's), which occupies until eleven. We then *wash our clothes, bring wood for the cook, also water* and various other things; dine at two, and again drill at four until dark; get our supper at seven; lie around until roll-call at nine; afterward go to bed to dream of home.

"General Bragg has just sent us word that we are to be exempt from hard labor at present."

It is not to be supposed that the men were confined to the rations here mentioned. All had money and could buy additional food; most of the messes had negro servants, who were excellent cooks, and boxes of goodies arrived continually from home. But, as I said before, the strict discipline, combined with deprivation of the glorious fighting in which they had expected to participate, was terribly irksome.

It was a most welcome order which transferred them to Virginia, and to the shady and delightful camping-ground which I have described in a former article (Introductory). An order to join the forces about to engage in the battle of Manassas was countermanded on account of a movement of the enemy which resulted in the "affair" at "Bethel Church." They remained upon the Peninsula under General McGruder, who was successfully holding McClellan in check by appearing at every point assailed by the Federals.

"The forces under General *McGruder* were the only obstacle in McClellan's road to Richmond.

"Under these circumstances, McGruder, with superb rashness, threw out his whole force as skirmishers, along a line of nine or ten miles.

"The Dreaux Battalion bore a conspicuous part in all the operations of this campaign." Later, the battalion went into winter quarters.

Because I wish to contrast the condition of these men during the first part of their service and when, later, they encountered inconceivable hardships and deprivations, I will here give entire a letter from one of the battalion, kindly placed at my disposal, describing the "house-warming" which was given when they moved into winter quarters on the Peninsula:

" CAMP RIGHTOR, November 29, 1861.

"I received yours of the 14th a few days since, and the 20th yesterday, both of which I will answer in one. The half-barrel of sugar was received long since, as you will see by looking over my letter to you about three weeks ago. The sugar came through in good order, also the white sugar, medicine, and coffee; the latter we use sparingly, mixing it with wheat,—one-third coffee and two-thirds wheat. The wheat does not seem to

20

change the flavor in the least. Sweet potatoes are also used in camp in place of coffee,—you dry it, then parch and grind it; we have not tried that method yet on account of the scarcity of potatoes. All our cabins are finished at last; the tents are used no more to sleep in. Our house-warming has taken place. We made about ten gallons of egg-nog for the occasion; we used about six dozen eggs. Walton's mess was over, and a good many from the rifles; various members from both companies of the guards. Also the major, doctor, adjutant, and Lieutenant Dunn, Grevot Guards. They say it was the best nog they ever drank; the house was crowded. The nog gave out, and we had to produce the jug. If we had had our sick messmate from Williamsburg, we would have had noise (Noyes) all night, but as it was it only lasted until one o'clock. Everybody in camp seemed to be trying to make more noise than his neighbor. Beard told us next day that it was a very well-conducted affair, that everything passed off *so quietly* with so much nog as that. He evidently went to bed early after he left us. I saw Posey yesterday, he was looking badly, seeming to have been troubled with the chills for some time. Since it has become so cold we have had to take the cook in the house, which makes eleven. This boy outsnores creation, beating anything you ever heard; he woke me up last night, and I thought it was the dog Cadet barking outside at the door.

" If you get this before ma sends off the expected-to-be-sent package, and if there is some room, you might put in *one* blanket. Since we sleep two in a bunk, we spread our blankets across the bunk. Brunet has three, and I have three, which makes it equal to six apiece. Send the blanket; it shall do its share of warming, I assure you. I suppose what ma sends will be my share of Christmas in New Orleans. Our turkeys look droopy, and there is no telling when they will peg out. We keep the gobbler's spirits up by making him fight. The camp is full of turkeys, and we make ours fight every day. *I have plenty of clothes and socks : I have over half a dozen of woollen socks.*

"The Gopher Mess send their best regards.
"Yours affectionately,
"Co. A, ORLEANS CADETS,
"Louisiana Battalion, Williamsburg, Virginia."

The formation of Fenner's Louisiana Battery was attended by tremendous difficulties and discouragements, patiently met, nobly overcome, by the gallant officer who found himself at last at the head of a company composed of men who, whether considered in the aggregate, or as individuals, had not their superiors in the Confederate armies,—intelligently brave, enthusiastic, patriotic, gentlemen by birth, breeding, and education, whom chivalrous devotion to duty forbade to murmur at any hardship which fell to their lot. As officers or private soldiers, looking to the future of the Confederacy as to something assured ; never despairing, ready to follow wherever and whenever a "hope" was led, no matter how "forlorn."

The record of this little band of devoted patriots has never been thoroughly known or understood as it deserves to be. Only once has its history appeared in print,—upon the occasion of a reunion of the command held in New Orleans, May 12, 1884. With great pride I transfer to these pages part of an article which then appeared in the *Times-Democrat* of that date :

"As the term of service (twelve months) of the corps began to approach its end, Captain Charles E. Fenner, commanding the company of Louisiana Guards, conceived the idea of raising a battery of artillery. He had no difficulty in getting the men, a sufficient number volunteering at once from the battalion, but he encountered other most disheartening obstacles. The War Department had not the means of equipping the artillery companies already in service, and authorized to be raised, and he could only obtain the authority to raise this battery on condition of furnishing his own armament of guns. He succeeded, however, in making arrangements with his friends in New Orleans to furnish the guns, and the battery had been made and was ready for him in New Orleans, when the city fell, and it was captured.

"Upon the discharge of the battalion, however, he changed his rendezvous to Jackson, Mississippi, and proceeded there to try and accomplish his object. Many of those who intended to join him looked upon his enterprise as so hopeless that they abandoned it and joined other commands. A sufficient number, however, rallied around him at Jackson, Mississippi, and, on the 4th of May, 1862, his company was organized by the election of officers, and on the 16th was mustered into service. Meantime, the chance of getting an armament was hopeless indeed. At last, however, Captain Fenner found, lying abandoned by the railroad, the ruins of a battery, which had been destroyed on the eve of evacuating New Orleans, under the apprehension that it would have to be left, but was subsequently brought off. The guns were spiked and rammed with wads and balls, the spokes and felloes of the wheels were cut, the trails hacked to pieces, and all the ordinary means of disabling a battery had been resorted to. The task of reconstructing this ruined battery was undertaken, and, after much difficulty, successfully accomplished.

"Then came the trouble of obtaining horses, harness, and other equipments, which had to be wrested from reluctant and ill-supplied quartermasters and ordnance-officers. At last, however, all difficulties were overcome. A few weeks of active drilling, and Fenner's Battery was ready for the field. On August 20, 1862, it received marching-orders for Port Hudson. Arrived there just after the evacuation of Baton Rouge by the Federal forces. Ordered on to Baton Rouge. Remained there a few days, when the battery returned to Port Hudson with the exception of one section, which was left with one regiment of infantry to occupy the city. Held it till retaken by the Federals in December, when our small force successfully evacuated it under the fire of the enemy's gunboats, and before the advance of their infantry, which had landed. The battery remained at Port Hudson, participating in all the operations of the forces there till May 1, 1863, when it was ordered to Williams's Bridge to intercept Grierson's raid, arriving there a few hours after the raid had passed.

"May 7. Ordered to Jackson, Mississippi, with Marcy's Brigade.

"Participated in the Big Black campaign of General Johnston.

"In position at Jackson, and engaged in the fighting around that place from 10th to 16th of July, losing several men killed and wounded.

"After the evacuation of Jackson, retreated with Johnston's army to Forrest and Morton. Thence to Enterprise, and from there to Mobile, and remained there till November 21, 1863, when ordered to the Army of Tennessee.

"Reached Dalton November 27, just after the defeat at Missionary Ridge.

"Spent the winter in building winter-quarters successively at Dalton and Kingston, which were evacuated before occupied.

"On the 1st of May, 1864, General Sherman advanced

20*

from Chattanooga toward Dalton, and the great Georgia campaign commenced. From that time till the 1st of September following, the Army of Tennessee was almost constantly engaged with the enemy.

" May 8 to 12. Battery in position at Mill Creek Gap, near Dalton, and engaged with the enemy. They fell back to Resaca. Engaged on the 14th of May in supporting charge by Stewart's Division upon the enemy.

" On the 15th, battle of Oostenaula. The battery was divided, one section on each side of a battery in a fortified work. The charge of the enemy was most desperate, and they captured and held the fortification, but were repulsed from the front of each section of Fenner's Battery, which held their positions till night, and then evacuated. Retreat of the army was continued to Calhoun, Adairsville, Cassville, Centerville; engaged more or less at each of those points.

" On the 25th of May occurred the battle of New Hope Church, one of the finest fights of the war. It was an assault of the whole of Hooker's Corps on Stewart's Division. The attack was almost a complete surprise. Fenner's Battery went into position at a gallop, had several horses killed while unlimbering, and fired canister at the first discharge. The engagement was continuous for two hours, during the whole of which time, owing to the thickness of the woods, the enemy's skirmishers were enabled to maintain their position within from fifty to one hundred yards, but their repeated charges were well repulsed. The enemy's loss was terrific, admitted to be over two thousand, far exceeding the number of our men engaged. Fenner's Battery lost twenty-three men killed and wounded, and nearly all of its horses, and was specially complimented in orders for gallantry and efficiency.

" From this point, in continual conflict with the enemy,

the army gradually fell back till it reached Atlanta, around which continuous fighting was kept up, until its evacuation on the 2d of September.

"1st September. Battle of Jonesboro', in which the battery was engaged.

"This may be considered the end of the Georgia campaign.

"After brief rest at Lovejoy's Station, the army commenced its long march to Tennessee by Centre, Jacksonville, Gadsden, and Florence.

"Left Florence November 20; arrived at Columbia, Tennessee, and struck the enemy there November 26. Enemy evacuate on the 28th.

"November 30. Battle of Franklin.

"December 2. Reached Nashville.

"December 6. Fenner's Battery was ordered to join General Forrest's command at Murfreesboro'; participated in the battle of Murfreesboro' on the 8th, and was still with Forrest when the battles of Nashville were fought, on the 15th and 16th, and the great retreat commenced.

"In this fight, which is called the second of Murfreesboro', it will be remembered that Bates's Infantry Division was stampeded early in the action, causing the loss of several guns of the Fifth Company, Washington Artillery. On this occasion (one of the few instances, if not the only one during the war) six pieces of field artillery, being four Napoleons of Fenner's Battery and two rifled pieces of Missouri Battery, placed in position by General Forrest,—their horses having been sent to the rear across Stone River,—held the line for three-quarters of an hour against the enemy's entire force until the infantry and wagons had safely crossed the river on the only bridge half a mile in the rear.

"As soon as the news reached Forrest, his command

started across from Murfreesboro' to join the main column at Columbia. There was no turnpike, the roads were in awful condition, the horses reduced and broken down, and a continuous rain pouring down. Two of the guns reached Columbia in safety; the other two would have been brought through but for the swelling of a creek by the rain, which it was impossible to cross,—the only guns the battery ever lost. The men remained by them alone till Columbia was evacuated by our forces and the enemy within a mile of them, when they destroyed their pieces, swam Duck River, and started after the army. The terrors of the retreat from Tennessee in midwinter, the men shoeless, without blankets, and almost without clothes, need not be recounted here.

"January 10. The battery reached Columbus, Mississippi.

"January 31. Ordered to Mobile. Remained there as heavy artillery till 11th of April, when it was evacuated; go up the river to Demopolis; from there to Cuba Station, Meridian, where, on the 10th of May, arms are laid down and the battery with the rest of General Taylor's army."

A member of the battery, who was an exceptional soldier, and who still cherishes and venerates everything that reminds him of the glorious past, has kindly placed in my hands some letters which I am permitted to copy and here subjoin, feeling sure that they will prove quite as interesting as the numerous documents of the kind published in the "lives" of those high in authority, although they contain only the experience of a young private soldier, conveyed in dutiful letters to his mother. Some of these will suggest the changes which befell the soldiers who gave the house-warming in Virginia, and the difference between the first and last years of the war.

"Near New Hope Church, Georgia,
" May 26, 1864.

"My Dear,—Knowing that you will be anxious to hear from me and the company after the late fight, I avail myself of the first opportunity to write. Stewart's Division of Hood's Corps arrived in the vicinity of the Church yesterday morning. Soon after skirmishes commenced, moving a mile off, and gradually approached us. By 3 P.M. it commenced to near us, and 5 P.M. found us galloping into position. Clayton's Brigade supported us behind log works, which served as an excellent shelter for us from the minies. The Yankees approached under cover of the woods to within two or three hundred yards, where they made their lines. As soon as we could see where they were we commenced firing into them, and kept it up until the ammunition of the limber was expended. They made several charges, but were repulsed by the infantry and artillery each time. Our loss was heavy (artillery), the infantry not being as much exposed as we were; their casualties were slight. At our howitzer Willie Brunet was killed after firing some fifteen rounds. He was killed in the act of giving the command to fire, the ball piercing him above the left eye. Early had four wounded,—viz., Vaudry, painfully in the breast; J. T. Pecot, painfully in the back; Eaton, in the wrist; Corporal J——, ball in the side. At Carly's piece none were killed, but McGrath and Joe Murphy were shot through the arm,— the latter it is thought will lose his arm,—and young Ford. At Woester's piece, R. A. Bridges was killed, Joe Bridges was shot in the leg; McCarty, in the foot; Dunbar, in the thigh; Lieutenant Cluverius, wounded in the side; Joe Reeves, through the leg; St. Germain, foot. The loss in horses was heavy. Woester had all eight horses of his piece killed, and his riding-horse.

Lieutenant Cluverius lost his horse 'Rebel,' who was shot in the head, and died. Our detachment had three wounded; the horses saved themselves by running away. In all, we lost twenty-three, and perhaps more. Stanford was on our left, they lost about fifteen killed and wounded; Oliver, sixteen. John Cooper has a welt on his shin from a spent ball; John was driving and lost both horses. I was number six at the limber until Willie was killed, when I acted as gunner. McGregor ranks me, and hereafter I expect to be caisson-corporal. General Clayton paid us the very highest compliment upon the manner in which the guns were managed; '*too flattering* to be repeated,' as Captain Fenner remarked. 'Owing to the loss in horses, men, and ammunition expended,' we were relieved and sent to the rear to replenish. A couple of days may right us, when we will again be in the front. Stewart did the fighting yesterday; I don't believe any other division was engaged. A part of Polk's (if not all) arrived about midnight. Since Polk's Corps joined us, I have found several acquaintances, among whom are John Butler, lieutenant of engineers; the two Spencer boys, in Cowan's Battery; and Ed. Hoops, in Tenth Mississippi. They were all apparently well when I saw them last, and inquired particularly of you.

"Respectfully Yours,

"——— ———"

I enclose a letter that we received from General Clayton on a copy of the letter to the captain, with an extract from the general's report of the battle of New Hope Church:

"HEADQUARTERS, CLAYTON'S BRIGADE,
"June 7, 1864.

"CAPTAIN,—I take pleasure in making for you the following extract from my report of the battle of New

Hope Church. With renewed expression of the profoundest acknowledgments for the signal service you did the country, and particularly my brigade, of which every officer and man speak in the highest terms,

"Believe me, dear captain,

"Yours always,

"A. D. CLAYTON,

".Brigadier-General."

(" *Extract.*")

" For its conduct in the engagement too much praise cannot be awarded to Fenner's Louisiana Battery, which occupied a position along my line. Although the enemy came within fifty or sixty yards of the guns, every officer and man stood bravely to his post."

The following letter describing a Christmas dinner in 1864 presents so true a picture of the situation, and at the same time so well illustrates the soldierly spirit of the battery, that I publish it in full:

"RIENZA, MISSISSIPPI, January 4, 1865.

"MY DEAR MOTHER,—An opportunity of writing now offers,—the first since our leaving Florence, before going on our Tennessee campaign, which has finally terminated so disastrously for us. Had orders been obeyed and carried out at Spring Hill, there never would' have been a fight at Nashville. By some misunderstanding, the Yankee army was allowed to cross at the above-named place without being attacked. We followed on their tracks to Franklin, picking up stragglers and prisoners all along the way, to the amount of several hundred.

" We left Columbia at daylight, marched twenty-three miles, and fought the battle of Franklin before dark. Our battery did not take part in the battle: we were in position, but, owing to the close proximity of the two armies, could not fire,—we were under fire, but no one was hurt. Stewart's and Cheatam's Corps with one division from our corps, fought the battle. I passed over the field next morning and saw *enough* for never wanting to see another such field. The men were actually lying in some portions of the trenches *three deep.* Ours being the attacking party suffered severely,—almost an equal loss to the Yankees. Our loss was about forty-five hundred, and theirs five thousand, including prisoners. Next day we started for Nashville, eighteen miles distant. Our battery remained there till the 5th, when we were ordered to Murfreesboro' to aid General Forrest in reducing that place. On the 6th we arrived there, took position, and built works. Next day, on account of a flank movement by the enemy, we had to move our position back a mile. Soon the enemy appeared in our front, and skirmishing commenced. The infantry fell back, leaving the artillery to do the fighting without one musket to protect us. We stayed as long as we could, when we finally had to follow the footsteps of the infantrymen. The fight—there was none—nothing but a big scare and run. General Forrest sent General Bateman with his division to Nashville, but kept our battery with him. We lost one man at Murfreesboro', I. T. Preston, brother of the Prestons of Carrollton. We stayed in camp for seven days when General Forrest determined to attack again and took one section of the battery with him,—the other section, the one I belong to, was sent to protect his wagon-train. Two days afterwards the army commenced its retreat from Nashville (the particulars of which no doubt you have already learned). Our march was over a muddy and rugged road for fifty miles to Columbia. It was the severest march I ever undertook: we pushed and worked at the wheels all the time. The horses finally broke down, and we had to take oxen and yoke them in and drive them. Can you imagine me up to my knees in mud, barefooted and muddy, with a long pole, driving oxen. It was a very picturesque scene, and no doubt the 'Yankee Illustrators' would pay a good price for such a picture. I was about on a par with two-thirds of the others, and we made as merry as possible under the circumstances. We had no rations, and lived entirely on the people : they treated us splendidly, gave us more than we could eat, and left us duly indebted to them for their many kindnesses. I for one will never forget the hospitality received in Tennessee. We recrossed the Tennessee on the 26th of December. Christmas day was quite an event to us. We were then out of Tennessee, in a poor country, and could get very little to eat. All day myself and mess were without food ; late in the evening we saw a butcher-pen and made for it ; all we could get was oxtails and a little tallow procured by a good deal of industry from certain portions of the beef. One of the boys procured a lot of bran and unbolted flour and at twelve o'clock at night we sat down at our Christmas dinner (oxtail soup and biscuit), and if I ever enjoyed a meal I enjoyed that one. The army is retiring to Okolona and the artillery to Columbus, Mississippi. The barefooted men were left here to go by rail. When we get away I cannot say. We had to leave two of our pieces stuck in the mud, the other side of Columbus ; the third piece was thrown in the river ; the fourth piece, the one I am interested in, was saved and represents the battery."

And here is the *last,* written from Demopolis, Alabama, April 15, 1865 :

"DEAR MOTHER,—You have heard ere this of the evacuation of Mobile, which happened on the day of the eleventh. After the fall of Spanish Fort and

L   q   21

Blakely, all hope of holding Mobile was given up. The works around the city were made to be manned by eight thousand, but, after the capture of the garrison at Blakely, our forces were too much reduced to hold the place. When evacuated, the place was not threatened, but might have been completely invested in a week's time. All the heavy guns were destroyed: we destroyed seven twenty-four pounders. The total loss of guns must have amounted to three hundred. We left Mobile by boat, and each man with a musket. It is a heavy fall for us who have been in artillery for three years, and now find ourselves as infantrymen, much to our displeasure. As much as I dislike it, I shall keep my musket until something better turns up. . . . "

The history of the battery, from first to last, is that of thorough soldiers, brave in battle, uncomplaining, cheerful, even *jolly*, under the most trying circumstances, bearing with equanimity the lesser ills of a soldier's life, with unshaken fortitude and undiminished devotion to " The Cause," indescribable hardships and discouragements.

Proud as I am of their whole record, I must admire the noble spirit which animated these patriots, when, at Mobile, having been deprived of their cannon, they *cheerfully* shouldered the muskets assigned to them, and were prepared to use them, never dreaming that the bitter end was so near. All soldiers will well understand that this was a *crucial test* of their devotion and patriotism.

The exceptional talent which, during the war, these young men freely gave in aid of every charity, was then only budding. Since the war, splendid fruit has appeared.

Perhaps no single company of veterans numbers among its members more talented and remarkable men, or more prominent and loyal citizens.

Of the "boys" who once composed Fenner's Louisiana Battery, a goodly number yet survive.

The ties of old comradeship bind them closely. Not one forgets the glories of the past. True,

> "*Some* names they loved to hear
> Have been carved for many a year
> On the tomb,"

but the survivors "close up" the broken ranks, and still preserve, in a marked degree, the *esprit du corps* which belonged to

> "The days that are no more."

CHAPTER X.

The Boy and the Man.

(Communicated.)

In the early summer of 1846, after the victories of Palo Alto and Resaca de la Palma, the United States Army, under General Zachary Taylor, lay near the town of Matamoras. Visiting the hospital quarters of a recently-joined volunteer corps from "the States," I remarked a bright-eyed youth of some nineteen years, wan with disease, but cheery withal. The interest he inspired led to his removal to army headquarters, where he soon recovered health and became a pet. This was "Bob Wheat," son of an Episcopal clergyman, and he had left school to come to the war. He next went to Cuba with Lopez, was wounded and captured, but escaped the garroters to follow General Walker to Nicaragua.

Exhausting the capacity of South American patriots to *pronounce*, he quitted their society in disgust, and joined Garibaldi in Italy, whence his keen scent of combat summoned him home in time to receive a bullet at Manassas. The most complete Dugald Dalgetty possible; he had "all the defects of the good qualities" of that doughty warrior.

Some months after the time of which I am writing, a body of Federal horse was captured in the valley of Virginia. The colonel commanding, who had dismounted in the fray, approached me. A stalwart, with huge moustache, cavalry boots adorned with spurs

244

worthy of a caballero, slouched hat and plume; he strode along with the nonchalant air of one who had wooed Dame Fortune too long to be cast down by her frowns.

Suddenly Major Wheat near by sprung from his horse with a cry of "Percy, old boy!" "Why, Bob!" was echoed back, and a warm embrace followed. Colonel Percy Windham, an Englishman in the Federal service, had parted from Wheat in Italy, where the pleasant business of killing was then going on, and now fraternized with his friend in the manner described.

Poor Wheat! A month later he slept his last sleep on the bloody battle-field of Cold Harbor. He lies there in a soldier's grave.

Gallant spirit; let us hope that his readiness to die for his country has made "the scarlet of his sins like unto snow."

21*

PART II.

CHAPTER I.

NELLY.

In the early autumn, on a lovely afternoon, a little girl sat upon the stile which led from a spacious farm-yard into a field of newly-mown wheat. In her hand she held a long switch, and her business was to watch the motions of a large flock of fowls, which, as is usual at harvest-time, had been kept in their coop all day, and only let out for an hour or two, just before sun-set, to run about in the grassy yard, seeking bugs and worms, or other dainties, which they alone know how to find.

Of course they could not be allowed in the field before the grain had been safely garnered, so Nelly had been permitted to mount guard upon the stile, the better to observe and control them. She quite felt the importance of the trust, and, holding her switch as proudly as if it had been a sceptre, was eager and quick to discover occasions to use it. Many a staid and demure-looking hen, or saucy, daring young chicken, had stolen quite near to her post, stopping every few moments to peer cautiously around, or to peck at a blade of grass or an imaginary worm, as if quite indifferent to the attractions presented

246

by the field beyond, but just as they had come close to
the fence, thinking themselves unnoticed, Nelly would
jump from her perch, and, with a *thwack* of the switch,
send them squawking back to their companions. At
length, however, the child seemed to grow weary of
her task. Slowly descending to the ground, she walked
toward the barn, and, returning with her apron full
of corn, opened the door of the chicken-house, and,
having enticed her charge within, shut them up for the
night. This done, Nelly wandered aimlessly about for
a while, then, sitting down upon a large stone, which
seemed to have been rolled under a tree just to make a
nice seat, she looked around in an impatient and discontented manner. The sights and sounds which surrounded her were very pleasant, and—one would have
imagined—exceedingly attractive to a child. The rays
of the declining sun, slanting across the grassy yard,
brightened up the low, brown farm-house until the old-
fashioned glass door and latticed windows on either
side seemed as if brilliantly lighted from within. One
might easily have imagined it an enchanted castle.
The mossy roof looked as if gilded. In front of the
house the well-bucket, hanging high upon the sweep,
seemed dropping gold into the depths beneath. On the
porch, upon a table scrubbed "white as the driven
snow," were set the bright tin pans ready to receive
the evening's milk. Within the house the maids were
singing gayly as they passed to and fro preparing a
substantial supper for the farmer. Outside, the creak-
ing wagons were being driven into the barn-yard.
Gentle oxen, released from their daily toil, stood
patiently waiting to be fed. Horses, with a great deal
of stamping and fuss, were led into the barn. Up the
lane came the ̄cow-boy, alternately whistling, singing,
and cracking his whip, until at length the drove of

sweet-breathed cows stood lowing at the bars, which, at milking-time, would be let down for them to pass each to her own stall.

Nelly seemed to see and hear nothing that was passing around her. The shadow upon her face deepened; the sweet blue eyes filled with tears. At last she rose, and, crossing the stile, passed rapidly through the wheat-field, climbed a low stone wall and presently came to a green knoll, shaded by a sycamore-tree, commanding a view of the public road. Here she stood, eagerly gazing down the road, while seemingly struggling to subdue a sorrow which, however, soon found vent in heart-broken sobs. Still searching the road with anxious, tearful eyes, she seemed to hesitate for a while, but at last, after casting many a fearful glance toward the farm-house, the little girl began to descend the high bank, slipping many times, and sadly scratched by the rough gravel and projecting roots of the trees.

Having reached the bottom, she did not pause a moment, but drew her light shawl over her head and ran swiftly away. And now let us try to discover the cause of all this trouble.

My dear young friends, have you ever heard of a disease called "nostalgia?" A long, hard word, and one which contains a world of terrible meaning. It is a kind of sickness which attacks not only children, but also strong and wise men, who have been known to suffer, nay, even to *die*, because they could not obtain the only remedy which ever does any good. Nostalgia means homesickness.

Poor little Nelly was homesick, and in desperation she had fled, hoping to find, not her own dear, Southern home, for that she knew she could never see again, but the house of her grandmamma, where she had some time before left her dear mother. The little girl had, ever since she could remember, lived very happily with her parents in their lovely Virginia home. An only child, she was petted to her heart's content, having scarcely a wish ungratified. But when the war began her papa became a soldier. Nelly thought he looked very grand in his uniform of gray with its red trimmings and bright buttons, and rather liked the idea of having a soldier papa. But after he had gone away she missed him dreadfully. Her mamma was always so pale and sad that the child also grew anxious, and could no longer enjoy her play. At first letters from the absent soldier cheered them, but as the months passed they ceased to hear at all, except the wild rumors which often frightened and distressed the anxious wife. "Maum Winnie," an old negro servant, who claimed to have "raised Mars Ned" (Nelly's papa), now proved a faithful friend and a great comfort to her mistress; but Nelly, missing the old woman's cheerful talk and the laugh that used often to shake her fat sides, thought she had grown cross and exacting.

The bright morning sunlight sometimes made the little girl forget to be sorrowful, and when her "Ponto" came frisking around her, she gladly joined him in a wild romp. Immediately Maum Winnie would appear, the very picture of dignified astonishment,—"Now, Miss Nelly, *ain't* you 'shame'? Yer pore mar she bin had a mity onrestless night, an' jes' as she 'bout to ketch a nap o' sleep, yere you bin start all dis 'fusion. Now, her eye dun pop wide open, an' she gwine straight to studyin' agin." The days passed, each made more gloomy by rumors of the near approach of the enemy. At last, one dreadful night, a regiment of Federal soldiers suddenly appeared, and at midnight Nelly and her mamma were compelled to seek shelter in Maum

Winnie's cabin. The next morning only a heap of smoking ruins remained to show where their sweet home had been.

The plantation owned by Nelly's papa was some three miles distant from the family residence; therefore, only the few servants necessary for household service lived upon the "home place." Their cabins, somewhat removed from the house, had escaped the flames. Maum Winnie's was larger and better furnished than any, and far more attractive in appearance. A rustic fence, built by her old husband, "Uncle Abe" (long since dead), enclosed a small yard, where grew all kinds of bright, gaudy "posies," with here and there a bunch of mint or parsley or sage, and an occasional stalk or two of cabbage. Over the little porch were trained morning-glories and a flourishing gourd vine. Beneath, on each side, ran a wide seat, where, in the shade, Maum Winnie used to sit with her knitting, or nodding over the big Bible which on Sunday evening she always pretended to read. The neat fence was now broken down, the bright flowers all trampled and crushed by the feet of men and horses. Inside also, the once spotless floor was muddy and stained with tobacco, all the old woman's treasures being broken and scattered. Amid all this confusion, in the little front room, once the pride of Winnie's heart, was carefully placed almost the only thing saved from the burning, an easy-chair, cushioned upon the back and sides, and covered with old-fashioned chintz. How the faithful soul had managed to get it• there no one could have told, but there it stood, and Winnie said, "Dat ar wos ole mistes' cheer, and she sot in it plum twill she die. Ole Winnie couldn't stan' an' see *dat* burn, nohow." Upon the little porch sat Nelly and her mamma on the morning after the fire, worn out with excitement, and feeling utterly forlorn. Soon Win-

nie appeared, bearing upon a gay red tray two steaming
cups of coffee. Mrs. Grey took only a sip or two, then
setting the cup upon the bench at her side, she grasped
the arm of her old servant, and, leaning her head upon the
faithful breast, began to sob and moan piteously. Nelly
at this also cried bitterly. Tears streamed down Winnie's fat black cheeks. But the faithful negro tried to
soothe and comfort her mistress, patting her shoulders
as if she had been a baby, saying, "Dah! Dah! honey,
don't take it so haad. Try to truss in de Lawd. He
dun promus, an' he aint gwine back on nobody. I's
dun sperience *dat*."

At last, won by Nelly's caresses and Maum Winnie's
coaxing, the weary lady consented to take some repose
in "ole missis' cheer," where, leaning her aching head
upon the cushioned side, she fell asleep.

Nelly greatly enjoyed the strong coffee (which she
never before had been allowed to drink). It made her
feel very wide awake. Presently she strolled off toward the adjoining cabins. These were quite empty,
the men-servants having disappeared with the Federal
soldiers the night before, the women had followed to
their camp not far distant. Not a living thing was to
be seen; even the chickens had disappeared. The whole
scene was very desolate,—the smoking ruins, the deserted
cabin, a cloudy sky. Soon the child remembered her
playfellow, Ponto, and began to call him. A doleful
whine answered her, seeming to proceed from under one
of the negro cabins. Nelly stooped to look, but could
only see two glowing eyes, and hear the knocking of the
dog's tail upon the ground. Ponto had been so badly
frightened that no coaxing or ordering would induce
him to come out. So his little mistress walked angrily
away, and, passing through the broken gate, stood looking up and down the road. Presently there came riding

along a Federal officer on horseback, who, discovering the forlorn child, stopped to speak to her.

Nelly's first impulse was to run away, but, instead, she stood clinging to the gate-post, kicking the ground with one foot and flashing angry glances at the "Yankee." The officer sighed deeply as his glance fell upon the ruined home, and then upon the little, tear-stained face before him. Dismounting, he approached more closely, and strove to take the unwilling hand. But the child now broke into a storm of sobs, crying out, "Go away! you're a naughty Yankee, and I hate you. 'You alls' have burnt up my mamma's pretty house, and all our things, and my mamma just cries and cries; but my papa is gone to fight the 'Yankees,' and I hope he will shoot them all!"

The soldier slowly paced back and forth. "Ah," said he, softly, "if this were my little Ida: God bless her! Little girl, where is your mamma? Perhaps I can help her. Will you lead me to her?"

The child had hidden her face upon her arm, but now looked up in affright. "You won't hurt my mamma? You ar'n't going to burn up Maum Winnie's house?" said she.

Gradually his kind face and gentle manner reassured her, and she was, at last, persuaded to convey to her mother a few lines which he pencilled on a card. To Nelly's surprise, Mrs. Grey consented to receive the "Yankee." The little girl was sent to conduct him to the cabin. The lady was standing at the door as the officer and his little escort drew near. Nelly thought she had never seen her mamma look so pretty. Her eyes were shining, a lovely red spot glowed upon each cheek, but she did not smile as she used to do when receiving a guest, and, while offering the stranger a seat, she remained standing, looking very tall and grand.

During the conversation which followed, Mrs. Grey learned that as a battle was imminent at the front it was impossible to pass her through the lines (which had been her hope when she consented to see the officer). It was equally impossible to remain where she was. Her only place of refuge was her mother's home in Maryland, where she had been raised, and had lived previous to her marriage.

Promising to arrange for her transportation to the nearest railroad station, the kind-hearted officer took his leave.

When Maum Winnie was told of the proposed journey, she was greatly troubled. But when Mrs. Grey further informed her that she was free and not expected to make one of the party, her distress knew no bounds. Rushing out of the cabin, she seated herself on a log at some distance, and, throwing her apron over her head, rocked her body to and fro, wailing out, "Oh, my hebbenly Marster, 'pears like I aint fitten to bar all dis trouble. An' how dem dar gwine to do 'out ole Winnie?"

After a while, drawing her pipe and tobacco from her pocket, she sought the comfort of a smoke. Just then, Ruthy, the cook, made her appearance with a large bucket on her head. Flaunting past the old woman, she entered the kitchen without a word, and set about preparing a supper for the hungry inmates of the cabin. Where the material came from she declared was "her bizness," and her saucy manner and independent talk so confounded Maum Winnie that she asked no more questions, concluding that "Mars Yankee sont 'em an' made dat gal fotch 'em."

Mrs. Grey and Nelly had few preparations to make for the morrow. The child, soon after sunset, threw herself across the foot of the high feather-bed which

22

stood in a corner of the cabin, and slept soundly. Maum Winnie, taking off her shoes, bustled about in her stocking-feet, apparently very busy. Her movements were for some time unobserved by her mistress, who was lost in thought. At last, kneeling before the fire-place, she reached up the chimney and brought out from its hiding-place an old, black tea-pot, with a broken spout. From this she took several papers of dried "yarbs," some watermelon-seed, an old thimble, a broken tea-spoon, a lock of "de ole man's ha'r," and lastly, the foot of an old stocking, firmly tied up.

This last it took some time to undo, but finally, approaching Mrs. Grey, she turned out into the astonished lady's lap what proved to be a collection of gold and silver coins, the hoarded savings of years, the gift of many whom she had served.

"Why, Winnie," said Mrs. Grey, "what does this mean? Where did you get this money, and why do you give it to me?"

"Wall, Miss Ellen, yo' see, ez fur back ez ole mass an' mistes' time, me an' my ole man usen to wait on de wite gemplums an' ladies wot come to de big house, an' de ole man he mity clus-fisted, an' nebber spen' nuffin, an' sence he die, an' ole mass an' miss dey gone, too, Mars Ned he dun tuk mity good keer of ole Winnie, an' I nebber bin had no excessity to spend dat money, so I's kep' it an' kep' it, ontwill 'pears like de Lawd he dun pint out de way fur it to go. 'Sides, we all's gwine way off yander, an' we can't 'pear *no ways* 'spectable 'dout little cash money."

"But, Winnie, only Nelly and I are going away. You are free now, and will find other friends, and——"

"Dah! dah! honey," broke in the poor old creature, "don' say no mo'! I's *'bleeged* to go 'long. Wat I want to be free for? Who gwine keer 'bout me? 'Sides,

I dun promus Mars Ned I gwine to see to you an' dat chile yander, an' I's gwine 'long *shuah*."

Wearied and exhausted with the discussion, and unwilling to grieve her husband's faithful old nurse, who still clung to her own fallen fortunes, Mrs. Grey ceased to object, but resolutely refused to take the money, which Winnie reluctantly gathered up and carried out of the room, to seek among the numerous secret pockets she always wore a secure hiding-place for her treasure. This decided upon, while Mrs. Grey sank into an uneasy slumber in the chair, the old woman made a little fire just outside the back shed, where, with her pipe now lighted and now "dead out," she nodded and dozed until morning.

Nelly awoke at sunrise, bewildered at her strange surroundings, then oppressed and sadly grieved by recollections of all that had happened. Catching sight of her mother's pale, suffering face, the child flew to her side, seeking to cheer her by fond caresses.

Just then the sound of wheels was heard as the ambulance-wagon, which was to convey them to the railroad, drew up before the door. The driver dismounting, announced that, as the camp was about to be broken up, Colonel —— desired the ladies to start at once, adding that "the colonel would ride over to see them off."

Their loss by the fire had been so complete that there was no baggage. Nelly was glad to wear a clean, white sun-bonnet of Winnie's, and Mrs. Grey was similarly equipped with a black one and a small black shawl. Maum Winnie appeared in full Sunday rig, her head crowned with a towering head-handkerchief. Her manner was lofty and imposing. Evidently she was aiming to support the family dignity, which had been quite lost sight of by the others, Mrs. Grey being far too sorrowful, and Nelly, in spite of everything, **gay** and excited at the prospect of a ride and a change. Putting on her brass-rimmed spectacles, the old woman inspected, with an air of supreme contempt, the "turn-out" before the door, occasionally rolling her eyes toward the driver in a manner that spoke volumes, but was quite lost upon "dat po' wite trash, who 'spected Miss Ellen to git in dat ole market-wagon." After the others were seated, Winnie disappeared within the cabin, and, after much delay, came out dragging an immense bundle. She had tied up in a gorgeous bed-quilt her feather-bed and pillows with,—nobody knows how many things besides.

The driver sprang to the ground in consternation.

"Hey, old nigger, what's in that great bundle? You can't lug *that* along. What you got in there, anyhow?"

"Dat my bizness," retorted Winnie. "You is too inquisity; 'sides, who you call nigga'? I's a 'spectable cullud ooman, and Mars Ned nebber 'low nobody to call me outen my name."

Mrs. Grey vainly tried to restore peace; her voice was not even heard; but just then Colonel —— rode up, and as Winnie seemed inclined to stand her ground, he gave her a choice between mounting at once to a seat beside the driver or being left behind. Then perceiving that Mrs. Grey seemed quite overcome by emotion, and wishing to remove her as quickly as possible from the desolate scene before her, he gave the order to drive on, and, raising his hat, rode off towards camp before the lady could find voice to express her gratitude. A few hours' ride brought the refugees to the railroad station, where they took the cars for ——, the home of Nelly's grandmamma. Here a warm welcome and entire comfort awaited them. Nelly had often spent weeks at a time with her grandmamma, and was delighted to find all her old haunts as pleasant as ever. Her dolls, toys, books, etc., had been carefully kept. Better than all, she discovered a fine Newfoundland puppy and a litter of pretty white kittens to console her for the loss of Ponto.

One day, when they had been at grandmamma's only a fortnight, Nelly saw a neighboring farmer drive up to the front gate, and ran gladly to meet him, for farmer Dale was a cheery old man, who had always seemed very fond of the child. Now, however, he looked very grave, merely shaking hands, then bidding Nelly tell her grandmamma that he must see her at once, "and, Nelly, you need not come back," said he, "I have business with your grandma." Soon after the farmer drove away, while grandmamma returned to the house, wearing a very serious face, and after sitting in the darkened parlor awhile, apparently thinking deeply, passed slowly into her daughter's room. Then Nelly heard a faint cry from her mamma, and hurrying into the house, found her excitedly walking up and down, wringing her hands, and crying, "I must go to him! I must, I must!" A letter received by farmer Dale from his son, who was a Confederate soldier, had contained the news that Mr. Grey was wounded and a prisoner. Just where was unknown, or whether his wounds were severe or perhaps fatal. This news rendered the poor wife almost frantic. All night she paced the floor in sleepless agony. Next day the farmer paid a second visit, and was for a long time closeted with the distressed ladies. Afterward, Mrs. Grey seemed more restless than before, requiring the constant attention of both grandmamma and Maum Winnie. Thus a week passed.

Suddenly, one morning farmer Dale again appeared, and this time very smiling and gracious to Nelly.

"Chatterbox," said he, "how would you like to ride home with me and stay awhile, until your mother gets

r 22*

better? You can run about over there, and make all the noise you want to; nobody will mind it."

Nelly could not tell whether she would like or not. It was very dull where she was, but she did not care to leave her poor mamma. Grandmamma, however, decided the matter by assuring her that Mrs. Grey needed perfect quiet, and would be better without her. So the little girl ran off to Maum Winnie to be dressed for her ride.

Arrived at the farm-house, the kindness of the family, and the novelty of everything she saw, so charmed the child that for a while she was quite content. Little tasks were, by her own request, assigned to her, easy and pleasant, but seeming to the child of great consequence. But, in spite of all, homesickness attacked her; she grew weary of everything, and begged to be taken to her mamma. The kind farmer and his wife tried to turn her thoughts from the subject, telling her she could not go just then; but day by day Nelly became more dissatisfied, the longing for home grew stronger, until, on the evening when this begins, she actually ran away. And now let us see what became of her.

Once on the road, Nelly ran very fast, until, almost breathless, she found herself compelled to rest awhile in a little grove by the roadside. Scarcely had she seated herself upon the grass when the steady trot, trot of a horse was heard. She had barely time to hide behind a large tree when one of the farm-hands passed on his way from the mill. It seemed to Nelly that the slight rustle of the leaves under her feet must betray her, and the loud beatings of her heart be heard. But the boy passed on, and soon his low whistle, as well as the measured beat of the horse's hoofs, grew fainter.

However, all danger was not over, for just as she was about to venture forth, the panting of some animal startled her. For a moment her terror was extreme. This changed to chagrin and vexation as Rover, the farmer's dog, ran to her hiding-place and fawned upon her. Having followed the farm-boy to the distant mill, the poor dog, growing weary with his long run, had fallen far behind. Now Rover and the little girl had been great friends, and had enjoyed many a romp together, but just then his presence made her very cross; so, seizing a large stick, she beat the poor fellow until he ran yelping away.

Left alone once more, Nelly set off in the direction of town. Having often, in her rides with grandmamma, passed along the same road, she thought she knew the way; but night was approaching. It appeared to the child that darkness must bring added danger. Besides, she would soon be missed at the farm, pursued, overtaken, and carried back. This dread gave her fresh courage, and again the young traveller walked rapidly on. Before she had gone far, a light wagon overtook her. In its driver she gladly recognized an old man who sometimes supplied her grandmamma with vegetables. He drew up in great astonishment as Nelly called to him, but at her request allowed her to climb to the seat beside him. As they approached the town, the heart of the runaway began to sink; a sense of her disobedience, and the knowledge that it would add to the grief of her dear mother, and, perhaps, greatly displease grandmamma, oppressed her sorely. She decided that she could not face them just then. Begging the old man to put her down at the nearest corner, the unhappy little girl approached the house by a back entrance, and, concealed amid the shrubbery, stood trembling and weeping. The lamps had been lighted, and from the windows of the dining-room a bright ray shone out upon the lawn, seeming almost to reach the place where the child was hidden. Within was a pleasant little group gathered around the tea-table. To her great surprise, Nelly discovered her mother busily engaged in arranging upon a waiter covered with a white napkin a nice supper, while grandmamma added a cup of steaming tea. Winnie stood by as if waiting to carry supper to somebody, but Nelly was puzzled to know for whom it was intended. Just then, however, the gate-bell rang loudly. Winnie hurriedly caught up the waiter and disappeared as the opposite door opened to admit farmer Dale. His first words seemed greatly to disturb and alarm the ladies. Grandmamma quickly arose with a cry of grief and horror. Mrs. Grey stood motionless, her eyes fixed on the farmer's face, her hands pressed to her heart.

Nelly could bear no more. Rushing impetuously into the house, she threw both her arms around her frightened mother, crying,—

"Oh, mamma, grandmamma, I am not lost, but I have been so naughty. I wanted you so, and I ran away. Oh, let me stay; please let me stay."

The mother sank into a chair, her arms instinctively enfolding her naughty child, but she did not kiss or welcome her. Grandmamma, too, looked very grave and troubled. After a few minutes of painful silence, the farmer took his leave, saying,—

"I'll leave you to settle with the little one. I must make haste to relieve my wife's anxiety."

After his departure, the penitent nestled more closely to her mother. She felt sure of her love and forgiveness, and hoped that grandmamma might not be too severe, although she fully expected a good scolding and some kind of punishment besides, which she meant to bear quite meekly. To her surprise, neither mentioned her fault. Her mother seemed to be thinking of something else, and Nelly did not at all understand the queer looks which passed between the ladies. At last Winnie put her head in the door, evidently to deliver some message, for she began, "Mars——," when Mrs. Grey started up suddenly, saying,—

"Oh, Winnie, here is our Nelly," while the child sprang forward to throw herself on the breast of her astonished nurse.

"De Lawd er Massy! Whar dat chile cum from dis time o' nite?"

"Why, Winnie," explained grandmamma, "she has run away from the farm, and here she is. Did you ever hear of such badness?"

"Dah, now!" cried the negro, "didn't I tole you dat? I jest know dat chile wasn't gwine to stay nowhar 'dout her mar an' me. Po' chile, she look mity bad, 'deed she do."

"Well, Winnie, never. mind that now, she is only tired; let her eat her supper and go to bed."

Nelly had expected, at the very least, to be sent supperless to bed, but instead, grandma gave her all she could eat, and, but for the strange preoccupied manner which so puzzled her, the child would have been very comfortable. When, led by her mamma and attended by Winnie, she went up-stairs she found that her couch had been removed into her grandmamma's room. "You will be better here," explained Mrs. Grey, "for I am very restless and might disturb you."

Nelly was just conscious of an unusual bustle in the passage outside, and of hearing voices and footsteps going up to the third story; but, too sleepy to pay attention, she soon ceased to hear anything.

When she awoke the morning was far advanced, and her grandmamma was not in the room. While she lay thinking over the strange events of the day before, Maum Winnie appeared with some fresh, clean clothes upon her arm.

"Mornin', little missy," said she, pleasantly; "is you gwine ter sleep all day?"

Nelly sprang up and was soon dressed. Running into her mamma's room, she found it all in order, the sweet wind and the morning sun coming in freely through the open windows. Mrs. Grey, however, was not there; nor did she find her in the breakfast-room, where only grandmamma sat waiting to give the child her breakfast. Upon the sideboard stood a tray which had contained breakfast for somebody; Nelly wondered who, and suddenly asked,—

"Is mamma sick?"

"No, she is quite well now," was the reply.

"Well, did she eat breakfast with you?"

"Yes."

The child again glanced toward the sideboard, and at last asked plainly,—

"Whose breakfast is that yonder, and who did you all send supper to last night?"

"Nelly," said her grandmamma, sharply, "eat your breakfast, and ask no more questions. Little girls should be seen and not heard."

The child obeyed, but remained curious, and determined to find out the mystery, if she could. Soon her mother came in, kissed her affectionately, and stood for a few moments by her chair, smoothing back her curls just as she used to do. Nelly thought gladly of the happy day she would spend at her mother's side, but Mrs. Grey disappointed her by saying,—

"My daughter, you must play as quietly as possible to-day, and don't run or romp near the house. I am far from well, and very nervous."

The little girl, however, drew her mother out of the room upon the vine-shaded gallery, where they walked up and down for a few moments. But Mrs. Grey still

seemed ill at ease, and soon returned within the house.
Then Nelly ran down the steps and across the lawn in
search of her old playmates, the kittens and the puppy,
visited the garden and summer-house, where she occupied herself in arranging a bouquet for her mamma.
At last it seemed to her that it must be nearly twelve
o'clock; so returning to the house, and finding the lower
rooms deserted, she wandered into the kitchen, where she
found Maum Winnie broiling some birds and preparing
some nice toast, while near by upon the kitchen-table
was a waiter ready to carry up the delicate lunch to
somebody. Nelly at once began,—

"Oh, Maum Winnie, who are those birds for? Where
is the cook? What are you in the kitchen cooking
for?"

Winnie seemed wonderfully flurried and confused by
all these questions, and Nelly was equally disconcerted
at finding the old woman so cross.

"Jes' listen to de chile!" cried Winnie. "Wot you
makin' all dis miration 'bout? I nebber seed nobody so
inquisity as you is. De cook she dun leff, an' I's cookin'
ontwill yer grandmar git somebody. Ef you don' be-
lieb me, ax yer mar. Ennyhow, I's gwine to 'quaint
yer mar with yer conduck, axin' so many perterment
questions."

"But, who are the birds for?" persisted Nelly. "I
know mamma never eats birds, and grandmamma isn't
sick."

"I 'clar, Miss Nelly, *I's* outdone wid you. Go outer
heah, 'fore I calls yer grandmar."

Nelly left, still very curious and dissatisfied.

Having wandered about aimlessly for a while, the
little girl at last strayed into the empty parlor, and
there sat down to consider. Suddenly she heard a
stealthy step upon the stairs. At the same time a faint

odor of broiled birds saluted her nostrils. Nelly crept softly to the door, just in time to see her grandma ascending the flight of stairs leading to the third story. "Now," thought the child, "I *will* find out what all this means."

Waiting until the old lady had passed out of sight in the corridor above, she stealthily followed. All the doors of the rooms in the third story were closed, but through an open transom came the sound of voices. Listening eagerly, she heard her mamma speaking, and in reply a voice which set her heart beating wildly and made her dizzy with surprise. In a moment she was vainly striving to open the locked door, screaming loudly, "Papa! oh, papa!" Instantly the door was opened, and she found herself dragged inside the room, her grandma's hand placed closely over her mouth, while her mother, in a hoarse whisper, said, "Nelly, for *pity's sake hush, no one must know.*" Gazing about her with wildly-distended eyes, the frightened girl beheld, reclining in an easy-chair by the bedside, her dear papa, but, oh, so pale, so changed. A small table drawn closely to his side so as to project over the arm of the chair held a large pillow covered with oil-cloth, upon this lay one arm, which, with the shoulder, was entirely bare; just under the collar-bone appeared a frightful wound, over which Mrs. Grey was preparing to lay a linen cloth wet with cool water. Nelly gasped for breath and turned very white, but when her papa held out his well hand towards her with the old sweet smile she so well remembered, she ran to his side and nestled there, still trembling and sobbing, for she had been frightened, first by the rough treatment of her grandma, and yet more by the changed appearance of the dearly-loved father, who, as it seemed to her, must be dying. As further concealment was useless, Nelly was taken into the confidence of the ladies, who, however, seemed almost in despair lest the child in some thoughtless manner should betray the *secret so anxiously guarded.*

A short time before the visit to the farm a dreadful battle had been fought in Virginia, not many miles from the State-line, near which stood the house of Nelly's grandma. It so happened that the regiment to which Mr. Grey belonged had participated in the fight, and at the conclusion he found himself badly wounded and a prisoner. Having been ill previously, the wounded soldier was unable to be marched off with other prisoners, but was left, as all supposed, to die. The tide of battle rolled on, leaving the field where the fight began strewn with the dying and the dead. A blazing sun poured its intolerable light and heat upon the upturned faces and defenceless heads of hundreds of suffering, dying men, adding frightful tortures to the pain of their wounds. When the dews of night came to moisten parched lips, to cool aching brows, Mr. Grey managed to drag himself to a stump near by, and placing his back against it, waited hoping to gain a little more strength. His mouth was parched and dry, but he had not a drop of water. Suddenly his eyes fell upon a canteen lying at no great distance, almost within reach of his hand; with infinite pain and trouble he at last possessed himself of it. It was not quite empty, but just as Mr. Grey was about to drink, he heard a deep groan, and turning, met the imploring eyes of a Federal soldier. He was but a youth, and had been shot through the body and mortally wounded. His parched lips refused to speak, only the earnest eyes begged for water. Mr. Grey at once handed him the canteen, although he felt almost as if he would die for want of the water it contained. Eagerly the dying boy drank. It seemed as if he must take all, there was so very little, but after a swallow or

M   23

two he resolutely handed it back, gasping, "God bless
———. Left you some." When the moon arose, its rays
fell upon the dead young face of the boy in his gory
blue, whose last words had been a blessing upon the
wounded, exhausted soldier in gray sitting beside
him.

Later came help,—old men who, starting when the
first news of the battle reached them, had ridden miles
guided by the sound of the firing. Most of them were
Marylanders, who had sent forth their sons to battle for
the Confederate cause, and who now sought among the
dead and dying with dim, anxious eyes for the loved
faces they yet prayed not to find. Among them came
farmer Dale, whose son was a Confederate soldier.
Eagerly he examined the faces of those who lay upon
the bloody field. All, however, were strange, until at
last he came upon Mr. Grey. Carefully assisting him
to reach an old cabin which stood near, he made the
suffering man as comfortable as possible, then, without
loss of time, set out to convey the news to Mrs. Grey.
Now, it would seem that the very easiest thing would
have been to carry the wounded soldier at once to the
house of his wife's mother to be nursed and *cared* for,
but it must be remembered that the Federal army had
been shown in many ways that they were considered as
invaders by the people of Maryland, and that their
presence was obnoxious and hateful. They, on the
other hand, considered all Southern sympathizers as
traitors to their flag and their country. Every open
expression of such feelings was severely punished. Had
it been known that any Confederate soldier was harbored
or concealed in any house within the Federal lines, the
owners would have been arrested together with the soldier they had hidden, their house would probably have
been burned. So it was necessary in the case of Mr.

Grey to observe great secrecy and to plan carefully his removal.

My readers will remember that Nelly was suddenly sent off to stay at the farm-house. Then Maum Winnie took occasion to pick a quarrel with the white servants, in which she succeeded so well that they both left in high displeasure. Shortly afterward, one dark night, Farmer Dale drove up to the carriage gate with a high-piled load of hay. There was a great deal of "geeing" and "hawing" and fuss, and then, instead of getting down, the farmer called out,—

"Say, are you all asleep?"

At once Maum Winnie's voice was heard inquiring,—

"Who dat?"

"Hey, old girl, come down here and open the gate. I've brought your hay, but I got stalled on the way, and it's too late to put it up to-night. I'll have to drive the wagon in and leave it. I'll unload it in the morning."

Maum Winnie shut the window, and soon was heard shuffling along the carriage-road, grumbling to herself.

"'Fore de Lawd, I *is* plum wore out. I dun wuk sence sun-up, an' dere dat ar fodder fotch here jes' es I gwine ter lie down."

This pretence of ill-humor was kept up until the wagon was well out of sight from the street and driven up under a shed close by the kitchen-door, when poor old Maum Winnie came up close and whispered,—

"*Is* you brung Mars Ned shure 'nuff? Oh, *whar* he? tell Winnie *whar* he!"

Just then the two ladies stole out from the house and came close to the wagon. Both seemed calm and self-possessed, save that the hurried breathing of Mrs. Grey showed her excitement. A light might have betrayed them, and they dared not run any risks. No time was now to be lost. Mr. Grey was, indeed, concealed among the hay, and needed immediate attention, for the long ride had greatly increased the pain and fever of his wound.

Slowly he crept out from his hiding-place, and, with the assistance of the farmer and Winnie, managed to reach an upper room, where he sank exhausted, yet with a contented sigh, on the comfortable bed which had been for days awaiting him.

Under the loving care of the ladies and Maum Winnie he slowly improved. No one had suspected his presence in the house until Nelly discovered him, as above related.

Mr. Grey scarcely dared to hope that the little girl would be able to keep the secret, but all was explained to her. She was made to understand the extreme danger to all concerned in case of discovery. The trust reposed in her made the child feel quite womanly. Every day she became more helpful, a greater comfort to her anxious mamma, better able to assist in nursing.

Weeks passed, bringing renewed health and strength to the soldier, who began to feel very anxious to rejoin his command. Various plans were discussed, but none appeared practicable. Rumors of an advance of the Confederate forces, and of an impending battle, became every day more like certainties. At last, one morning all were startled by the sound of heavy guns; later, volleys of musketry could be plainly heard. Federal troops marched at double-quick through the town, on their way to the scene of strife. All day the fight raged. Sometimes the sound of firing would seem nearer, then farther off; at nightfall it ceased. When it became quite dark, Mr. Grey, bidding them all farewell, hurriedly left the house, hoping to join some detachment of Confederates during the night, and to participate in the battle next day.

The next day was fought the battle of ——, which raged almost in sight of the town. Nelly was, of course, in a state of great alarm and excitement, but both her mamma and grandma were carefully preparing the house for the reception of the wounded. Soon every room was occupied, and the ladies had their hands full in attending to them. On the second day a wounded Federal was brought to the house. While nursing him, Mrs. Grey learned that he was a private in the regiment commanded by Colonel ——, the officer who had so kindly assisted in her time of need. He told her that the colonel had been terribly wounded and carried to a hospital on the battle-field. Mrs. Grey at once determined to find him, and, if still alive, to do him all the good in her power. So, summoning farmer Dale, she rode with him to the hospital. Being an officer, Colonel —— was easily found. He had just suffered amputation of an arm, and was weak from loss of blood, but recognizing Mrs. Grey, smiled and seemed glad to see her. It was impossible to move him, but from that time he lacked nothing that could add to his comfort. Later, Nelly was allowed to visit him, frequently bringing flowers, and in many pleasant ways cheering his loneliness.

Meanwhile the Confederate forces had swept on into Pennsylvania, but, alas, were forced back. When they returned to Virginia, Mrs. Grey and Nelly went with them, for both preferred to risk all chances rather than to remain within the Federal lines, cut off from all communication with the husband and father who might at any time need their services. So they became " refugees," living as did thousands of homeless ones, as best they might. Maum Winnie having proved her skill as a nurse, found plenty of employment. Her wages, added to the little Mrs. Grey could earn by her needle, kept them from absolute want.　At last came the sad day of "the surrender."

Nelly was yet too young to understand the sorrow and despair of her mother, nor could she refrain from exceeding wonder when one day Mr. Grey appeared, looking like an old and haggard man, and without a greeting to his wife and child, tottered to a seat, throwing his arms upon the table, burying his face within them, while he moaned and sobbed as only a man can. Kneeling by his side, his wife tried to soothe and comfort him, but although he was able at last to restrain his grief, it was many a day before he was seen to smile.

There was nothing left for the impoverished family but to return to the old Virginia home, and try to make the best of it.　They were compelled to travel as best they could, sometimes walking many miles, sometimes taking advantage of a passing wagon.　At last one evening, just as the sun was setting, they approached the home-place, once a blooming paradise, now a desert waste.　The cabin of Maum Winnie with a few of the servants' houses were still standing, but deserted and desolate.　Doors, log fireplaces, etc., had been torn down for firewood, and in many places patches of charred wood, or dead embers, showed where camp-fires had been lighted.　The little garden in front of Maum Winnie's cabin, made and carefully tended by " de ole man," was a wilderness of weeds among which flowers of rank growth still struggled for a place.　Where the chimneys of the " house" still stood, and all over the half-burned trunks of once beautiful trees crept and clung sickly-looking vines, springing from the roots which had once nourished a luxuriant growth and were not wholly dead.

As Mr. Grey surveyed the scene, a deep groan burst from his lips; but the wife laid her hand upon his shoulder, saying, " Courage, dear, we will make a home even here." Maum Winnie here stepped to the front, briskly leading the way to the little cabin, followed by Nelly, who, child-like, entered readily into any plan that promised to be novel and exciting. Everything of value had been carried off, but a few chairs and a bed with a shuck mattress remained, together with a few pots and pans. The fireplaces were also ready for use. Winnie soon had a cheerful fire, while Nelly set out on the top of a box the remains of the rations they had brought along, and which with some steaming coffee of parched corn formed the evening meal.

Ten years later a plain but tasteful cottage occupied the site of the ruined home. Fast-growing vines were doing their best to rival the luxuriant foliage which once almost hid the old house. A well-kept garden perfumed the air and delighted the eye. Fields ripe for the harvest occupied the land where the negro cabins had stood, forming an effective background to the newly-repaired and whitewashed house of Maum Winnie, which stood, a pleasant feature of this scene of peace and plenty, its fences intact, posies blooming as of old. On the little porch sat the old woman, dozing over her knitting. The gallery of the house was occupied by a family group, who were enjoying the fresh coolness of the evening out of doors. Mrs. Grey sat upon the upper steps arranging some flowers, which were supplied to her as she called for them by a lovely boy, who had just brought his apron full of them. Nelly, swinging in a hammock, was a picture of lazy enjoyment. The attention of all was attracted by the sound of wheels, which ceased as a carriage drove up containing a gentleman and lady, and a young lady who sat by the driver (an old negro who was often employed as a driver and guide by strangers). Nelly ran down to the gate, followed by her mother. The gentleman had by this time descended. One glance at the empty sleeve was enough, even if the kindly face had not been so little changed. It was Colonel ——, who, having business in Richmond, had "stopped off" at the wayside station for a few hours, that he might endeavor to find the Greys, and introduce to his wife and daughter the kind friends who had so faithfully nursed him when wounded, and also show them the scene of incidents often related to them.

The ladies having been introduced, the strangers accepted a cordial invitation to alight. While they were chatting pleasantly upon the vine-shaded gallery, Mr. Grey rode into the yard upon a strong-looking white mule. The greeting of the soldiers was courteous and pleasant. The contrast between them was striking indeed.

The one clad elegantly and fashionably, his shirt-front blazing with diamond studs, his hair and beard luxuriant and carefully kept. The pleasant eyes untroubled and smiling. The other in the plain garb of one who must earn his bread, coarse but scrupulously neat. The face bronzed from exposure, the hair damp with the sweat of toil, and yet, when the brown, hardened hand of the Virginia gentleman met the white clasp of the rich man of the North, Mr. Grey lost nothing by comparison. Colonel —— having laughingly inquired after Maum Winnie, the whole party repaired to her cabin. The old woman received her guests with stately politeness, holding her turbaned head high, as she *majestically* stalked before them to show, at their request, her chickens, ducks, and pigs. She omitted nothing that was due to her visitors, but there was a strained politeness, and a rolling of her eyes toward them, which made Mrs. Grey uneasy and quite prepared her for what followed. While Colonel —— was in the act of saying something which he thought would quite win the old creature's heart, she looked up at him over her glasses, saying,—

"Yer ain't seen nuffin er dat ar fedder-bed yet, is yer? Kase ole Miss she dun giv' me dat ar bed too long to talk about, an' ebery one ob dem fedders was ris rite on dis yere place. 'Fore de Lawd, if ole Miss know I dun. loss dat ar bed she gwine ter rise rite outen de grabe."

Colonel ——, remembering the scene of the disaster to Winnie's feather-bed, felt inclined to laugh heartily, but wishing to mollify the old creature preserved his gravity while he offered her quite a handsome sum "to buy some more feathers." A look from Mr. Grey put a stop to the old woman's talk. Soon the visitors took their leave, having given and received most pleasant impressions. Their visit recalled so vividly their time of trial and adventure that the Greys sat talking far into night.

The next morning Mr. Grey walked over to the cabin to administer a rebuke to Maum Winnie. As he drew near the gate the quavering voice of the old woman was heard singing jerkily, and with a pause between every few words,—

> "Aldo yer sees me gwine 'long so,
> I has my troubles heah below. "

At last, discovering Mr. Grey, she rose and dropped a courtesy.

"Mornin', Mars Ned."

"Well, Winnie, you forgot your Virginia raising yesterday. What is all this about your feather-bed?"

"Well, Mars Ned, dey dun stole it."

"Who stole it?"

"Dah, honey, de Lawd only knows, an' he ain't gwine

ter tell. I dun loss it anyhow, an' my pore ole bones
mity sore sleepin' on dem shucks."

Mr. Grey, finding that the old creature's grievance was
very real to her, refrained from scolding, and, passing
out through the little flower-garden, proceeded to the
stable to feed the stock, a piece of work which before
the war had employed many hands, but which now was
performed by himself, assisted only by one negro man.

Upon the summer air rang the sweet voice of Nelly
as she sang at her work. In the scented garden Mrs.
Grey with her little boy weeded and trimmed and twined
the lovely flowers, feeling really a greater delight in the
fruit of their labor than if they had no real acquaintance
with the flowers, but only received them from the hands
of a gardener.

Dear reader, we must now say farewell to our Nelly.
Let us hope that the clouds which darkened her childhood and early youth have passed never to return, and
that although "into each life some rain must fall," *her*
rainy days may be few and far between.

CHAPTER II.

BRAVE BOYS.

I BELIEVE I may safely say that no cause ever fought for, no army ever raised, numbered among its adherents and soldiers so many *mere boys* as rallied around "The Bonnie Blue Flag," bringing to its defence the ardor of youth, added to unquestioning loyalty and Spartan bravery. Aye, *more* wonderful, *more* worthy of admiration than the bravery of the Spartan youth, because our Southern boys had, up to the beginning of the war, known nothing of hardship or danger. Yet they met with splendid courage all that fell to their lot as soldiers, fighting with an impetuosity and determination which equalled that of the oldest veterans. My book contains already many instances of lofty courage and patient endurance as shown by boys. I will add one or two incidents worthy of record.

In one of the companies of the Third Lee Battalion was a bright Irish boy named Flannagan, who had been brought to Virginia by one of the officers as his attendant. During the seven days' fight around Richmond this child, having procured a small shot-gun, fought with the best of them, coming out safe and sound. I learned this little history from a soldier who knew the boy. Flannagan now lives in Texas.

It is well known that the boys of the Virginia University did excellent service under "Stonewall" Jackson. Here is a story of some other school-boys, related to me by their teacher, himself a brave soldier who lost an arm in one of the battles around Richmond.

When Wilson's raiders reached Charlotte County, Virginia, preparations were made by the Home Guards, aided by a few veterans who happened to be home on furlough, to check their further progress. Breastworks were thrown up on the south side of Stanton River, the railroad bridge was blockaded, and a gun placed in position to defend the passage. Colonel Coleman, who was at home on furlough, gave it as his opinion that these precautions must be supplemented and supported by rifle-pits on the north side, or no successful defence could be made. The pits were hastily dug, but, when volunteers were called for, the extreme danger prevented a hearty response. None appeared except a few old soldiers and six or seven school-boys, whose ages ranged from fourteen to sixteen. The Yankees advanced in line, in an open plain, about two thousand strong. A rapid fire was opened from the rifle-pits and from the gun on the railroad bridge.

After a few minutes the enemy retired, reformed, and came on again, but were again routed as before. Although the boys held a place where many a veteran would have quailed, they stood their ground nobly, and did a soldier's duty.

After the fight was over, two of them had a quarrel regarding a Federal officer whom both shot at and both claimed to have killed.

These were Virginia boys, the sons of veterans, and attending a local school.

The raid came to grief soon after, being routed by Fitz-Hugh Lee.

Thomas Hilton, of Uniontown, Alabama, volunteered

in the "Witherspoon Guards," Twenty-first Alabama Regiment, at the tender age of fourteen. He was too small to carry a musket, and was detailed as a drummer boy. At the battle of Shiloh he threw away his drum and so importuned his captain for a gun that it was given him.

Shortly after, while in the thick of the fight, he was shot through the face, the ball entering one side and passing out at the other.

Rev. N. I. Witherspoon (chaplain of the regiment) found him lying upon the ground, bleeding to death as he then supposed, and knelt beside him to pray. To his surprise the boy looked up, the fire in his eyes unquenched, and gasped out while the blood gushed afresh at every word,—

"Yes—chaplain—I'm—badly hurt—but—I'm—not—*whipped.*"

Thomas Hilton still lives in Uniontown, Alabama, respected by all who know him. His fellow-citizens regard the ugly scar which still appears upon his face with pride and reverence.

The battle of Mansfield, Louisiana, was one of the most hotly-contested and bloody of the war, the loss in men and officers being terrific. The tide of battle rolled on, through lofty pine forests, amid tangled undergrowth, and over open fields, where the soldiers were exposed a to storm of shot and shell, and where, on that beautiful Sunday morning, hundreds of the dead and dying strewed the ground. While the battle was at its height it became necessary, in order to secure concerted action, to send dispatches to a certain point. The only way lay across a ploughed field, exposed to a terrific fire from the enemy, whose target the messenger would become: and it seemed as if certain death must be the

24

fate of any one who should attempt to run the gauntlet. And yet the necessity was met. *A boy of eighteen years* stepped forth from the ranks of Company G, Crescent Regiment, Louisiana Volunteers, and offered to perform this dangerous service.

Dashing on through a perfect hail of shot and shell, stumbling and falling over the furrowed ground, struggling up and on again, he passed unharmed, successfully executing his mission. His escape was so miraculous that one can only account for it by the belief that God gave his angels charge concerning him.

The name of this valiant boy—James V. Nolan—should live in history. He still lives, and has been for years secretary of the Cotton Exchange at Shreveport, Louisiana.

CHAPTER III.

THE story of "The Little Apron" was written up by Major McDonald, of Louisville, to be read at a meeting of veterans of Association Army of Northern Virginia, Kentucky Division. It is true in every particular,—indeed, a matter of history.

I have given it a place here because I feel sure that many of my young readers will remember having seen the apron in question, and will like to read its full history. It was very kindly loaned to me, during the New Orleans Exposition, by Major McDonald, and was on exhibition at my tent ("The Soldiers' Rest"), among many other Confederate relics, where it never ceased to be an object of profound interest and veneration. Hundreds of people handled it. Veterans gazed upon it with moistened eyes. Women bedewed it with tears, and often pressed kisses upon it. Children touched it reverently, listening with profound interest while its story was told. The little apron was of plain white cotton, bordered and belted with "turkey red,"—an apron of "red, white, and red," purposely made of these blended colors in order to express sympathy with the Confederates. It yet bears several blood-stains. The button-hole at the back of the belt is torn out, for the eager little patriot did not wait to unbutton it. There is another hole, just under the belt in front, made when the wounded boy tore it from the staff to which he had nailed it to conceal it in his bosom. The story as told by Major McDonald is as follows:

279

In the spring of 1863, while the Army of Northern Virginia was encamped on the Rapidan River, preparing for that memorable campaign which included the battle of Gettysburg, there came to it, from Hampshire County, Virginia, a beardless boy, scarcely eighteen years of age, the eldest son of a widowed mother. His home was within the enemy's lines, and he had walked more than one hundred miles to offer his services to assist in repelling a foe which was then preying upon the fairest portions of his native State. He made application to join Company D, Eleventh Virginia Cavalry, which was made up principally from his county, and, therefore, contained many of his acquaintances, and seemed much surprised when told that the Confederate government did not furnish its cavalry with horses and equipments. Some members of the company present, who noticed his earnestness and the disappointment caused by this announcement from the officer, said,—

"Enroll him, captain; we will see that he has a horse and equipments the next fight we get into."

On faith of this promise he was enrolled,—James M. Watkins, Company D, Eleventh Virginia Cavalry, Jones's Brigade. Shortly afterward the campaign opened with the fight at Brandy Station, in which twenty thousand cavalry were engaged from daylight to sundown. Before the battle was over Watkins, mounted and fully equipped, took his place with his company. It was not long after this engagement that General Lee advanced the whole army, and crossed into Maryland, Watkins's command covering the rear. During the battle of Gettysburg, on the 3d and 4th of July, we were engaged several times with the enemy's cavalry on our right, upon which occasions he was always found in the front, and while on the march was ever bright and cheerful.

On the evening of the 4th, General Lee, in preparation for his retreat, began to send his wagons to the rear in the direction of Williamsport, when it was found that the enemy's cavalry had gone around our left and taken possession of a pass in South Mountain, through which lay our line of march. To dislodge them required a stubborn fight, lasting late into the night, in which General Jones's brigade was engaged, and he himself, becoming separated from his men in the darkness, was supposed to have been captured or killed.

Finally the Federals were repulsed, and the wagon-train proceeded on its way to Williamsport. In the morning Watkins's command was ordered to march on the left flank of the train to prevent a renewal of the attack upon it, and on approaching Hagerstown those in the rear of the column heard loud and repeated cheering from the men in front. After having been in an enemy's country fighting night and day, in rain and mud, those cheers came to those who heard them in the distance as the first rays of sunshine after a storm. Many were the conjectures as to their cause: some said it was fresh troops from the other side of the Potomac; others that it was the ammunition-wagons, for the supply was known to be short; while others surmised that it was General Jones reappearing after his supposed death or capture. Whatever the cause was, its effect was wonderful upon the morale of those men, and cheers went up all along the line from those who did not know the cause in answer to those who did. When the command had reached a stone mill, about three miles southeast of Hagerstown, they found the cause only a little girl about fourteen years of age, perhaps the miller's daughter, standing in the door wearing an apron in which the colors were so blended as to represent the Confederate flag. A trivial thing it may seem to those

24*

who were not there, but to those jaded, war-worn men
it was the first expression of sympathy for them and
their cause that had been openly given them since they
had crossed the Potomac, and their cheers went up in
recognition of the courage of the little girl and her
parents, who thus dared to give their sympathy to a
retreating army, almost in sight of a revengeful foe.
When Company D was passing the house the captain
rode up and thanked the little girl for having done so
much to revive the spirits of the troops, and asked her
if she would give him a piece of the apron as a souvenir
of the incident. "Yes, certainly," she replied, "you
may have it all," and in her enthusiasm she tore it off,
not waiting to unbutton it, and handed it to the officer,
who said it should be the flag of his company as long
as it was upon Maryland soil.

"Let me be the color-bearer, captain," said young
Watkins, who was by his side; "I promise to protect
it with my life." Fastening it to a staff he resumed his
place at the head of the company, which was in the front
squadron of the regiment.

Later in the evening, in obedience to an order brought
by a courier, the Eleventh Cavalry moved at a gallop
in the direction of Williamsport, whence the roll of
musketry and report of cannon had been heard for some
time, and, rejoining the brigade, was engaged in a desperate struggle to prevent the Federal cavalry from
destroying the wagons of the whole army, which, the
river being unfordable, were halted and parked at this
point, their principal defence against the whole cavalry
force of the enemy being the teamsters and stragglers that
General Imboden had organized. The Eleventh Cavalry
charged the battery in front of them, this gallant boy
with his apron flag riding side by side with those who
led the charge. The battery was taken and retaken,

and then taken again, before the Federals withdrew from the field, followed in the direction of Boonsboro', until darkness covered their retreat. In those desperate surges many went down on both sides, and it was not until after it was over that men thought of their comrades and inquiries were made of the missing. The captain of Company D, looking over the field for the killed and wounded, found young Watkins lying on the ground, his head supported by the surgeon. In reply to his question, " was he badly hurt ?" he answered, " Not much, captain, but *I've got the flag!*" and, putting his hand in his bosom, he drew out the little apron and gave it to the officer. When asked how it came there, he said that when he was wounded and fell from his horse the Federals were all around him, and to prevent them from capturing it he had torn it from the staff and hid it in his bosom.

The surgeon told the captain, aside, that his leg was shattered by a large piece of shell, which was imbedded in the bone; that amputation would be necessary, and he feared the wound was mortal. "But," he added, " he has been so intent upon the safe delivery of that apron into your hands as to seem utterly unconscious of his wound."

After parting with his flag the brave boy sank rapidly. He was tenderly carried by his comrades back to Hagerstown, where a hospital had been established, and his leg amputated. The next morning his captain found him pale and haggard from suffering. By his side was a bouquet of flowers, placed by some kind friend, which seemed to cheer him much. The third day afterward he died, and was buried in a strange land, by strangers' hands, without a stone to mark the place where he sleeps.

Thus ended the mortal career of this gallant youth, who had scarcely seen sixty days' service; but though he lies in an unknown grave, he has left behind a name which should outlast the most costly obelisk that wealth or fame can erect. Gentle as a woman, yet perfectly fearless in the discharge of his duty, so sacred did he deem the trust confided to him that he forgot even his own terrible sufferings while defending it. Such names as this it is our duty to rescue from oblivion, and to write on the page of history, where the children of our common country may learn from them lessons of virtue and self-sacrifice. In his character and death he was not isolated from many of his comrades: he was but a type of many men, young and old, whose devotion to what is known as the "lost cause" made them heroes in the fullest acceptation of the term, flinching from neither suffering nor death itself if coming to them in the line of duty.

CHAPTER IV.

BRAVERY HONORED BY A FOE.

The following story was written out for me by Eddie Souby, of New Orleans, while I was acting as assistant editress of the *Southern Bivouac.*

It was related to him by his father, E. J. Souby, Esq., formerly a gallant soldier of the Fifth Regiment, Hay's Brigade, and now an honored member of Association Army of Northern Virginia, Louisiana Division. It is a true story in every particular, and the name of the youthful hero is given, that it may live in our hearts, and be honored as it deserves, though he who so nobly bore it is now dead. I wish that I could also give the name of his generous foe,—no doubt as brave as generous,— the Federal officer who interposed his authority to preserve the life of this gallant boy. They should be recorded, side by side, on the same page of history, and be remembered with pride by the youth of our land, no matter whether their fathers wore the blue or the gray during the late civil war.

Nathan Cunningham was the name of this young hero. He was a member of the Second Company Orleans Cadets, afterwards Company E, Fifth Regiment, Louisiana Volunteers, Hay's Brigade, Army of Northern Virginia, and color-bearer of the regiment at the time the incident narrated below occurred. The story is as follows:

It was a dark and starless night. Tattoo-beat had long been heard, and Hay's Brigade, weary after a long day's march, rested beneath the dewy boughs of gigantic oaks in a dense forest near the placid Rappahannock. No sound broke the stillness of the night. The troops were lying on nature's rude couch, sweetly sleeping, perhaps, little dreaming of the awful dawn which was soon to break upon them. The camp-fires had burned low. The morrow's rations had been hastily cooked, hunger appeased, and the balance laid carefully away; but that which was most essential to life had, unfortunately, been neglected. No provision for water had been made. The springs being somewhat distant from the camp, but few had spirit, after the day's weary march, to go farther. The canteens were, for the most part, empty.

Though thirsting, the tired soldiers slept, oblivious to their physical sufferings. But ere the morning broke, the distant sound of musketry echoed through the woods, rudely dispelling the solemn silence of the night, and awakening from their broken dreams of home and kindred the whole mass of living valor.

The roll of the drum and the stentorian voice of the gallant chief calling to arms mingled together. Aroused to duty, and groping their way through the darkness, the troops sallied forth in battle array.

In a rifle-pit, on the brow of a hill overlooking the river, near Fredericksburg, were men who had exhausted their ammunition in the vain attempt to check the advancing column of Hooker's finely equipped and disciplined army, which was crossing the river. But owing to the heavy mist which prevailed as the morning broke, little or no execution had been done. To the relief of these few came the brigade in double-quick time. But no sooner were they intrenched than the firing on the opposite side of the river became terrific, and the constant roaring of musketry and artillery became appalling.

Undismayed, however, stood the little band of veterans, pouring volley after volley into the crossing column.

Soon many soldiers fell. Their agonizing cries, as they lay helpless in the trenches, calling most piteously for water, caused many a tear to steal down the cheeks of their comrades in arms, and stout hearts shook in the performance of their duty.

"Water!" "Water!" But, alas! there was none to give.

Roused as they had been from peaceful dreams to meet an assault so early and so unexpected, no time was left them to do aught but buckle on their armor.

"Boys!" exclaimed a lad of eighteen, the color-bearer of one of the regiments, "I can't stand this any longer. My nature can't bear it. They want water, and water they must have. So let me have a few canteens, and I'll go for some."

Carefully laying the colors, which he had conspicuously borne on many a field, in the trench, he leaped out in search of water, and was soon, owing to the heavy mist, out of sight.

Shortly afterwards the firing ceased for a while, and there came a courier with orders to fall back to the main line, a distance of over twelve hundred yards to the rear. It had, doubtless, become evident to General Lee that Hooker had crossed the river in sufficient force to advance.

The retreating column had not proceeded far when it met the noble youth, his canteens all filled with water, returning to the sufferers, who were still lying in the distant trenches. The eyes of the soldier-boy, who had oftentimes tenderly and lovingly gazed upon the war-worn and faded flag floating over the ranks, now saw it not. The troops, in their hurry to obey orders and owing, probably, to the heavy mist that surrounded them, had overlooked or forgotten the colors.

On sped the color-bearer back to the trenches to relieve the thirst of his wounded companions as well as to save the honor of his regiment by rescuing its colors.

His mission of mercy was soon accomplished. The wounded men drank freely, thanked and blessed him. And now to seize the flag and double-quick back to his regiment was the thought and act of a moment. But hardly had he gone ten paces from the ditch when a company of Federal soldiers appeared ascending the hill. The voice of an officer sternly commanded him to " Halt and surrender!" The morning sun, piercing with a lurid glare the dense mist, reveals a hundred rifles levelled at his breast. One moment more and his soul is to pass into eternity, for his answer is, " Never while I hold these colors."

But why is he not fired upon ? Why do we still see him with the colors flying above his head, now beyond the reach of rifle-balls, when but a moment before he could have been riddled with bullets ? And now, see! he enters proudly but breathlessly the ranks, and receives the congratulations of his friends in loud acclaim.

The answer comes, because of the generous act of the Federal officer in command of that company. When this noble officer saw that the love of honor was far dearer to the youth than life, in the impulse of a magnanimous heart he freely gave him both in the word of command,—

" Bring back your pieces, men! don't shoot that brave boy !"

Such nobility of character and such a generous nature as that displayed by this officer, must ever remain a living monument to true greatness; and should these lines perchance meet his eyes, let him know and feel the proud satisfaction that the remembrance of his noble deed is gratefully cherished, and forever engraved in the heart of the soldier-boy in gray.

CHAPTER V.

ON a bright Sunday morning Sally sat upon the gallery of her uncle's house slowly swaying backward and forward in a low rocking-chair. In her hand was her prayer-book, but I greatly fear she had not read as she ought, for while her finger was held between the shut covers, marking "the Psalms for the day," her bright eyes wandered continually over the lovely scene before her. Above her head branches of tender green were tossing merrily in the March wind, at her feet lay a parterre bright with spring buds and flowers. Beyond the garden-fence the carriage-road described a curve, and swept away under the lofty pines which here bounded the view. On either side lay fields of newly-planted cotton. Behind the house, seen through the wide-open doors and windows, the orchard gleamed pink and white. Still beyond, blue smoke curled upward from the cabins of the negroes in "the quarter,"—almost a village in itself. The noise of their children at play was borne upon the wind, mingled with the weird chanting of hymns by the older negroes. The family, with the exception of Sally, had gone to church,—a distance of twelve miles.

For weeks it had been known that "Wilson's raiders" would be likely at any time to appear; but continued security had lulled the apprehensions of the planters hereabouts, and, besides, they depended upon Confederate scouts to give timely warning. But suddenly on this peaceful Sunday a confused noise from the direction of "the quarter" startled Sally, and directly a crowd of frightened negroes ran to the house with the tale that a party of scouts had been driven in, reporting the Yankees approaching and only ten miles away.

The sense of responsibility which at once took possession of the girl's mind overmastered her terror. She, as well as a few servants considered worthy of trust, had received clear instructions how to act in such an emergency; but before anything could be accomplished a party of horsemen (Confederates) rode up, and hastily giving information that the Federals had taken the "Pleasant Hill road," dashed off again. This knowledge did not relieve Sally's mind, however, for on the Pleasant Hill road lay the fine plantation of another uncle, Dr. ——, who was, she knew, absent. The overseer, unaware of the approach of the raiders, would, unless warned, not have time to run off the valuable horses. By the road the enemy had taken the distance was several miles, but there was a "short cut" through the woods, which would bring a rapid rider to the plantation much sooner, and at once it occurred to our heroine to send a boy on the only available animal, an old white mule, which had long enjoyed exemption from all but light work as a reward for faithful services in the past. Alas! Sally found she had "reckoned without her"—negro. Abject terror had overcome even the habitual obedience of the servants, and not one would venture; they only rolled their eyes wildly, breaking forth into such agony of protestations that the girl ceased to urge them, and, dismayed at the peril she was powerless to arrest, sat down to consider matters. She knew that the family had that morning driven to church, and so the carriage-horses were safe for the present.

But there was the doctor's buggy-horse, a magnificent

iron-gray, and Persimmon, her cousin's riding-horse, a beautiful cream-colored mare with black, flowing mane and tail, and *Green Persimmon*, her colt, which was like its mother, and scarcely less beautiful. Besides, there were horses and mules which, if not so ornamental, were indispensable. Oh, these must be run off and saved,—but how? Goaded by these thoughts, and upon the impulse of the moment, the girl ordered a side-saddle to be put upon old "Whitey," and, hastily mounting, belabored the astonished beast until, yielding to the inevitable, he started off at a smart trot.

Once in the woods, Sally's heart quailed within her; her terror was extreme. The tramp, tramp of her steed she thought was as loud as thunder, and felt sure that thus she would be betrayed. The agitation of the underbrush caused by the wind seemed to her to denote the presence of a concealed enemy. She momentarily expected a "Yank" to step from behind a tree and seize her bridle. As she rushed along, hanging branches (which at another time she would have stooped to avoid) severely scratched her face and dishevelled her hair; but never heeding, she urged on old Whitey until he really seemed to become inspired with the spirit of the occasion, to regain his youthful fire, and so dashed on until at length Sally drew rein at the bars of the horse-lot, where the objects of her solicitude were quietly grazing, with the exception of Green Persimmon, who seemed to be playing a series of undignified capers for the amusement of her elders. To catch these was a work of time: Sally looked on in an agony of impatience. But, forunately, a neighbor rode up just then with the news that for some unknown reason the Federal soldiers had, after halting awhile just beyond the forks of the road, marched back to the river and were recrossing. With the usual inconsistency of her sex,

Sally now began to cry, trembling so violently that she was fain to dismount, and submit to be *coddled* and petted awhile by the old servants. She declared that she never could repass those dreadful woods, but later, a sense of duty overcame her nervousness, and (the family having returned), escorted by her cousins and followed by a faithful servant, she returned to her anxious friends, who in one breath scolded her for having dared so great risks and in the next praised her courage and devotion.

*   *   *   *   *   *   *   *

The visit of the raiders was, alas! not long delayed, but its attendant horrors may not here be described. The terrible story may, perhaps, be told at another time, —for the present, *adieu.*

CHAPTER VI.

The following story, originally written by me for the *Southern Bivouac*, is strictly true. The successful forager was once a patient of mine, and is well known to me. I also know that he perpetrated the joke as described. The article is intended to appear as if written by a soldier's son.

HIGH PRICE FOR NEEDLES AND THREAD.
By Walter.

My father was once a private soldier in the Confederate army, and he often tells us interesting stories of the war. One morning, just as he was going down town, mother sent me to ask him to change a dollar. He could not do it, but he said,—

"Ask your mother how much change she wants."

She only wanted a dime to buy a paper of needles and some silk to mend my jacket. So I went back and asked for ten cents. Instead of taking it out of his vest-pocket, father opened his pocket-book and said,—

"Did you say you wanted *ten dollars* or ten *cents*, my boy?"

"Why, father," said I, "whoever heard of paying ten dollars for needles and thread?"

"I have," said he. "I once heard of a paper of needles, and a skein of silk, worth *more* than ten dollars."

His eyes twinkled and looked so pleasant that I knew there was a story on hand, so I told mother and sis' Loo, who promised to find out all about it. After supper that night mother coaxed father to tell us the story.

We liked it ever so much: so I got mother to write it down for the *Bivouac.*

After the battle of Chickamauga, one of "our mess" found a needle-case which had belonged to some poor fellow, probably among the killed. He did not place much value upon the contents, although there was a paper of No. 8 needles, several buttons, and a skein or two of thread, cut at each end and neatly braided so that each thread could be smoothly drawn out. He put the whole thing in his breast-pocket, and thought no more about it. But one day, while out foraging for himself and his mess, he found himself near a house where money could have procured a fine meal of fried chicken, corn-pone, and buttermilk, besides a small supply to carry back to camp. But Confederate soldiers' purses were generally as empty as their stomachs, and in this instance the lady of the house did not offer to give away her nice dinner. While the poor fellow was inhaling the enticing odor, and feeling desperately hungry, a girl rode up to the gate on horseback, and bawled out to another girl inside the house,—

"Oh, Cindy, I rid over to see if you couldn't lend me a needle! I broke the last one I had to-day, and pap says thar ain't nary 'nother to be bought in the country hereabouts!"

Cindy declared she was in the same fix, and couldn't finish her new homespun dress for that reason.

The soldier just then had an idea. He retired to a little distance, pulled out his case, sticking two needles on the front of his jacket, then went back and offered one of them, with his best bow, to the girl on the horse. Right away the lady of the house offered to trade for the one remaining. The result was a plentiful dinner for himself; and in consideration of a thread or two of silk, a full haversack and canteen.

After this our mess was well supplied, and our forager began to look sleek and fat. The secret of his success did not leak out till long afterward, when he astonished the boys by declaring that he "had been 'living like a fighting-cock' on a paper of needles and two skeins of silk."

"And," added father, "if he had paid for all the meals he got in Confederate money, the amount would have been far more than ten dollars."

I know other boys and girls will think this a queer story, but I hope they will like it as well as mother and Loo and I did.

CHAPTER VII.

BUNNY.

ONE bright morning I sat in the matron's room of the
"Buckner Hospital," then located at Newnan, Georgia.
Shall I describe to you this room—or my suite of rooms?
Indeed, I fear you will be disappointed, dear young
readers, for perhaps the word "hospital" conveys to
your mind the idea of a handsome and lofty building
containing every convenience for nursing the sick, and
for the comfort of attendants. Alas! during the war
hospital arrangements were of the roughest. Frequent
changes of location were imperative, transportation
was difficult. So it became a "military necessity" to
seize upon such buildings as were suitable in the towns
where it was intended to establish a "post." Court-
houses, halls, stores, hotels, even churches had to be
used,—the pews being removed and replaced by the
rough hospital beds.

The "Buckner Hospital" was expected to accommo-
date nearly one thousand sick and wounded, and embraced every building for two solid squares. Near the
centre a small store had been appropriated to the matron's use during the day. Here all business relating to
the comfort of the sick and wounded was transacted.
The store as it stood, shelves, counters, and all, became
the "linen-room," and was piled from floor to ceiling
with bedding and clean clothing. The back "shed-room"
was the matron's own. A rough table, planed on the
top, stood in the centre. With the exception of one

large rocking-chair, kindly donated by a lady of Ring-gold, Georgia, boxes served for chairs. A couch made of boxes and piled with comforts and pillows stood in one corner. This served not only as an occasional rest-ing-place for the matron, but, with the arm-chair, was frequently occupied by soldiers who, in the early stages of convalescence, having made a pilgrimage to my room, were too weak to return at once, and so rested awhile.

Here I sat on the morning in question looking over some "diet lists," when I heard a slight noise at the door. Soon a little girl edged her way into the room.

Her dress was plain and faded, but when she pushed back the calico sun-bonnet a sweet, bright face appeared. She came forward as shyly as a little bird and stood at my side. As I put out my hand to draw her closer, she cried, "Don't, you'll scare him!"

And then I perceived that she held close to her breast, wrapped in her check apron, something that moved and trembled. Carefully the little girl removed a corner of the apron, disclosing the gray head and frightened eyes of a squirrel. Said she, "It's Bunny; he's mine; I raised him, and I want to give him to the sick soldiers! *Daddy's a soldier!*" And as she stated this last fact the sweet face took on a look of pride.

"What is your name, and how did you get here?" I said.

"My name is Ca-line. Uncle Jack, he brung in a load of truck, and mammy let me come along, an' I didn't have nothing to fetch to the poor soldiers but Bunny. He's mine," she repeated, as she tenderly covered again the trembling little creature. I soon found that she desired to give the squirrel away with her own hands, and did not by any means consider *me* a sick sol-dier. That she should visit the fever-wards was out of the question, so I decided to go with her to a ward where were some wounded men, most of whom were convalescent. My own eyes, alas! were so accustomed to the sight of the pale, suffering faces, empty sleeves, and dreadful scars, that I did not dream of the effect it would have upon the child.

As we entered she dropped my hand, clinging convulsively to my dress. Addressing the soldiers, I said, "Boys, little Ca-line has brought you her pet squirrel; her father is a soldier, she says." But here the poor child broke down utterly; from her pale lips came a cry which brought tears to the eyes of the brave men who surrounded her: "Oh, daddy, daddy; I don't *want* you to be a soldier! Oh, lady, *will* they do my daddy like this?"

Hastily retreating, I led the tortured child to my room, where at last she recovered herself. I gave her lunch, feeding Bunny with some corn-bread, which he ate, sitting on the table by his little mistress, his bright eyes fixed warily upon me. A knock at the door startled us. The child quickly snatched up her pet and hid him in her apron. The visitor proved to be "Uncle Jack," a white-headed old negro, who had come for "little Missy."

Tears came to my eyes as I watched the struggle which at once began in that brave little heart. Her streaming eyes and heaving breast showed how hard it was to give up Bunny. Uncle Jack was impatient, however, and at last "Missy" thrust the squirrel into my hands, saying, sobbingly, "*Thar*, you keep him to show to 'em, but don't let nothin' hurt him." I arose and placed Bunny in the deep pocket of an army overcoat that hung by the window, where he cuddled down contentedly. Ca-line passed out with a lagging step, but in a few moments ran back, and, drawing a box under the window, climbed upon it to peep into the pocket at her pet, who ungratefully growled at being disturbed. She then ran out without a word to me, and I saw her no more.

Bunny soon attached himself to me. Creeping into my pocket, he would always accompany me in my rounds through the wards. The sick and wounded took the greatest delight in his visits. As soon as I entered the door the squirrel would run up on my shoulder; from thence, jumping upon the beds, would proceed to search for the treasures which nearly every patient had saved and hidden for him. His capers were a source of unceasing amusement to his soldier friends,— I cannot describe to you how great. The story of little Ca-line's self-sacrifice went the rounds among them. All admired and truly appreciated her heroism and her love for " the poor, sick soldiers."

Bunny lived happily for a long time. One day, however, as I was passing along the street, he began as usual to run from out my pocket to my shoulder, and back again to nestle in his hiding-place.

Just then a large dog came by. The frightened squirrel made a vain attempt to reach a tree by the road-side. Failing, he was at once seized and instantly killed. My regret was shared by all the soldiers, who long remembered and talked of poor Bunny.

CHAPTER VIII.

BEAUREGARD.

ONE very cold day in the winter of 1862 there came to the Third Alabama Hospital, in Richmond, Virginia, a sick soldier, belonging to the Third Alabama Regiment. He was shivering, and so hoarse that he could only speak in whispers. Instead of going at once to bed, however, he sat down upon a bench by the stove, keeping his blanket drawn closely over his chest. His teeth were chattering, and continued to do so until I ordered him to go to his bed immediately, meanwhile hastening down-stairs to prepare for him a hot drink. Upon my return, my patient was in bed, closely covered up,—head and all. As soon as I turned down the bedclothes from his face, I was startled by a furious cr-r-r-r bow-wow, wow, wow, which also attracted the attention of every one in the large ward. Of course it was impossible longer to conceal the fact that the new patient had brought with him a dog, so he showed me—nestling under his arm—a young Newfoundland puppy, looking like nothing so much as a fluffy black ball. His bright eyes gleamed fiercely and he continued to bark in a shrill tone, which could not be allowed to continue, as it excited and disturbed the sick. I am a lover of dogs, and now offered to take charge of this little waif. His master was unwilling to part with him, but there was no alternative, so I carried him off down-stairs, where, installed in comfortable quarters and petted by everybody, the ungrateful little dog seemed to forget the sick

300

master who had cherished him so fondly, and, far from grieving or moping at the separation, grew every day more frolicsome. From the soldier I learned the history of his dog. He said,—

"Shortly before I was sent to the hospital our regiment captured a Federal camp. Among the plunder I found that little fellow curled up in a camp-bed that some Yankee had just got out of, and as warm as toast. He seemed to take to me right off. I reckon the Yankee had a name for him, but I call him 'Beauregard.' The poor fellow has had a hard time since I got him, for rations in the valley are poor and scant, but *I've* done with less so *he* could have a bite, and I tell you he has kept me warm a many a night."

However, when the soldier was ready to return to camp, Beauregard had grown quite too large to be carried in his master's bosom. So he was given to my little son, and remained to claim our care and to become an object of interest to all inmates of the hospital. It became so much a matter of course for me to take the dog with me on my morning rounds through the wards that whenever he was left behind, my patients never failed to miss him, and to inquire, "Where's the general to-day?" He was very intelligent, easily learning to trot quietly along down the rows of beds. If he ever grew too frisky, I had only to stop short, pointing to the entrance, when down would drop his tail, and he was off like a shot to the yard. There he awaited my coming, always looking anxiously in my face to see if I was still angry. When I would ask, "Are you sorry, Beau?" he would whine and come crawling to my feet. As soon as he heard me say "All right," he began to bound and run around in a circle and in other ways to show his joy.

Among the patients he had many warm friends who

used to take great pleasure in saving scraps to feed him with. They also loved to tease him by wrapping some nice morsel in many papers. The parcel was then hidden. Beauregard knew just which beds to stop at, and, greatly to the delight of his friends, would put his paws upon the bunks and "nose about" under the mattress or pillows for the bundles there hidden. After many attempts to get through the many papers in which lay a coveted morsel, he would grow impatient and disgusted, and would at last sit down, looking earnestly first at the inmate of the bed, then at the parcel on the floor. Then, if he was not helped, he would push the bed with his paw, until at last he succeeded in gaining his wish.

Early in the spring Beau fell into some disgrace, for while romping with my little boy he threw him down and broke his arm. Everybody scolded the poor dog, crying shame on him wherever he appeared, until he got a habit of slinking out of sight. Before the broken arm was quite well, little Wally grew very ill of typhoid fever, so ill that his papa was sent for, for it seemed that he must die. Beauregard attached himself very closely to my husband, rarely leaving his side. When his new master returned to camp, I went down to the boat to see him off. The dog followed us. The boat was crowded with soldiers going to reinforce McGruder, so I did not go on board, but when ready to return discovered that Beau was missing. The first letter from my husband announced that the dog had followed his master on the boat, where he must have hidden, for his presence was not discovered until some time after the boat had left the wharf. In camp he became a terrible nuisance. No matter how securely he was tied, the dog always managed to escape and *attend the drill.* Here he would sometimes sit down and gravely watch the proceedings, cocking his head first on one side, then on the other, but usually he would rush into the ranks to find his master, getting under the feet of the men, who in consequence lost step and got out of line, of course becoming very angry. The shells frequently exploding in the vicinity became a constant terror to this unfortunate, who knew not how to avoid them. He soon learned to distinguish the shriek of a coming shell, and would race off in one direction, looking fearfully back over his shoulder, until a similar sound in another quarter would so puzzle and terrify him that he would stand still awhile until the noise of an explosion *utterly* demoralized him, when he would frantically dig up the ground, as if trying to bury himself.

I am afraid I must acknowledge that my dog was not strictly honest. In fact, his depredations upon their larders won for him the undying hatred of the colored cooks of various messes, who were always seeking revenge. Their dislike culminated one day in a dreadful scalding, inflicted upon the poor dog by the cook of an officers' mess, who poured a whole kettle of boiling water upon his back, causing him weeks of suffering and the loss of part of his beautiful glossy coat. This seemed to have implanted in his mind a profound distrust of negroes, which he never ceased to entertain until the day of his death. After this Beauregard was sent up to Richmond that I might cure his wound; this I was more easily enabled to do, as my friends among the surgeons kindly advised and assisted me. He was soon quite well, the growing hair nearly concealing his scars. When I left Richmond with my little boy, Beau accompanied us, and found a permanent home upon the plantation of a relative in Alabama. It was here that he first showed his extreme dislike for negroes, which attracted attention and became unmistakable.

At first it gave much trouble, but gradually he grew tolerant of the servants upon the "home-place," although he never took kindly even to these. He never forgot that he had been scalded. At any time steam arising from a boiling tea-kettle or pot would send him yelping away. I remember hearing the youngsters say that once when Beauregard had followed them miles into the woods, seeming to enjoy the tramp and the hunt, they having decided to have a lunch of broiled birds, heated some water in a camp-kettle to scald them preparatory to picking off the feathers. As soon as the birds were dipped into the water and taken out steaming, the dog set out for home, where they found him, upon their return, hiding under a corn-crib.

Although, as I said before, Beau became used to the servants whom he saw every day upon the home-place, no strange negro dared to come inside the big gate unless accompanied by one of the family. Whenever the deep, hoarse bark of Beauregard announced the appearance of strangers, it was known that the dog must be chained. Not once, but many times, I have seen a load of "fodder" or "garden-truck" driven into the yard and immediately *surrounded* by this one big dog, who would keep the black driver crouching at the very top of the load with "ashy" face and chattering teeth, while his besieger walked growling around the wagon, occasionally jumping up upon the chance of seizing an unguarded foot. Until the dog was securely chained nothing would induce his prisoner to venture down. No chicken-thieves dared to put in an appearance so long as this faithful beast kept watch upon the premises. And for his faithfulness he was doomed to destruction. Such a state of security in any place could not long be tolerated. The would-be thieves, exasperated by the impunity with which fine, fat turkeys, geese, ducks, and chickens walked about before their very eyes, and smoke-houses, melon-patches, and wood-piles remained undisturbed, at last poisoned faithful Beauregard, whose death left the home-place unprotected, for not one of his successors ever followed his example or proved half as watchful.

PART III.

CHAPTER I.

"MY BOYS."

Address to the Wives and Children of Confederate Veterans.

I **HAVE** been often and earnestly requested by "my comrades" to address to you a few words explanatory of the tie which binds me to them and them to me. They tell me, among other things, that you "wonder much, and still the wonder grows," that I should presume to call grave and dignified husbands and fathers "my boys." Having promised to meet their wishes, I must in advance apologize for the egoism which it is quite impossible to avoid, as my own war record is inseparable from that of my comrades.

Does it seem strange to you that I call these bronzed and bearded men "my *boys?*" Ah, friends, in every time-worn face there lives always for me "the light of other days." Memory annihilates the distance between the long-ago and the present.

I seem to see them marching, with brave, bright faces and eager feet, to meet the foe. I hear the distant boom of cannon, growing fainter as they press the retreating enemy. And then, alas! many come back to me mutilated, bleeding, dying, yet with ardor unquenched, re-

---

* These articles, originally prepared for *The Southern Bivouac* and "South Illustrated," are here republished by special request.

pressing moans of anguish that they may listen for the shout of victory: wrestling fiercely with the King of Terrors, not that they fear to die, but because his chill grasp palsies the arm that would fain strike another blow for the right.

I stood among the sick and wounded lying in a hospital in Richmond, Virginia, while the magnificent Army of Northern Virginia was passing from the scene of their late glorious victory at Manassas to meet the invaders under McClellan, who were marching upon the Peninsula. Around me lay many sick and wounded men, gathered under the immense roof of a tobacco factory, which covered nearly a whole square. Its windows commanded a full view of the legions passing on both sides.

The scene I can never forget. As the strains of martial music fell upon the summer air, pale, gaunt forms struggled to their feet, feebly but eagerly donned clothes and accoutrements, and, staggering under their weight, crept to the office of the surgeon in charge, piteously begging that they might "get to go on with the boys." Many, too weak to rise, broke into bitter sobs: tears poured from eyes bright with fever or dim with the shadow of death. Passing among these, I was startled to see a patient, whom all had supposed to be dying, sitting up in bed. Stretching his arms toward me, he cried out, "Lady, lady, come here!" He was a boy of sixteen years, one of the glorious Third Alabama, and he begged so hard to be allowed to see "the boys" that I had his bunk drawn up to an open window, supporting him in my arms so that he *could* see. When his own regiment passed, he tried with faltering breath to cheer, but, failing, waved his feeble hand, gasping out, "*God knows*, I wish I could be with you, boys, but 'pears like the heavenly Master ain't willing."

His comrades passed on. The boy was borne back to his place, whence, in a few hours, he passed beyond all pain and disappointment.

I need not mention here the magnificent record of the army that passed that day the streets of Richmond. The pages of history are ablaze with the glory of it. Not less glorious to me are the records written in my heart of heroic fortitude, patient endurance, sublime resignation. Alas for my poor, worn, shattered, suffering, dying boys! how their souls were tried, *yet never found wanting!*

The fortunes of war led me from the scenes of my first service to rejoin my husband, who had been ordered to the Army of Tennessee. On my journey, and while waiting to be assigned to duty, I lingered for a while among the homes of Southern soldiers. How can I convey to you the impressions there received?

Here lay the main-spring of the valor which then and long afterward astonished the world. In the towns and near the front thousands of women daily ministered to the sick and wounded. When a battle ended, these could soon know the fate of loved ones, perhaps were permitted to nurse them, to attend their dying hour, or—inestimable privilege—reclaim the precious casket which had enshrined a gallant soul. But in many a country home women endured, day after day, crucifixion of the soul, yet heroically, patiently, toiled and prayed on. Startled by flying rumors, tortured by suspense, weary with unwonted labor, they never dreamed of leaving the post of duty or of neglecting the interests confided to their care. No comforter had they save their God, no resource but unwearied prayer.

Memory brings back to me a scene which sadly illustrates the exalted courage and faith of these noble women. I was present one night when, at a plantation home, the family and servants were assembled, as usual, for prayers. The aged father led the worship, but, while praying for the absent sons, two of whom had already fallen in battle, he faltered and ceased. Instantly the clear, sweet voice of the mother was heard as she prayed fervently, not only for the dear ones at the front, but for the holy cause, for *other* parents, *other* sons, and for *strength* to *submit* to *God's will.*

I have, sitting by the bedside of sick or wounded soldiers, read to them letters from just such homes, breathing lofty courage, full of cheer, although I knew that the hearts of the writers had been almost breaking, the fingers that penned them stiff and trembling with toil hitherto unknown. God bless the women of the South.

If from every wreath that ever adorned the brow of a hero the brightest laurels were plucked, all would not form an offering too resplendent to lay at their feet.

Soon after the battle of Shiloh began my service with the Army of Tennessee. How shall I make you understand, dear friends, how strong, how dear, how imperishable are the ties which bind me to these grand and noble heroes,—the true, brave boys with whom I shared until the bitter end their trials and glory. Heroic souls who bore with equal fortitude and transcendent bravery alike the shock of battle, the pangs of "hope deferred," the untold hardships which soon became their daily portion. Their bleeding feet dyed alike the snows of Georgia and the rocky mountain paths of Tennessee.

As their ranks were decimated by battle, disease, starvation, death, the hearts that were left swelled higher and higher with holy zeal, sublime courage. Night after night, with lagging, unwilling feet, they made the hated retreat.

Day after day the sun shone on those defiant faces as they presented a still unbroken front and hurled themselves again and again against the invaders, contesting every inch of the land they loved.

Ah, the horrors of those latter days, when daily, almost hourly, brought to me ghastly wrecks of manhood, when my ears were always filled with the moans of the dying, or irrepressible agonizing shrieks of those who were undergoing the torture of the surgeon's knife without the blessed aid of chloroform, for that was contraband of war. Do you wonder, then, that I love to call those comrades of mine " my boys"? Whether they served in the Army of Northern Virginia or the Army of Tennessee, they were all alike my comrades. Their precious blood has often dyed my own garments. I have gone down with them to the very gates of death, wrestling with the death angel every step of the way, sometimes only to receive their last sighs as they passed into the valley of the shadow, sometimes permitted to guide their feeble feet once more into the paths of glory.

I have shared their rations, plain but plentiful at first, at the last only a mouldy crust and a bit of rusty bacon. I have been upon an ambulance-train freighted with human agony delayed for hours by rumors of an enemy in ambush. I have fed men hungry with the ravening hunger of the wounded with scanty rations of musty corn-bread; have seen them drink eagerly of fœtid water, dipped from the road-side ditches. Yet they bore it all with supreme patience; fretted and chafed, it is true, but only on account of enforced inactivity. I have packed haversacks with marching rations for forty-eight hours, a single corn-dodger split and with only a thin slice of bacon between the pieces. This was a *Confederate sandwich.* And on such food Southern soldiers marched incredible distances, fought desperate battles. The world will never cease to wonder at the unfailing devotion, the magnificent courage, the unparalleled achievements of the Southern armies. Scarcely less admirable is the heroic spirit in which they have accepted defeat; the industry which has hidden the desolation of our land with bountiful harvest, the honesty of purpose which now seeks to restore the constitution framed by our forefathers as it was, the patient yet invincible determination which has driven out tyranny and oppression, and reclaimed for posterity this beautiful Southland, rich with historic memories, made sacred and beautiful by the graves of heroes.

And these are *my boys*—still—always my boys. From the highest places of the land they turn to give me a comrade's greeting. I glory in the renown of these, but just as dear and precious to me is the warm grasp of the toil-hardened hand and the smile which beams upon me from the rugged face of the very humblest of " the boys who wore the gray."

Dear friends, this subject is to me inexhaustible; but I may no longer trespass upon your patience. With loving, reverent hands I have lifted the veil of the past. Let the transcendent glory streaming through penetrate the mask which time and care and sorrow have woven for the faces of my boys, and show you the brave, un-faltering hearts as I know them.

CHAPTER II.

THE CONFEDERATE REUNION AT DALLAS.

On the morning of August 6, 1885, a small party of ladies and gentlemen set forth from Shreveport to attend the Confederate reunion at Dallas, Texas.

The gentlemen of the party were veteran soldiers, and your correspondent claimed like honors. (Place this admission to my credit, for, believe me, it is a ruthless sacrifice of womanly vanity to dearer memories.)

In congenial companionship the day passed quickly. Its close brought us to Dallas. And here began at once an emotional experience which might well be called "a tempest of the heart,"—glimpses of glory once real. "Forms and scenes of long ago" appeared in such constant succession that it seemed like a resurrection of the dead and buried past.

The first object that met our view was a large Confederate battle-flag, suspended from a conspicuous building on one of the principal streets, surmounted, surrounded by "star-spangled banners," large and small, but still there, to set our hearts throbbing wildly, to call forth a rain of blinding tears. This was but the beginning. Borne swiftly onward to the hotel, we momentarily started forward with streaming eyes and bated breath to gaze upon the phantom legions ever passing. Squads of cavalry dashed by, manly, weather-beaten boys in gray, and elegant-looking officers wearing the well-remembered slouched hat with cord and feathers, and full Confederate uniforms. Infantry and artillery officers and privates thronged the sidewalks, arm in arm, walking in half embrace, or standing with hand grasping hand. Those not in uniform wore the badges of their respective commands, and frequently some faded remnant of "the gray."

In the large dry-goods establishment of Sauger & Brothers an immense show-window was skilfully and beautifully arranged in honor of the occasion. Confederate soldiers (life size), so natural and life-like as to startle one, were grouped around a camp-fire anxiously watching a large kettle containing a tempting-looking "mess" of green corn, potatoes, other vegetables, and the rations of pork and beef. Blankets neatly rolled and strapped, canteens, haversacks, etc., lay near upon the ground. In the background, a deck of cards and two piles of Confederate money had evidently been thrown down and deserted to "watch the pot." We learned that this most realistic arrangement was the work of a "Yankee boy," whose father had served in the Federal army,—a loving tribute to the people among whom he had come to make his home.

Arrived at the hotel, where a crowd of people waited in the parlor to be assigned rooms, we witnessed many a touching scene between veterans who met now after twenty years. An anxious face would look in at the door, a manly form would advance irresolutely into the room, furtively scanning the new-comers. Suddenly,— "Jim, can this be you?" "Why, Dave, old fel! great God, is this Dave?" Then as hand met and grasped hand these strong men would often break into sobs which forbade all speech, while every heart of those who looked on thrilled with responsive feeling.

From what I learned of the intended evening festivities at the camp-ground (music and dancing under the glare of the electric light), I felt disinclined to be present.

o   27

All day I had walked hand in hand with memory, turning again and again to clasp her closely and to feel the throbbing of her sad heart upon my own. The dear presence still enthralled me, and I could imagine no counter-charm in the laughing face and airy form of Terpsichore.

On the following morning, Amy and I, escorted by a gallant Missouri veteran, set out for the rendezvous, where we found assembled three or four thousand people, among whom hundreds wearing more or less of the gray were conspicuous. The perfect and magnificent arrangements for the comfort and entertainment of guests inspired one with genuine admiration for those who had so well accomplished the grand results everywhere apparent. Did one thirst? In a hundred cool, pleasant nooks were placed casks of ice-water, with dippers and gourds of all sizes attached by long chains. If hungry, at "Headquarters" requisitions were furnished and duly honored by the commissary, who seemed to have a never-failing supply of delicious barbecued beef and mutton, also generous rations of fresh bread.

These were supplemented by elegant refreshments of all kinds, served under shaded tents by ladies, whose entire cordiality made them charming hostesses.

Bands of music continually enlivened the scene. One of these (Gauche Brothers, of Dallas) was of rare excellence, rendering "Bonnie Blue Flag," "Dixie," and an exquisite nocturne, "The Soldier's Dream" (composed for this occasion by the leader of this band), with so much expression and skill as to elicit great applause. The speaker's stand was beautifully ornamented. Hanging on either side of the rostrum was a Confederate battle-flag. Above them, in the centre, floated a new and very handsome United States banner in graceful undulations.

From its blue field not a star was missing. All had been restored, and the bunting waved proudly as if instinct with knowledge of this fact. But, oh, those other flags! sacred emblems of a cause so loved, so nobly defended, yet, alas, lost! shattered and torn by shot and shell, begrimed with the smoke of battle, deeply stained with precious blood; as the summer breeze dallied with their ragged folds, they seemed to stir with a feeble, mournful motion, like the slow throbbing of a breaking heart. Pictures illustrating camplife, battle scenes, etc., ornamented the stand, which was also decorated plentifully with red and white, with a sufficient admixture of blue to make one remember to be loyal to the present. The attempt to depict camplife, cannon, camp-fires, tents, stacked guns, sentries, etc., was utterly upset by the presence of hundreds of ladies and children, with the inevitable paraphernalia necessary to their comfort. "The front of grim-visaged war" was constantly being smoothed into beauty by baby fingers. Men, lured by siren voices, deserted the tented field, and were happy, in entire forgetfulness of duty (so called). Soldiers who did *not* bring ladies enjoyed hugely living in tents and once more " messing" together. Many eloquent speakers addressed the crowd. Pearls of eloquence were sown broadcast, and brought forth a generous harvest of applause.

The number of officers present was surprising. Generals, colonels, majors were pointed out to me by the score, and at last I began to wonder whether in the portion of the Confederate army here represented there were any " privates," at least I *might* have so wondered had I not *known* that, after many of the battles now being recalled with honest pride and merited applause, my own eyes had been too dim with tears to see the glory, my ears had failed to catch the sounds of triumph, because so filled with awful death-groans or the agonizing cries of the wounded. Men whose parting breath was an ascription of praise to the god of battles, whose last earthly joy was the knowledge of victory, and others who, shattered and torn and in throes of agony, yet repressed their moans that they might listen for the music of the fount which "springs eternal," whose bright waters (to them) mirrored the cause they loved so well.

All honor to those who planned the glorious campaigns of the late war—who dauntlessly led heroic legions. Their record is without a parallel in the history of nations. Equal honor to the rank and file—whose splendid valor and self-sacrifice made success possible even when further efforts seemed but a "forlorn hope."

I believe I have omitted no important detail of the reunion. Each day was just like the preceding one. Meetings and partings "tried men's souls," and women's hearts were stirred to their depths.

At last the end came; afterwards to many painful reaction. Still it was passing sweet to meet old friends and comrades, and to find that memory had not proven faithless to her trust. For many a day in the future we shall stand in the light of the surpassing glory which streamed through as the curtain, which has so long obscured the past, was lifted again and again by tender, reverent hands, under the oaks at Dallas.

An Incident of the Dallas Reunion.*

(The scene here described is to me a "*memory*" passing sweet, and one which I desire to perpetuate. This feeling is far removed from vanity. Had the "Lost Cause"

---

* Written at the time for the Shreveport paper by Colonel Henderson, a true and gallant soldier, who has since died.

been triumphant, my lips would have been sealed as to my own service. As it is, I glory in having served it, and cherish fondly even the slightest token that " my boys" do not forget me.)

" On the last day of the Southern Soldiers' Reunion at Dallas, and when sentiments had been read in honor of this and that officer of distinction in the service of the Lost Cause, a lady occupying a somewhat retired position on the platform handed to General Gano a slip of paper on which was traced the following noble sentiment as read by General Gano in a clear, distinct voice, and in tones that expressed his entire concurrence.

" The sentiment and the name subscribed are sufficient of themselves. We give it as follows :

" ' THE PRIVATE SOLDIER OF THE CONFEDERATE STATES ARMY.

" ' He bore in his bosom a heart of oak ; he withstood the brunt of battle and sustained the heat and burthen of the day. His blood nourished the laurels which otherwise had never bloomed to grace the brow of Lee and Jackson. For myself, no blessing has ever crowned my life more highly prized than the God-given privilege I enjoyed during four years of the war, of ministering to the boys who wore the ragged, unornamented gray.

" ' Your devoted friend and comrade,

" ' MRS. FANNY A. BEERS,

" ' Late of the Confederate Army.'

" To this sentiment came the response of three cheers and a regular rebel yell, repeated and repeated for the space of twenty minutes.

" But the most touching feature followed. A number of old Confederate soldiers, who had in wounds and

27*

sickness received gentle and healing ministrations from the hands of Mrs. Beers, and learned just then that she was present, in defiance of all order, rushed to the stand and gathered about her. Each and every one bore the mark of some wound received in the war, and wore about their person some fragment of Confederate uniform—a hat, a coat, or other article—as souvenirs of the days of trials and glory.

"Like old children they gathered around her, grasping her hand and blessing her and testifying to all the world what a blessing she had been to them.

"It was, indeed and truly, the most touching and striking incident of the late reunion of Confederate veterans at Dallas."

CHAPTER III.

The Louisiana Soldiers' Home.

I MUST begin with a digression, for, as thought concentrates itself upon this pleasant subject, one is irresistibly impelled to remember the delightful ride thitherward, and to wonder if any other city in the United States can boast of street-car routes so beautiful. The visitor to "Camp Nichols," taking on Canal Street a car of the Esplanade and Bayou Bridge line, is borne smoothly along for miles under cool, green arches of oak-trees, a broad street on either side, bordered by elegant residences and lovely, fragrant gardens.

Looking back, where the green arcade narrows away in the distance, or forward, to observe how the rough track is made beautiful by the shadows of dancing leaves and boughs,—glancing at the rapidly-succeeding pictures of beauty and comfort on either side, inhaling the mingled perfume of flowers,—one is placed under a spell of enchantment which lasts until, at "Bayou Bridge," the end of the route is reached. Leaving the car, a very short walk along the banks of the Bayou brings the visitor to the "camp." Upon entering the gate the first thought is, "How pleasant, how peaceful, how homelike." The comfortable-looking house is beautifully shaded by large live-oaks. Under these green grass is diversified by neatly-kept walks. Midway between the outer gate and the house a small stream is spanned by a rustic bridge. As I stood upon this

319

bridge and saw, upon the pleasant galleries in front of their rooms, the maimed and scarred veterans sitting in groups or apart, tranquilly smoking and chatting or reading, the dying words of our "Stonewall" Jackson came into my mind,—"Let us cross the river and rest in the shade of the trees." To him was given eternal rest. The weary spirit even then stood by the river of death and viewed beyond the trees of paradise. Less happy those who remain to witness the downfall of hope. Ah, what can be more glorious, yet more deeply sorrowful, than the story of their past. The strength and beauty of their youth and early manhood was freely given to the cause they deemed sacred. It was, alas! lost; and, the tempest of war subsiding, left upon a desolate shore these wrecks.

Returning after the war to find only ruined homes and shattered fortunes, those who had retained health and strength found them taxed to the utmost. Necessity held them in bonds of iron, and the demands of helpless families absorbed them. All the same, manly hearts have been often and painfully stirred by the silent appeals of maimed and suffering comrades, and the faithful few have never ceased to hope and strive for the result now attained in the "Soldiers' Home."

It is pleasant to feel that the first rays of the newly-arisen sun of prosperity have dispelled the darkness wherein these poor fellows have wandered so long, revealing to them the kindly faces of brothers, who, having gone in search of them, will lead them to home and rest.

As I said before, the "Home" viewed from the bridge, a few hundred yards in front, suggests ideas of comfort which are fully realized upon a closer investigation. The rooms are delightfully situated (opening upon a shaded gallery), perfectly ventilated, and very cool, furnished with iron bedsteads, comfortable and cleanly bedding, wardrobes or bureaus, and washstands. The library and reception-room is a charming nook, embellished with many gifts from loving hands.

Immediately opposite the entrance is placed an excellent portrait of General Francis T. Nichols, a hero whom all (Louisianians especially) delight to honor. From the bloody battle-fields of Northern Virginia he brought back a mangled and shattered body, but enough to hold and enshrine a powerful, active brain, and a heart as brave and generous as ever beat in human bosom.

He is idolized by his comrades and beloved by us all. By a unanimous vote of the board of directors the home has been called "Camp Nichols," and from a gracefully-proportioned flag-staff, placed directly in front of the reception-room (the gift of the Army of Tennessee), floats a banner whereon this honored name was embroidered by the daughters of Generals Lee and Jackson during their recent visit to New Orleans.

The dining-room is very large, well lighted, and fairly shines with cleanliness. In short, every appointment is excellent, and every effort of managers and officers is directed toward making the disabled veterans feel that they are honored inmates of a home which they have earned and deserved, not recipients of charity. Camp Nichols may well be called a trysting-place of heroes. Here old comrades meet as comrades and friends. In the warm grasp of hands there is no suspicion of patronage. Right down in these brave, long-suffering hearts shine glances full of the unforgotten "light of other days," causing eyes dim and clouded by care and sorrow to beam with a responsive brightness. Ah, who shall undertake to estimate the value and blessedness of this work!

The Legislature of Louisiana organized this enterprise in 1881, making a yearly appropriation for its support. It is designed for all soldiers of Louisiana who have been disabled by wounds received in her service or have become incapacitated by age or disability; is controlled by a board of directors, also created by the State, consisting of the president, three vice-presidents, and recording secretary of the Army of Northern Virginia, and the president, three vice-presidents, and recording secretary of the Army of Tennessee.

The harmonious action of this board is nobly sustained by the members composing both organizations.

The president of the Army of Tennessee, Judge Walter Rogers, is an indefatigable worker, as he was once a brave and faithful soldier. He may with perfect truth be written "as one who loves his fellow-men" (especially his fellow-soldiers). I believe he will, as long as he lives, stand a faithful sentinel upon the sands of time, watching lest the ever-encroaching tide of years may obliterate sacred foot-prints.

All arrangements having been nearly completed, the Home was opened January 1, 1884. Eight soldiers were at once admitted, and since the number has been increased to fifty. Under the rules of the institution no compulsory labor is allowed except that necessary to properly police the quarters. Yet all feel so deep an interest in their Home that they yield willing assistance whenever asked. They choose such occupations as they are physically able to perform, and take delight in keeping things in order.

The Home has many friends outside of the Confederate organizations, none more zealous and truly kind than the officers and members of the Grand Army of the Republic, "Mewer Post." These are frequent and welcome visitors to Camp Nichols, and have shown both generosity and thoughtfulness in their contributions to the comfort of its inmates. The superintendent, Captain William Bullitt, was selected on account of his soldierly qualities and excellent administrative abilities, and by a unanimous vote of the board elected to fill the position.

His record is untarnished and excellent. At the inception of the war, having assisted in raising the First Company Louisiana Guards, he went out as first lieutenant of the same, won by promotion the rank of captain and afterwards of major, which he held at the close of the war. Used, therefore, to command, he also brings to his work a thorough love for it, and an amount of intelligence in interpreting, and skill in carrying out arrangements and improvements proposed by the board of directors, which insures success and the satisfaction of all concerned.

" God bless our Home," and let the light of His countenance shine upon it and bless it.

And may God strengthen the kindly hands which have led these weary ones away from thorny pathways " through green pastures and beside still waters." May they never falter nor fail until the all-merciful Father shall himself provide the " rod and staff" which shall guide all through the dark valley to rest eternal.

CHAPTER IV.

THE MARCH OF TIME.

Thoughts suggested while witnessing the ceremonies attending the unveiling of a statue of General Albert Sydney Johnston, erected upon their tomb by the Louisiana Division, Army of Tennessee, in New Orleans, Louisiana, April 6, 1887.*

LITTLE more than three years ago there came a day long to be remembered by every man, woman, and child resident in New Orleans, and by all strangers then sojourning within her gates. A day when the souls of thousands held but a single thought, when all hearts beat as one, when one impulse, strong, thrilling, irresistible led willing feet to where, upon a pedestal, raised stone by stone by love and self-sacrifice, stood the shrouded figure of General Robert E. Lee. Above hung heavy clouds, alas! too suggestive of the hopes that perished forever at Appomattox, but ever and anon the struggling sun broke through, lingering awhile as if to recall the matchless glory which, even in the hour of disaster and defeat, gilded and made immortal the untarnished swords, the stacked arms, then and there surrendered.

To me the terrific storm which soon broke, upsetting all arrangements, abolishing all ceremonies, hushing all oratory, seemed to solemnize and mark in a most fitting manner this great occasion. For no tongue of man or angel could have evoked a feeling so strong, a sentiment

---

* The article was first published in "The Illustrated South."

so lasting, as that written, as it were, by the finger of Heaven that day upon the hearts of that awe-stricken multitude. Years hence, those who were boys then will remember the lesson there learned. They will tell you of the soldierly figures standing at the foot of the monument, exposed to the pitiless storm, immovable, unshrinking ON DUTY, and these were men who, following where duty led, had won an imperishable record under the immortal Lee.

They will describe how, in the storm-swept streets outside the enclosure, legions of soldiers, the Blue as well as the Gray, calmly faced the howling tempest, standing "at rest," awaiting the moment when the form of the great commander should be revealed to their reverent gaze. Among these, the veterans of the Army of Tennessee bore a conspicuous part. In their true, brave hearts, second to none in allegiance to their commander-in-chief, there yet lay enshrined another image, there burned another purpose equally high and holy. Hope pointed down the long vista of the future to where lay—a tomb! only a tomb! nay, more—a "bivouac of the dead," where, life's battle fought, the toilsome march ended, weary comrades might gather to their rest. And so far distant, yet always in sight, gleamed their Mecca; steadily towards it marched the pilgrims of memory, unfaltering, undismayed, led by a few brave, faithful spirits, through deserts of discouragement, when oases were few and far between, patiently bridging chasms which seemed impassable, until to-day they stand at the goal so hardly won. There lie the veterans who one by one have stolen to the bivouac. "After life's fitful fever they sleep well." Above, faithful comrades keep watch and ward. Here is a solemn but glorious trysting-place.

On the morning of the 6th of April, twenty-five years
28

ago, a sky as bright and beautiful as that which to-day bends above us, became obscured and darkened by the smoke of battle. Of the Confederate forces then and there engaged it has been said, "Their splendid valor has been rarely equalled, never surpassed, on any field of any war." Alas! why must it be that grief and glory always go hand in hand? Up through the heavy clouds which hid the face of nature that terrible day sped hundreds of gallant souls, straight to the light wherein was made clear *to them* the awful Providence which even now disquiets our hearts and clouds our earthly vision. Among them, one whose sudden taking off filled every breast with gloom, and wrested from the Confederacy the fruits of a splendid victory.

So many and so grand are the eulogies which have been pronounced upon Albert Sydney Johnston that nothing remains for me to add. Who does not remember the sorrow of a nation at his death? Who can forget the lava tide of indignation which spread over our land when the "conquered" were forbidden to mourn their fallen hero, when a stricken people were compelled to "lay their hands upon their mouths, their mouths in the dust," when even the mournful voices of the bells were silenced?

Viewed in the glorious light of to-day, how like a prophecy fulfilled appear the beautiful lines of Father Ryan,—

> " There's a grandeur in graves, there's a glory in gloom,
>   For out of the gloom future brightness is born,
>   As after the night looms the sunrise of morn,
>   And the graves of the dead, with grass overgrown,
>   May yet form the footstool of Liberty's throne."

Years of bitter strife have left sad traces all over this beautiful Southland. In lovely valleys, upon every hill-

side, in the majestic forests, lie, side by side, the Gray
and the Blue. The sun clothes every mound with equal
glory, the sky weeps over all alike. Standing beside
these graves, angry passions die in the hearts of brave
men; "one touch of nature" moistens manly eyes,
softens obdurate hearts. Involuntarily hands meet in
a firmer clasp, which expresses respect as well as sympathy.

The soldiers on both sides have learned to appreciate
and understand each other, so, in spite of those who
would fain prolong the strife, the long-oppressed people
of the South are free to mourn their dead, and

> "The graves of the dead, with grass overgrown,"

indeed

> "Form a footstool for Liberty's throne."

To-day the veterans who met and fiercely battled at
Shiloh unite in doing honor to the memory of General
Johnston and of the men who, with him, won immor-
tality upon that bloody field.

To-day imperishable laurels bloom afresh upon the
upturned brows of the men who hail with loud acclaim
the image of their chieftain placed here to guard forever

> "War's richest spoil,—the ashes of the dead."

It is fitting that, on this day of memory, rich strains
of martial music should awaken long-silent echoes in
this city of the dead,—fitting that nature should be
despoiled of her floral treasures to deck this sacred
place which, indeed, is "not so much the *tomb* of virtue
as its shrine."

The flowers that yield their beauty and fragrance to
grace this scene will fade and die. Yon radiant sun

will set, but not before it has burned an indelible record upon the young hearts of thousands to whom, ere long, we must trust this precious spot.

Of the remnant of the once magnificent Army of Tennessee gathered here it will soon be said,—

> " On Fame's eternal camping-ground
> Their silent tents are spread."

But the figure of their chieftain will be left to tell the story of a patriotic purpose long cherished in faithful hearts, at last accomplished by patient hands.

> " Nor wreck, nor change, nor winter's blight,
> Nor Time's remorseless doom,
> Can dim our ray of holy light
> That gilds this glorious tomb."

CHAPTER V.

A WOMAN'S RECORD.*

(From the *Southern Bivouac*.)

THIS record will be found to substantiate in every particular my own history of the period referred to.

Being inspired by an ardent zeal or a high sense of duty, not a few noble women during the war arose conspicuous to view. Their gentle deeds, though done in humble spheres, yet shone like "a bright light in a low world."

Fair exemplars they were of patriotic virtue, whose acts of devotion helped much to enshrine in our memories a melancholy past; and they should not be forgotten. In the March number of the *Bivouac* was given a short sketch of a lady who, during the war, tenderly cared for the sick and suffering Confederates in a Northern prison. It is now proposed to give the record of one who, animated with a romantic love for the cause of the South, left a luxurious home and spent nearly four years in nursing the sick and wounded in Confederate hospitals.

Mrs. Fannie A. Beers was a native of the North, and the child of fond parents, who gave her every educational advantage, and the means of acquiring all the accomplishments usual in refined circles.

When very young she was married to her present husband, and before the war came South to reside at New Orleans. By nature ardent and susceptible, she

---

* Written in 1883 by Major McDonald, of Louisville, Kentucky, then editor *Southern Bivouac*.

readily adapted herself to the surroundings of her new life, and soon grew to love the people and the land of her adoption. A few years of happiness passed and then came the sectional storm. Full well she knew that it threatened to sunder cherished ties, but it did not move her from the side of her choice.

When the struggle came at last, and her home was broken up in New Orleans by the absence of her husband in the field, she returned to the parental roof, to beguile the time in the companionship of her mother. But the separation, with the anxiety it brought, became intolerable; besides, from the positiveness of her opinions and the warmth of her zeal, she soon became ill at ease in the land of her birth. So, with her mother's approval, she resolved to face all perils, and to return and share the fortunes of the Confederacy. Taking her little boy she set out for "Dixie," and, after many trials, arrived at Richmond, Virginia, just after the battle of Bull Run. Here she was kindly cared for by some old acquaintances, among whom was Commodore Maury, a friend of her family, and who had dedicated his "Geography of the Sea" to her uncle, George Manning, of New York. Through his introduction she made many dear friends among the ladies of Richmond, some of whom pressed her to come and dwell with them; but she neither needed nor was seeking roof and shelter. If she so wished, she might have found them with her husband's relatives in Alabama. What she felt the want of was occupation,—work in behalf of the cause to which, in spite of selfish reasons, she felt impelled to devote herself.

In order that she might have this work, and at the same time be where assistance could be rendered her husband and friends at the front, she asked to be appointed a hospital matron.

Commodore Maury for some time protested against

such a step, saying that she was too young, and had been too tenderly raised; but she persisted, so he finally yielded, as appears from the following letter:

"RICHMOND, August 10, 1861.

"MY DEAR FANNY,—You bear the heart of a true and tender woman, in the breast of a noble patriot. I will no longer oppose your wishes, and mean to help you all I can. Command me at any and all times.
"Yours truly,
"MATTHEW F. MAURY."

At first she assisted in a private hospital maintained by some Richmond ladies, who, by turns, sent in all the food required. Permission was applied for to enter the Louisiana hospital, but it was refused.

In a few weeks she was appointed matron-in-charge of the Second Alabama Hospital, with liberty to receive a limited number of her friends, who might be taken care of there.

Soon after she entered upon her regular duties the sick and wounded began to pour in, and from this time forward she was constantly employed till within a few weeks of the battle of Shiloh. With the departure of her husband's command to Tennessee, she was disposed for a like change of field-duty. She now left Richmond, and for a few weeks only was occupied with a visit to her husband's relatives. Then she resumed her hospital work at Gainesville, Alabama.

Her subsequent career is best related in the following letters from surgeons of high rank, and whose official positions gave them abundant opportunities of estimating the work she performed and the strength of the spirit which animated her. The letters were called from their authors in the spring of 1883, nearly twenty years after the close of the war, upon the occasion of a musical and literary entertainment being tendered Mrs. Beers by her soldier friends in New Orleans. So profound was the gratitude for her former services to sick and wounded Confederates, that all the military organizations exerted themselves to make it a success, and at the meeting of the members of the " Army of Tennessee," complimentary resolutions were passed, and the letters read.

" NEW ORLEANS, March 8, 1883.

" JUDGE ROGERS :

" DEAR SIR,—Understanding that the members of the 'Army of Tennessee' have tendered Mrs. F. A. Beers an entertainment, I feel anxious to aid in securing its success.

" I am well qualified to testify to the valuable and disinterested services which this lady rendered in the Confederate hospital during the late war. In truth, aside from officers and soldiers who may be now living and still holding in remembrance the kind and skilful nursing which she gave them personally while wounded or sick, I know of only four persons whose positions made them fully cognizant of the heroism, devotion, and self-sacrifice which she brought to the discharge of her duties. These are, first, Dr. T. H. McAllister, now of Marion, Alabama, in whose admirably-conducted hospital she was the only matron during the greater part of the war; second, Dr. C. B. Gamble, now of Baltimore; third, Dr. S. H. Stout, now of Roswell, Georgia, medical director of hospitals of the Army of Tennessee; fourth, the writer.

" I know that I can venture to speak in behalf of these gentlemen and for myself in declaring that the skill and efficiency with which she nursed and fed our sick and wounded soldiers, and the coolness and bravery

with which she faced danger in discharge of these duties do merit suitable recognition from the survivors of
those rapidly-diminishing numbers who fought under
the Confederate flag.

"Very respectfully,

"S. M. Bemiss, M.D.,

"Late Assistant Medical Director and Medical Director
of Hospitals, Army of Tennessee."

"Marion, Alabama, March 11, 1883.

"Dr. S. Bemiss, New Orleans,—Having heard an entertainment was to be given in your city on March 29
for the benefit of Mrs. Fannie A. Beers, I feel it to be
my duty, as well as pleasure, to add my testimony to
her worth and to the part she played in the late war.

"During the three years she was with me as a Confederate hospital matron, she conducted herself as a
high-toned lady in the strictest sense of the term, and
to every word I may say of her there are hundreds,
yea, thousands, of Confederate soldiers scattered all
over the South who would cheerfully testify to some
facts if opportunity were offered them.

"After the battles of Shiloh and Farmington, and
then the evacuation of Corinth, I was ordered to establish hospitals (in June or July, 1862) for the sick and
wounded of General Bragg's army, at Gainesville, Alabama. With scarcely any hospital supplies I began
preparations for the same, and in answer to a card published in the Selma (Alabama) papers, asking for supplies and a suitable lady to act as matron, she promptly
responded. At first sight her youthful, delicate, refined,
and lady-like appearance, showing she had never been
accustomed to any hardships of life, caused me to doubt
her capacity to fill the position of matron.

"She said she desired to do something while her husband was at the front defending our Southern homes. I soon found what she lacked in age and experience was made up in patriotism, devotion to the Southern cause, constant vigilance, and tenderness in nursing the Confederate sick and wounded. I soon learned to appreciate her services and to regard her as indispensable.

"She remained with me as hospital matron while I was stationed at Gainesville, Alabama, Ringgold, Georgia, Newnan, Georgia, and Fort Valley, Georgia, embracing a period of nearly three years. She was all the time chief matron, sometimes supervising more than one thousand beds filled with sick and wounded, and never did any woman her whole duty better. Through heat and cold, night and day, she was incessant in her attentions and watchfulness over the Confederate sick and wounded, many times so worn down by fatigue that she was scarcely able to walk, but never faltering in the discharge of her duties.

"At one time, while at Newnan, Georgia, the Federal forces under General McCook were advancing on the town, and it became necessary for every available man —post officers, surgeons, convalescents, and nurses—to leave the town and wards in order to repel the invading enemy. I was much affected while hurrying from ward to ward giving general orders about the care of the sick during my absence in the fight, to see and hear the maimed begging Mrs. Beers to remain with them, and they could well testify to how well she acted her part in remaining with them and caring for their many wants, while the able-bodied men of all grades went to battle for all they held dear.

"At the same time, all the citizens and officers' wives sought refuge in some place of safety. After the battle, which resulted in victory to the Confederates, and the wounded of both armies were brought to our wards, and the Federal prisoners (about one thousand) to the town, her attention and kindness was, if possible, doubly increased, extending help and care as well to the boys in blue as to those in gray. In her missions of mercy she made no distinction. There she was daily seen with her servant going into the prison of the Federal soldiers with bandages and baskets of provisions to minister to the wants of such as were slightly wounded or needed some attention. Many a Federal officer and soldier would doubtless bear willing testimony to these acts of unselfish kindness.

" While Atlanta was invested and being shelled she, contrary to my advice and urgent remonstrance, took boxes of provisions to her husband and comrades in the trenches when the shot and shell fell almost like hail. While at Fort Valley her courage and patriotism were put to the severest test in an epidemic of smallpox.

" When all who could left, she remained and nursed the Confederate soldiers with this loathsome disease. I desire to say she was a voluntary nurse, and did all her work from patriotism alone, until it became necessary for her to remain as a permanent *attaché* of the hospitals that her name should go upon the pay-rolls. After that she spent her hard earnings in sending boxes to the front and dispensing charity upon worthy objects immediately under her care.

" She was with me as voluntary nurse, or matron, for more than three years, and during that time she conducted herself in every respect so as to command the respect and esteem of all with whom she came in contact, from the humblest private to the highest in command, and the citizens of every place where she was stationed gave her a hearty welcome, and invited her into the best of society.

"Feeling this much was due to one who suffered so many privations for 'Dear Lost Cause,' I send it to you for you to use as you think proper in promoting her good. You know me well, and can vouch for anything I have said.　　　　　Very respectfully,

"Wm. T. McAllister, M.D.,

"Late Surgeon P. A. C. S."

After such testimonials of worth and work, anything more would seem out of place. Yet we cannot refrain from mentioning some of the sayings of soldiers who, though forgotten, yet recall her with affection for the tender nursing received at her hands. Says one, "She was the moving spirit in the hospital, officially and practically. The first object of her ministrations was to relieve suffering and save life. The next was to fit men for service. When health was restored she would brook no shirking, but with the power of kindly words impelled patients to the field. Her zeal sprang from profound convictions of the righteousness of the Cause, and with the vehemence of sincerity she wielded a great influence over those who had recovered under her care."

Another declares that he has seen her "not only bathing the heads of soldiers, but washing their feet."

So the evidence accumulates, and it is no wonder she is called by many "The Florence Nightingale of the South."

THE END.

1

THE

LIVERPOOL AND LONDON AND GLOBE

INSURANCE COMPANY.

Fire Assets $15,014,725.47

Total Fire Liabilities 5,614,692.11

Surplus for Policy Holders . $9,400,033.36

Assets in United States . . . $6,639,780.55

Liabilities in United States . 3,562,242.30

Surplus in United States . . $3,077,538.25

HENRY V. OGDEN,   CLARENCE F. LOW,

Resident Secretary.   Assistant Secretary.

**LOSSES CASHED UPON ADJUSTMENT WITHOUT
DISCOUNT.**

194 GRAVIER STREET.

NEW ORLEANS.

2

3

5

7

YALE & BOWLING,

WHOLESALE

DRY GOODS AND NOTIONS

17, 19, and 21 Magazine St.
AND
88 Common St.,

NEW ORLEANS, LA.

THE LOUISIANA NATIONAL BANK,
OF NEW ORLEANS.

Capital	$500,000.00
Surplus	200,000.00
Undivided Profits	140,000.00
	$840,000.00

R. M. WALMSLEY,   A. LURIA,   LEON F. JANIN,
President.   Vice-President.   Cashier.

M. HACKETT,
WHOLESALE AND RETAIL GROCER,
Importer, Wine and Liquor Dealer,
223 TO 227 MELPOMENE STREET,
BARONNE STREET SIDE OF DRYADES MARKET,
NEW ORLEANS.

JNO. P. RICHARDSON,

WHOLESALE

DRY GOODS AND NOTIONS

CORNER

Magazine and Common Sts.,

NEW ORLEANS, LA.

8

9

ANNOUNCEMENT FOR 1888.

The complete novels that have already been arranged for to appear in

LIPPINCOTT'S MONTHLY MAGAZINE

for 1888 are as follows:

"**CHECK AND COUNTER-CHECK.**" By Brander Matthews and George H. Jessop (January).

"**THE SPELL OF HOME.**" **After the German.** By Mrs. A. L. Wister (February).

"**HONORED IN THE BREACH.**" By Julia Magruder (March).

"**THE QUICK OR THE DEAD?**" By Amélie Rives (April).

THIS series of novels, it will readily be seen, will be of great literary value and interest. Miss Amélie Rives has excited universal admiration by the short stories and poems that she has contributed to current magazines, and a novel from her pen will be eagerly welcomed by a wide circle. Edgar Saltus, a brilliant young author, whose "Mr. Incoul's Misadventure" was excellent in itself and gave promise of still more brilliant performance in the future, is another rising name. William H. Bishop and Brander Matthews have an established position among contemporary novelists, and the new novels from their pen will be equal to any of their former work. Mrs. A. L. Wister's adaptations are known to all readers of American fiction. Miss Julia Magruder, whose "Across the Chasm" and "At Anchor" (in *Lippincott's Magazine*) were hailed as among the most charming of modern Southern novels, is another writer with an audience already created. Miss M. Eliott Seawell is the author of "Maid Marian," a delightful little extravaganza in the December, 1886, number of *Lippincott's*, and the novel which she has written for this magazine will add another star to the galaxy of Southern novelists.

In addition, Albion W. Tourgee will contribute a notable series of stories, illustrating the interesting and exciting phases of the legal profession, under the general title of "With Gauge & Swallow." Each story will be complete in itself, though all will revolve around a common centre of interest.

Stories, essays, and poems may be expected from Amélie Rives, Edgar Fawcett, Thomas Nelson Page, H. H. Boyesen, Joaquin Miller, Walt Whitman, Will Carleton, M. G. McClelland, Helen G. Cone, Mrs. S. M. B. Piatt, J. J. Piatt, C. L. Hildreth, Will H. Hayne, Lucy C. Lillie, Edith M. Thomas, and many others; and autobiographical articles, dealing with interesting phases of their career, from Lotta, Fanny Davenport, H. H. Boyesen, Edgar Saltus, Clara Barton, Belva Lockwood, Frances E. Willard, etc., etc.

A number of ideas new to periodical literature will be exploited during the year. For example, the February number will be written entirely by women for women, and will contain a novel by Mrs. Wister; a novelette by Miss Amélie Rives; poems by Mrs. Piatt, Helen G. Cone, Edith M. Thomas, and Ella Wheeler-Wilcox; autobiographical sketches by Belva Lockwood, Fanny Davenport, etc.; and articles of general interest by other famous women of the country.

Subscription per Annum, $3.00. *Single Number, 25 Cents.*

J. B. LIPPINCOTT COMPANY, Publishers,

715 and 717 Market Street, Philadelphia.

FIRE.   RIVER.   MARINE.

Incorporated April, 1857.

Reorganized April, 1882.

HOPE

INSURANCE COMPANY

OF

NEW ORLEANS,

No. 188 Gravier Street.

Cash Capital **$250,000.00**

Assets **403,766.98**

PROGRESSIVE AND LIBERAL.

J. A. CHALARON, PRESIDENT.   MAURICE STERN, VICE-PRESIDENT.

LOUIS BARNETT, SECRETARY.

14

Library of Congress Cataloguing in Publication Data

Beers, Fannie A.
Memories: a record of personal experience
and adventure during four years of war.
Reprint. Originally published: Philadelphia:
Lippincott, 1888.
1. Beers, Fannie A.
¯2. United States—History—Civil War, 1861-1865—
Personal narratives, Confederate.
3. United States—History—Civil War, 1861-1865—Hospitals.
4. United States—History—Civil War, 1861-1865—Medical care.
5. United States—History—Civil War, 1861-1865—Women.
6. Southern States—Biography.
7. Nurses—Southern States—Biography.
I. Title.
E605.B41   1985   973.7'82   84-16139
ISBN 0-8094-4471-2 (library)
ISBN 0-8094-4470-4 (retail)

Printed in the United States of America

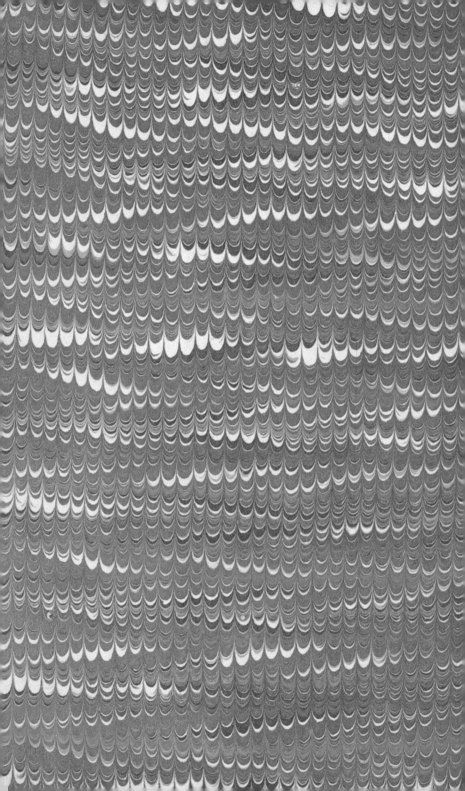